Searching For

The Dutch Partridge Dog

Searching For The Dutch Partridge Dog

Peter Sedgwick

ARDRA PRESS

First published in 2006 by

Ardra Press
PO Box 78
Cottingham
HU16 4WT
United Kingdom
www.ardrapress.co.uk

ISBN: 0-9548678-3-1

British Library Cataloguing in Publication Data
A CIP record for this book can be obtained from the British Library

Designed and typeset by Julie Martin

Printed and bound by TJ International Ltd, Padstow, Cornwall

Cover design by Ciaron Lee Marlow
www.rockers-going-starwars.co.uk

To Mum and Dad

For everything

CONTENTS

ACKNOWLEDGEMENTS

I would like to thank my son, Tom, for inspiring me to write this book, for his wit and wisdom throughout life and for questioning me to keep me on track. Also my wife, Alison, for incredible patience, for many hours spent over the keyboard, for putting up with my constant absences and for seeing the funny side of having holidays, anniversaries and other events 'dog-jacked'.

My three dogs – Jake, Molly and Stan – have not only taught me so much but inspired my all-consuming love for, and interest in, dogs. Every day I share with them is a privilege.

Many friends and colleagues have given me support and encouragement throughout this project. My heartfelt thanks to each and every one of them.

Many thanks to Ronan Fitzsimons at Ardra Press, for seeing past the mess of ideas and having faith in this book.

I have tried to acknowledge sources and people as I go in this text. If I have missed you, please be assured that this is through cock-up rather than conspiracy!

As I say in the book, the internet is a great tool for so many purposes. One of these is for finding out information, and I would like to acknowledge the following sites gratefully. Each is worth a visit in its own right.

General dog breed information and information on health conditions:

www.pedigreedogs.co.uk and **www.dogbreedinfo.com**

Site opposing the European Convention:

www.saveourbreeds.org.uk

Site campaigning against breed-specific legislation: **www.dominodogs.org**

And on the canine 'holocaust': **www.angelfire.com/biz6/dogholocaust/olfen.html**

Information on Bedlington and the surrounding areas: **www.bedlington.co.uk**

And on Bedlington's industrial heritage: **www.pitwork.net**

Information on Rye: **www.visitrye.co.uk** and **www.whitecliffscountry.org.uk**

Travelling and staying in Ischia: **www.ischia.it** and **www.ischiaonline.net**

Dog-related charity websites:

Guide Dogs For The Blind: **www.guidedogs.org.uk**

Canine Partners for Independence: **www.caninepartners.co.uk**

And Endal's amazing story: **www.milleniumdog.freeserve.co.uk**

Pets As Therapy: **www.petsastherapy.org**

The Cinnamon Trust: **www.cinnamon.org.uk**

Dogs For The Disabled: **www.dogsforthedisabled.org**

Hearing Dogs For Deaf People: **www.hearing-dogs.co.uk**

The docking debate:

In favour, The Council for Docked Breeds: **www.cdb.org/**

Against: **www.rspca.org.uk** and **www.anti-dockingalliance.co.uk**

Details of Clicker Challenges, courses, *Teaching Dogs* magazine: **www.learningaboutdogs.com**

All-round canine website with details of Crufts, Hero Dogs (Friends for Life) etc:

www.the-kennel-club.org.uk
(Also a great provider of statistics and holder of breed standards, etc.)

The International Sheep Dog Society **www.isds.org.uk**

And for sheep dog handling experiences **www.bordercollies.co.uk**

Kamp Westerbork:
'Westerbork: Portal of Auschwitz', created by Hans Vanderwerff at: **www.cympm.com/westerbork.html** and **www.kampwesterbork.nl**

And finally, Marjaan's beautiful Dutch partridge dogs at: **www.bolognezer.nl**

Peter Sedgwick
March 2006

CHAPTER 1

Life Begins at 40

And so, this is how it all began …

It was my 40th birthday. As I had expected, I woke up feeling exactly the same as when I was 39. I never had believed the propaganda anyway. I couldn't detect any extra aches or pains and a quick look in the mirror didn't seem to reveal any more grey hairs than the day before. So that was all OK, then.

I was particularly relieved that I had got away without the dreaded party. I still find it difficult to believe that people actually choose to hold these things of their own accord. If I did have one, I would spend all my time worrying that people had just attended to be polite and couldn't wait to get away. Or picturing the rows between the married couples before they came – especially where you only really know one of them (usually through work) and their partner doesn't know anyone at all, just spending the evening smiling but slowly dying inside.

Anyway, my 'do' had been a quiet one, just six or seven of us – all family. I had emerged completely unscathed.

And now it was time for the presents.

I'm really lucky, I get excellent presents. It is so rare for me to get something I don't want, even though comedy sketches tell me that this is far from the norm. But then, on the other hand, I also spend ages looking for presents for people to make sure they get something they like, which again seems quite unusual, especially for men! So, I like to think that this is karma.

Most of my presents tend to have one theme – dogs. So I had a wonderful silk dog tie (quite subtle, with a small dog motif all over) and some Scooby Doo socks (less subtle motif). I also had some presents relating to my other passions: CDs and DVDs to reflect my love of music and a season ticket for the other love of my life – my local non-league football club.

I was particularly thrilled to receive a couple of rare old dog books: *The Book of the Dog* edited by Brian Vesey-Fitzgerald (a 1040-page, monster first edition from 1948) and *Black Bob – The Dandy Wonder Dog*, an old soft-backed cartoon-strip dog book of four stories about Black Bob, the wonderful black and white sheepdog. Read these stories and you realise that Lassie is for wimps. Cor, the things that Black Bob can do!

I've got a pretty good collection of dog books, both old and new. I'm particularly interested in those about training and about how we live with our dogs, although I have plenty of books on individual breeds, sports and activities, collections of photographs and some pretty strange dog-themed books, such as a book of 'dogs of famous owners'. I even have modern comic strips about dogs and kiddies' books of dog stories, as well as books of breed standards (the blueprints for the various breeds) and novels in which dogs play a prominent part. Obsessed? Well, maybe a little.

It's amazing to read these books and see how attitudes towards dogs (and indeed people) have changed and just how society has moved along. Even the names of the authors are a bit of a giveaway if you go back a little in time. How about *Disobedient Dogs* by Lieutenant Colonel G. H. Badcock? I wonder what that one's like? Or *Dogs of Every Kind* by Sir Reginald St Johnston. How about *The Mating and Whelping of Dogs* by Captain R. Portman Graham? It's all very different nowadays!

Training books are my favourites – real barometers of how our interaction with dogs has changed. If you read a few of them you can pick up the movement in values over the years – in terms of our expectations of, and our whole relationship with, our animals.

Consider this from Colonel Konrad Most's book *Training Dogs – A Manual* (1954):

> 'The switch should be employed until the animal submits and his will to resist, and the exasperation which accompanies it, is replaced by fear. So long as the dog does not submit, but continues to resist, a flexible switch should be used, if necessary, on the head and the jaws, but not on the top of the nose. It may also be used on the neck, ears, legs and tail, but not on the sexual parts or on the lower regions of the belly and chest. Apart from such exceptional cases *heavy* cuts should only be applied to the powerful muscles on the fore- and hindquarters and on the back.'

The last present I opened was one of Tom's. Tom is my thirteen-year-old son and he's excellent at getting things you want which you didn't know you wanted – the fun I've had with the dog-themed magnetic poetry set he bought me! Unfortunately, even after hours of trying – not all in one go – my best effort so far is:

> 'My intelligent canine friend
> He gambols and plays in the park
> He investigates my butt with his nose
> And passes right out with a bark'

Now I know it's not Shakespeare and I don't want to be defensive, but have you seen those magnetic poetry sets? Really. I even took the set with me when I was on a course for a few days and sat in front of it and the TV for a couple of evenings, but still couldn't do any better.

This time, Tom's little surprise was a book: *The Usborne Spotter's Guide – Dogs*. What a fantastic little book! If, like me, you were brought up with *I Spy* books, you'll get the idea. There is a list of different things – in this case breeds of dogs – and you simply tick each one off on your spotter's chart when you see it (of course, you could cheat, but then like they say at school, 'you'd only be cheating yourself!'). There are lots of other books in the series, such as birds, shells, wild flowers and dinosaurs (although I'm not too sure how you go about 'spotting' them).

There's more to the book than that, though. The chap who has put it together – H Glover – has managed to pack it full of information on markings, pedigrees, different types of tail and ear carriage, a few basics on training and dog care and even found space to list some useful websites. All this for £2.99! No fewer than 148 dogs are listed to be spotted. I was immediately hooked – like the proverbial dog with two whatsits just at the thought of it.

I couldn't help winding Tom up.

'This is easy – I've already seen most of them,' I said.

'Well it starts today, so that won't count,' said Tom.

'Okay, then, Crufts is coming up soon, so I'll get them all there,' I tried.

'That won't count either,' replied my resolute son, with a tinge of menace, I thought.

It was soon clear that we needed some ground rules for this challenge and they became the subject for some negotiation over the rest of the day.

In the end we agreed that:

- This was 'day zero' – dogs seen previously didn't count (I was gutted because I had just had a Bassett Griffon Vendeen in one of my training classes and probably wouldn't get another one for ages, if ever).
- A maximum of five dogs could be seen at Crufts.
- Dogs I trained would get an asterisk as well as a tick (this of course had no purpose or benefit, but it made me feel better and Tom was wise enough to spot that this concession cost him nothing).
- Wherever possible I should get someone to confirm my sighting, a photo or other evidence (I thought this was going a bit far and suggested full-blown DNA profiles, but Tom pointed out that sarcasm was the lowest form of wit).

Still, I was confident. I spend a lot of time with dogs – running a couple of training classes a week, attending some shows and helping to run others, walking my own three dogs and grooming quite a few in addition. In fact, dogs are a huge part of my life. Quite simply, they are my survival mechanism for a day job spent in a potential Kafkaesque nightmare of bureaucratic life.

So, I was pretty confident that this challenge would be easy – until I took a closer look at the list. Most of the old familiars were there, German shepherd dog (known as an 'Alsatian' when I was a kid and the 'devil dog' of the press before the Doberman and the Rottweiler became popular), the boxer, the cocker spaniel and so on. But where had this list come from? Certainly not the Kennel Club – where was I going to see a Griffon Brabancon or a Large Münsterlander … and what the hell was a *Drentsche Patrijshond* …?

CHAPTER 2

Teaching People, Teaching Dogs

My day job is to train humans – well, lawyers, anyway. In the evening and at weekends I teach people to teach their dogs. Both very satisfying and guess which one I prefer?

I generally avoid calling myself a dog-trainer, not least because of the tweed-skirted images the term puts in people's minds – and that's strictly my private stuff I don't want them thinking about. I also think the title is a bit misleading. Unsurprisingly, people think it means that I train *dogs*. I don't though, not really. My whole aim is to teach owners to train their own dogs. After the initial two-hour session in the owner's home, I actually do very little training with any particular dog – I leave it to the owners. What good is it if the dog does things for me and not for them?

To be honest, alarm bells tend to ring when I answer the phone and someone says (normally either hysterical or at least panting heavily), 'I've got a dog I want you to train'. Often, it's just the way they have worded it, but I do need to make sure that their expectations are realistic and that they will be met – i.e. that *they* will be training their dog and it will be what they do between the classes with me that will determine their success.

Sometimes, people will have been told all sorts of things about their dog and start off with all manner of negative preconceptions about their dogs, which will just get in their way. They will start the call with 'I know you can't train a shih tzu

/chow/bulldog/bull terrier (delete as applicable), but I have a twelve-week-old puppy and I need some help…' It always upsets me when I hear that sort of thing, especially as it has often been put into their heads almost proudly by the puppy's breeders and others 'in the breed'. Perhaps these people haven't really tried to 'train' their own dogs or maybe they have used completely inappropriate, probably force-based methods and failed. Worse still, it's sometimes other trainers who have put this in their heads – presumably competitive types in body warmers and combat trousers with Border collies, German shepherds or other canine 'high performers' glued to their leg, who then look down on all other breeds.

My own aims are pretty modest. I only really offer basic 'good manners' training – sit, down, stay, walking on a loose lead, manners through the doorway, letting go of objects and so on. And yet these basic things are apparently exactly the things that a lot of breeds 'won't do'.

In fact, the reason I first got involved in dog training is that I want all dogs to have homes where they are relaxed and happy because their owners are relaxed and happy with them – which means that they must be able to do these basics. From this point of view at least, it's a real disservice to these breeds to say they won't be able to manage it. Can you imagine the scandal if you said these things about particular races of humans? ('Well, of course he's French, so he won't be able to work for more than 10 minutes at a time without a break.') Come to think of it, though…

People do forget that breeds of dogs have been developed for particular reasons and with different jobs in mind over many generations. It follows then that you might have to take a different approach with these different breeds, taking their anatomy into account, and treating each dog as an individual (there are, after all, huge variations in personality between dogs of the same breed), but to say that 'they can't be trained' is just not true. It makes me wonder how many people don't even try (and maybe end up getting rid of the dog because they can't cope) because their heads have been filled with this nonsense?

One frightening fact spurred me on to offer training classes: by far the greatest reason for young dogs to die is lethal injection because their behaviour is inappropriate. This is usually due to a lack of socialisation and/or training.

Right, now that I've got that righteous indignation out of my system, let's have some fun with stereotyping. We all love it really, don't we? You are no doubt familiar with the 'light bulb' jokes? You know: 'How many psychiatrists does it take to change a light bulb? One, but the light bulb must want to change.' 'How many surrealists does it take to change a light bulb? A fish.' 'How many PE teachers does it take to change a light bulb? Ten – one to hold the light bulb and nine to rotate the ladder.' Well, these are in circulation about dog breeds, too. Now although it's never the sign of a good joke that you have to explain it, I'll put one or two words after each answer to tell you which breed characteristic is being teased.

So, how many of each breed does it take to change a light bulb?

Labrador: 'Oh me, me!! Pleeeeeeze let me change the light bulb! Can I? Huh? Huh? Huh? Can I?? (Very enthusiastic and eager to please)

Dachshund: 'You know I can't reach that damned stupid lamp!' (Testy, with short legs!)

Border collie: 'Just one, and then I'll replace any wiring that's not up to standard.' (Extremely clever workaholic)

Poodle: 'I'll just blow in the Border collie's ear and he'll do it.

By the time he finishes rewiring the house my nails will be dry.' (Glamour puss, manipulative)

Greyhound: 'It isn't moving, so who cares?' (Chase-stimulated, otherwise lazy)

Boxer: 'Who cares, I can still play with my toys in the dark!' (Clown with little interest in anything but fun and play)

Golden retriever: 'The sun is shining, the day is young, we've got our whole lives ahead of us and you're wasting your time inside, worrying about a light bulb?' (Live life to the full, enjoy the moment)

Rottweiler: 'Make me!' (Tough and potentially aggressive)

Irish setter: 'It only takes one, but it will put in a really dim bulb!' (Not the brightest light in the firmament)

Afghan hound: 'What light bulb?' (Even dimmer)

Pomeranian: 'I don't change light bulbs but I'll ask my agent to get a German shepherd in to do it while I'm out.' (Arrogant and bossy)

Jack Russell terrier: 'Two, but the job never gets done – they just keep arguing about who is doing it and how it's supposed to be done.' (Argumentative, likes a scrap)

Springer spaniel: 'Light bulb? That thing I just ate was a light bulb?' (Lives in the moment, acts before thinking. Full of beans)

And so it goes on…

People often ask me what the most intelligent type of dog is and I really don't know where to start. I'm big on the idea of multiple intelligences for people and dogs. A bloodhound is often considered stupid, but can track someone or something for days and miles. Isn't that a form of intelligence? How do you measure intelligence anyway? In people it seems to be a narrow measure of language and number ability – not allowing for the intelligence of a great sculptor or even a footballer who can look up for a split second and use his body and spatial awareness to plant a ball on the foot of a team-mate 70 yards away. There are now (primarily fun) IQ tests for dogs and some more serious books around. Stanley Coren's *The Intelligence of Dogs* is quite learned. Melissa Miller's *The Definitive IQ Test For Dogs* offers a whole batch of tests to do with dogs. (Don't tell Tony Blair; he'll have league tables for dogs at 3, 6, 9 and 24 months before you can say 'meaningless exercise in bureaucracy.') You can even buy little test kits with exercises and a stopwatch now to test your dogs with. The trouble is, my three always come out as canine geniuses. Of course, you do your best for your dogs, give them everything you can in life and just hope that they follow after you…

I have two collie crosses: Jake, who is 15 and crossed with a Springer spaniel (a high- octane mix!), and Molly, who is 11 and is crossed with probably a bulky terrier type of dog. They are both rescues. Finally, I have Stan, an 8-year-old pedigree Border collie. Stan's education has even included Tom and me buying him a poster showing different breeds of sheep, which we pinned to the wall for several weeks at his eye level. Ungrateful as he was, he paid next to no attention to it and yet still comes out as a genius. Jake, incidentally, is now largely blind (apparently his view of the world is like permanently peering through the frosted glass of a bathroom window, not that I would know what that was like), largely deaf (although I really suspect this to be 'cognitive' rather than physical deafness, in other words he just can't be arsed) and he's had any number of operations to remove suspicious growths. And yet, just like some of those orange-disabled-badge-holders at

Tesco, he can still outsprint you to the doors of the shop when they open on Christmas Eve. One thing is for sure: crossbreeds and mongrels are at least as intelligent as pedigree dogs (and a damn sight healthier).

Another top question is: 'is it better to have a dog or a bitch?' I don't know. Is it better to have a BMW or a Mercedes? Is petrol better than diesel? It depends what you want and there is no general answer. It has to be an individual discussion and decision. For my part it is always worth having at least one female, though, so you can get up at work and say with impunity things like 'I'm going home to work my bitch.' I just need some bling now.

I run three or four classes per week, depending on demand and the time of the year. Everyone who comes to the class gets a home visit for a couple of hours first. This means that I go into about 150 homes each year. It's like an extended version of *Through the Keyhole*. Perhaps unsurprisingly, the dog's behaviour is usually a reflection of the way in which the people live with and interact with each other. Where the kids run the household, so does the dog. Where people are calm in their language and manner, so is the dog. It's just fascinating. I remember watching a dog training programme on Channel 4, *It's Me or the Dog*, followed by *Supernanny*, where an expert helps a family to deal with 'problem' children. You could have just swapped the presenters and the commentary from one to the other and got equally impressive results.

Happily, there were no such problems with my current classes. It was not long after I had taken on Tom's challenge that I received not one but two calls from owners of bulldog puppies. I was really pleased – I love bulldogs. People often tell me that their faces are ugly. I just can't see it – in fact when I see them I have to restrain myself from squidging their faces and giving them a big hug. When I got the calls I was also pretty pathetic in being delighted because this would allow me not just a tick but also an asterisk next to the bulldog in my *Spotter's Guide*, according to the rules agreed with Tom.

Morgan lived in a house with three other bulldogs and an awful lot of bulldog memorabilia – statues, pictures, cushions, even soft toys. Because the house was in the Black Country I didn't just get offered a cup of tea, but also a piece of cake and sandwich of my choice. They're always amazing, welcoming people in that part of the world. Morgan was 15 weeks old and had that permanently sad expression of the breed. He was broad already – but nothing compared to the other members of his new bulldog family who seemed to be as wide as they were long. Morgan was a light brindle in coat colour. He was also fairly far up the scale of the 'stubborn/can't be trained' stereotype!

How different little Arnie was. He was a 'red' bulldog – that's brownish to you and me by the way, not the colour of a pillar box. He was quite 'petite', although only three weeks younger than Morgan. He was narrower and, to be honest, able to move a lot more easily than Morgan, who already waddled and laboured his way around, panting as he went. He was also a lot more 'biddable' – quick to respond and keen to learn. Both were absolutely beautiful dogs, but how different these two dogs of the same breed were – in appearance and conformation and their early behaviour. Arnie was more like a picture of the breed from thirty years ago.

In fact, the bulldog is one of many breeds 'enjoying' the close scrutiny of Europe at the moment. Much as I hate to admit it, I have to say that you can see Europe's point of view this time. It may be that 'those Eurocrats meddling with our breeds' and particularly the bulldog, that very symbol of Britishness, rankles with us, but is what they're trying to do really so bad?

For years now the Council of Europe has been trying to bring in The European Convention for the Protection of Pet Animals. Some countries have signed up, but (not unusually) the UK has not. The Convention sets out basic principles for the keeping of pet animals – such as not abandoning them, not causing unnecessary pain or suffering, giving them food, water, exercise and so on. All pretty uncontroversial so far.

Where it seems to have caught people's interest and caused a bit of a furore, though, is in the section on breeding and on surgical operations. With regard to breeding, the convention states (Article 5): 'Any person who selects a pet animal for breeding, shall be responsible for having regard to the anatomical, physiological and behavioural characteristics which are likely to put at risk the health and welfare of either the offspring or female parent.'

Again, you're probably thinking, like me, that this does not seem unreasonable. What's the problem, then?

Well, taking the bulldog as an example, over the years through selective breeding (often done to emphasise the 'bulldogness' of the bulldog), exaggerations have taken place which mean it is often no longer possible for a bitch to give birth naturally. The puppy's head is too big in proportion – and delivery has to be by caesarean section. Probably, like me, this makes you wonder how on earth we could have let this happen.

At least part of the responsibility for this must lie with the 'breed standard', in effect a blueprint for what the breed should look like and, to some extent, behave like. Judges judge dogs in dog shows against their own interpretation of the breed standard. Prior to 1988 the breed standard for the bulldog almost made exaggeration a plus point, in fact a necessity. For the head, the standard used to say 'the bigger the better'. Quite a clear message there, then – if you wanted to succeed with bulldogs in the dog world there was only one way to go.

As recently as September 2003, further revisions have been made to the standard to modify this position. I think I smell a garlic-scented rat. It is surely no coincidence that this should happen when the EU was showing so much interest in breeding in the form of the European Convention for Pet Animals.

It's not just the size of the head which poses a problem for bulldogs, though. There are eye problems such as 'cherry eye', which is a red swelling on the third eyelid and is treated by removal under local anaesthetic. Also in the eye, there are problems with 'tear stains', brown stains on the dog's face caused by faulty drainage in the eyes. Then there is the double whammy of 'ectopian', a condition where the lower eyelid turns outwards exposing the conjunctiva, causing the eyes to water continuously and for which the treatment is surgery. The other half of the double whammy is a condition called 'entropian', where the eyelid this time turns inwards causing the eyelashes to rub against the cornea, leading to corneal ulcers.

If you are Churchill the bulldog, though, your potential problems don't end there. There are also breathing problems to be dealt with, such as Brachycephalic (short face) Syndrome. This is a term for chronic airway obstruction caused by constricted nostrils, excessive tissue in the mouth and pharynx, crowded nasal cavities, an elongated soft palate or an underdeveloped trachea. If a dog suffers from this, symptoms include the dog regurgitating food and bringing up frothy mucus. Unfortunately, the condition is made worse by factors such as stress and heat. This is because the dog is simply not able to reduce its body heat, resulting in a cycle of increasing breathlessness and even, in the worst case, death.

In addition, Churchill can have problems with the tail and the skin, where eczema can occur.

Of course, I'm not suggesting that these conditions will occur in every bulldog. The most experienced breeders and owners may well be able to avoid any or many of these problems – but the fact is that these dogs are not bred or owned only by the most fastidious.

This is not a new problem. These dogs were originally intended for bull-baiting, but when this was outlawed in 1835 the breed found a new life as a companion and a show dog. Even as early as 1927, one writer on dogs, Edward Ash, was writing in *Dogs: Their History and Development* that 'characteristics desired at earlier times for fighting and baiting purposes were exaggerated so that the unfortunate dog became unhappily abnormal. In this translation state, huge, broad, ungainly heads were obtained, legs widely bowed were developed and frequently the dog was a cripple.'

This wasn't the end of it, though, and other features began to be overemphasised and exaggerated, including the wrinkles on the face (originally intended to channel the baited bull's blood away from the dog's eyes), the shape of the face (originally allowing the dog to breathe while holding on to the bull's nose) and the loose skin on the body (originally intended to protect the dog's internal organs). You can see many links between these factors and the medical conditions listed earlier. Put simply, if you breed primarily for one characteristic, statistically you are much more likely to have an adverse effect on others, whether they be related to health or temperament.

The UK Government is currently looking at animal welfare matters in general and has decided to include the Convention in those discussions. The Kennel Club has been keen to meet with the relevant Government Department and to emphasise the work on 'voluntary' revision of Breed Standards, no doubt hoping that voluntary self-regulation will fend off the need for signing up to the Convention.

Changing breed standards and 'educating' breeders is something which the Convention is keen on, to the extent that if this is not done or if this does not work, there is a suggestion that the breeding and selling of certain types of breeds with harmful defects should be banned.

The sorts of revision to breed standards which the Convention wants to see are:

- Setting maximum/minimum values for height and weight for very large or very small dogs (to prevent joint problems).
- Setting maximum values for the proportion between length and height of short-legged dogs (such as the dachshund) to avoid vertebral problems.

And

- Preventing the occurrence of abnormal position of teeth and eyes, and markedly folded skin (to avoid skin infections).

As you would probably expect from any other area of life, there are always interest groups with opposing views. The main group working against the Convention – Save Our Breeds – would have us believe that 'The Convention wants us to breed only one euro style dog!'

They list 107 breeds as being affected by the Convention's provisions. In reality, though, this is pretty alarmist stuff, as 55 of these 107 are affected by a ban on tail-docking alone and a further 22 by a ban on the removal of dewclaws alone (the additional claw on the inside of – usually – the front leg). This leaves around 30 dog breeds with a 'named fault'.

I suppose my argument is that, if you really love dogs and want what is best for them rather than for yourself, is it really so awful to have pressure put on breeders and breed clubs to change breed standards which lead, no doubt unintentionally, to dogs that cannot give birth naturally, dogs whose joints degenerate leading to pain and arthritis, whose skin is so wrinkled that it leads to soreness and infection, to dogs with eyelashes growing inwards and rubbing on the eyeball – just to name a few of these conditions?

And yet Save Our Breeds makes the comment, after listing some of these apparently unconcerning problems, 'what would happen to pedigree and working dogs in the UK if the above was adopted? We dread to imagine.'

I can't help reading that comment with a certain amount of irony. Of course, the ideal is that, under fear of legislation, sensible revisions and changes are made to the breeding of some of these dogs on a voluntary basis. Quite rightly, there is a fear of legislation after the many ludicrous problems caused by the poorly drafted Dangerous Dogs Act.

So, by now, you've probably gone off the idea of a bulldog. Maybe you'll go for something a little more exotic-sounding? Well, don't think that this is a problem only for the 'British breeds'. Let's just take a moment to consider the Chihuahua.

The Chihuahua is a very small dog which most people would recognise – weighing a maximum of only 6 lbs (2.7 kg). Some of the potential health problems the breed has – resulting from selective breeding for miniaturisation, appearance and temperament – are collapse of the trachea again, patellar luxation, pulmonary artery sterosis and hydrocephalus.

Tracheal collapse happens in a number of toy breeds. The trachea is the large upper airway or windpipe. Collapse can appear in the first instance as an intermittent cough or, more alarmingly, as an extreme difficulty in breathing and an intolerance to exercise. This is a truly debilitating condition.

The next condition, patellar luxation is also known as 'trick knee'. It is an orthopaedic condition and it causes the dog to carry its rear leg abnormally. It is a largely inherited condition, where rotation and bowing of the shinbones allow the patella (the kneecap) to slip out of its groove towards the inside of the leg. As you can imagine, this leads to lameness, pain and arthritic conditions. As far as treatment is concerned, depending on the severity of the condition, drugs can be used or surgery may be required.

Another potentially inherited condition is narrowing (stenosis) of the pulmonary artery. This restricts blood flow to the lungs, especially when the dog is exercising. In severe cases the dog's stamina is affected, breathing can be difficult and fluid can be retained in the abdomen. Heart failure can result. Nice, eh?

Perhaps the worst of all of these potential Chihuahua health problems though is hydrocephalus (water on the brain). This is a condition which affects many of the toy breeds, but notably the Chihuahua. Depending on what you read and whom you ask, this is definitely or definitely not linked to the presence of a permanent soft spot on the top of the head (like human babies have) called a fontanelle. Whilst some experts claim there is no link between this and hydrocephalus, others say that there is! What appears to be the case, however, is that selective breeding for appearance and temperament has given this particular little dog an increased risk of developing hydrocephalus.

The effect of this abnormal accumulation of fluid in the brain may or may not be apparently obvious. When it is severe, a Chihuahua puppy may have a sphere-shaped skull, with eyes pointing outwards. It may be depressed, have fits or seizures or show odd behaviour. The dog may walk abnormally or even be paralysed. In other cases, the condition may only become apparent after an accident or other trauma.

Diagnosis of the condition has to be by ultrasound, CAT

scan (ironically for a dog) or other advanced method. Treatment can then be by drug treatment or even surgical drainage of excess fluid.

The Chihuahua gets a special mention in the European Convention for the Protection of Pet Animals, which calls for a revision of breed policies to 'prevent the occurrence of a persistent fontella (e.g. Chihuahua) to avoid brain damage'. Currently the breed standard calls for a 'well-rounded, apple-dome skull' and so it could be argued that an inappropriate focus on achieving this may inadvertently have contributed to the breed's problems in this area.

Hydrocephalus is a congenital disease and dogs with the condition, or dogs who have a family history of hydrocephalus, should not be used for breeding. This in itself would go a very long way to eradicating the problem.

Not surprisingly, breeders get very angry with all of this. They will say that reputable breeders work hard to screen out these problems and breed carefully. Still, the fact remains that by selective breeding for particular attributes – the shortest nose, wrinkled skin, most 'apple-domed' skull (Chihuahua) – features have been bred into dogs that have been very damaging to them. As a dog-lover I think that the health and welfare of the dog – whatever breed – surely has to come before the collection of rosettes, trophies and 'tickets' (challenge certificates leading to champion status).

What is more, I just wonder how many puppies are bred and discarded in one way or another before the right 'show' specimen is found? Remember, these breeds are the creation of man, from originally very limited genetic stock. There is nothing 'pure bred' about them – all breeds have been created by picking dogs for attributes and crossing them. In truth, all dogs are mongrels! Some committee deciding that a dog is now a 'breed' doesn't change that.

I've got to say that I love dog shows. I love all the 'breeds' and the diversity of dogs. I always love Crufts and go to Best in Show. I help to organise dog shows. Even so, it's absolutely clear to me that the well-being of every individual dog has to come first. If that demands some radical action to stop breeding dogs that cannot give birth naturally, suckle from their mother, breathe, see and hear, then bring it on. Breeders and fanciers have rights, of course, but how do these match up with the dog's right to exercise even moderately without collapsing? Or to blink without damaging their eyes?

Steps to improve the situation are being taken by the Kennel Club and different breed clubs and associations. The problem is, though, that there are so many vested interests in keeping things fundamentally as they are and many of these people are in denial, refusing to face up to the problems in front of them. If it takes a scare from Europe to make people think hard about breeding dogs with a length of back which is so extreme that slipped disks regularly occur, causing pain and requiring surgery, then I'm not sure that's such a bad thing!

Anyway, back to the training class with Arnie and Morgan the bulldogs. In this particular class was a little shih tzu (no jokes please!) called Daisy, two beautiful crossbreeds called Henry and Monty, a Labrador (my most popular customer) called Tessa and a splendid Rottweiler pup called Tia. (Oh, OK then, seeing as you asked, 'what do you get if you cross a bulldog with a shih tzu? Yes, you guessed it: a bullshit!)

People's reactions are funny. Even now, I see grown men blanch at the word 'Rottweiler' and yet those Rotties who have attended my classes have been really clever, gentle giants with none of the characteristics attributed to them by the 'devil dog' stories in the press over recent years. Of course they can be made aggressive and, yes, there can be a tendency for the wrong type of owner to be attracted to them, but this certainly doesn't make the breed bad, just what some people do to it and with it.

So, just a few days after I took on the challenge, I had a few ticks in my book and even some crosses, so I was off to a good start in achieving Tom's challenge … only about 140 breeds to go …

Having got this heavy stuff on my chest, I'd think I better go and have a lie down… Meanwhile, here are:

Ten Favourite Dogs I've Trained:

I'm bound to have forgotten some fantastic dogs and it's a bit off to choose between them all anyway, but what the hell, here are some favourites:

1 Ojay

Ojay was an enormous Dalmatian. He had lived with a disabled lady for ten years before being re-homed on her death. He was like a barrel, the size of a small horse. He had been overfed and never been out for a walk. Alongside his size, the other consequence of his lifestyle was that he couldn't deal with other dogs at all and exhibited that classic mix of fear and aggression.

His new owners were moving to Wales to open a Bed and Breakfast and wanted to be able to welcome guests and their dogs peaceably. This was quite a challenge. Still, Ojay proved that you can teach an old dog new tricks. We worked hard using the clicker and treats to associate the presence of other dogs with lovely rewards rather than fear. Over the weeks he began to meet the other dogs, move around them at a distance and ultimately weave in and out of them happily.

It was a really brilliant result and fantastic to see. Ojay had a new life and his owners were optimistic about their new business.

2 Bronson

Bronson was quite a different dog. He was a beautiful black adolescent Staffordshire bull terrier. His coat shone with health and his muscles rippled under the skin. He didn't walk, he swaggered. I feared the worst when I met his owners – a couple in their late teens.

Working with Bronson and his owners was a true pleasure. They were kind but firm and did everything I asked them to. Bronson was a fantastic dog – when he went into the down the whole hall would shake with the force of him hitting the floorboards!

He was a friendly and playful dog with people and tolerant of other dogs. One particular cocker spaniel pushed his luck with Bronson on an outdoor session and I had to intervene. The spaniel's owner really couldn't see that Bronson was feeling stressed – putting up with being jumped on and nipped.

Bronson was a wonderful ambassador for his breed and showed why some Staffies do so well in formal obedience. That didn't mean you could 'take the Mick' with him, though.

Shortly after Bronson had finished his training I got a call from the couple's sister-in-law, wanting me to work with their massive bull mastiff, Bailey. That dog turned out to be great to work with, too.

3 Daisy

Now not being personal, but Daisy was a little shih tzu. I had never been particularly attracted to these furry little dogs, but Daisy certainly wasn't a lazy little lapdog. If she'd been the size of a German shepherd or Rottweiler she'd have been terrifying! She was all spirit and 100% dog.

Daisy was also incredibly intelligent – quicker on the

update than her owner, certainly a confident little dog who soaked up learning like a sponge. Her larger than life attitude just had to be channelled appropriately. I still have a picture of Daisy sitting on the grass in her outdoor session. The photo makes it look like she was wearing a nearby dandelion in her hair. Nothing would have surprised me.

Tragically, Daisy died at about 18 months old. It wasn't just her owner, Elaine, that was heartbroken.

4 Alfie

Alfie was a big, boisterous Weimaraner – a large, powerful, multi-purpose hunting dog. These can be a real handful. Alfie was a lot more biddable than most but maintained his 'clown' personality throughout. He was one of those dogs who always shows the trainer up by not doing a single thing he's asked to when demonstrating! Still, he did everything for Mum, Dad and the kids, so that was the main thing.

His strangest foible, though, was his refusal to work for the all-conquering baked pig's liver. He also then turned his nose up at little pieces of cheese and sausage. Dog treats and doggy choc drops got me nowhere.

Luckily, the youngest daughter of the family had Alfie weighed up. She found out exactly which treat to use in the early days and – this is the absolute truth – Alfie turned up with a packet of cheesy Wotsits every week and got straight down to work.

5 Millie

Millie was a puppy West Highland white terrier (Westie). She was a 'we'll have to let her go if we can't sort her out soon' dog. The sort of call that really bothers me. I know I shouldn't fall for emotional blackmail, but I sometimes do.

Basically, Millie was with a couple with a young family who had found themselves in a real catch-22 situation.

When Millie was in the house with the family she was like a little tornado – over-excited, running around, nipping, weeing on the floor, jumping up on people and furniture. The family was soon tired of this and put her in her own area (utility room and garden) very quickly.

This, of course, meant that the next time she came in she was so excited to see people and be in strange places that she reacted even more excitedly, so that she was then put out again. The real problem was that her owners didn't really know what to do with her when she did come in.

This was one of the most satisfying visits I've ever done. We introduced Millie – who was an incredibly quick learner – to the clicker and taught her some basic sits and downs, gradually adding a little time in each. To start with, we did a little on the lead, but soon took that off.

There was no looking back. From nearly being at the end of their tether, over the next few weeks of the course, Millie's owners became so proud of their dog and huge advocates of dog ownership – Millie was a real star.

Annoyingly, they seemed to forget how desperate they had been and thought all this dog-owning lark was very easy! Still, you shouldn't be a dog trainer if you want thanks!

6 Barnum and Bailey

This is a cheat, since (as you will have noticed) there were two of these Standard poodles (those are the big ones).

Bailey was the colour of Bailey's Irish Cream. Barnum (so named, very appropriately as it turned out, to complete the name of the circus act) was jet black. These were two very big dogs and were litter brothers. They were also both entire (not castrated). Often, having two entire males this close in the hierarchy can lead to serious fighting. There was no sign of this in these two, even though you could almost smell the testosterone when they were around.

These two big dogs were owned by a lovely retired couple who (thankfully) found everything in life very funny. The pair of them coming through the hall doors was like a cyclone arriving! They had taken on the poodles as they had always had German shepherd dogs (Alsatians) and wanted a quieter life!

These dogs were a handful, but through perseverance and good humour a lot was achieved. In fact, they came back for more and shone like little (well, big) stars through the more advanced class, earning a Kennel Club Good Citizen Award.

7 Phoebe

I first met Phoebe when she was just about 12 weeks old. She was a lovely chocolate Labrador. The family consisted of Mum and Dad and a ten-year-old daughter.

From the beginning this family was completely consistent with their pet, setting boundaries and making rules for the puppy to live by. They really enjoyed the home session, asking loads of questions.

I never doubted that Phoebe would be a complete star, taught with calmness, love and consistency. The folks always put the time in and did everything asked of them and more. They got the dog they deserved – an excellent family pet.

8 Brizo

Brizo was an extremely heavy, well-built, muscle-laden Rottweiler.

It's always a relief when you get to meet these dogs and find that the owners are sensible and well intentioned. The worst thing about Brizo, in fact, was his best friend, a 15-foot python. Even with him in his tank I had to ask to do the home visit in a different room.

Brizo turned out to be a real gentle giant. He picked things up really quickly, always responded (in time) and used to go into the down with a big sigh and huge, slightly watery eyes.

You just knew that if Brizo were human, he'd be really good company in the pub and he'd always get his round in.

9 Beau

Beau was a rescued lurcher – about 3 years old. He was quite a slight dog, whose ribs you could clearly see through the flesh. This is not usual with these dogs, though. He was really happy lying in front of an open fire. He didn't want much more out of life.

He was very laid back and a gentle soul. He wasn't the most obedient dog, but learnt quickly through gentle training (any sign of force and this dog would have disappeared inside himself).

His owners were looking to retire to the country. One little request they had was that their dog should bark when someone came to the door instead of standing there like a chilled-out dude. The problem was, Beau never barked.

We had to spend ages getting him really excited with a toy before he would bark at all. When he barked, we marked it with a 'click' and a treat and then began to label it with the word 'speak'.

On the last night of his course, Beau came in in his normal quiet way. 'Dad' told everyone that Beau had something to show us all. On the command 'speak', Beau let out two loud barks. Everyone was delighted.

At least now Beau could be sent to the front door and be told to 'speak' even if he was never going to bark of his own accord.

10 Archie and Amber

Archie and Amber were two Border terrier puppies. By chance, although the owners didn't know each other, they ended up in the same class and it turned out that they were litter brother and sister. Young children were involved in the training of them both – fantastic kids who were consistent and calm with their dogs. One of the two sisters was just 6 years old. The parents were always there, of course, but the kids did all the training in the classes and practised hard in between. Seeing the dogs with the kids was great – watching the relationship between them grow and the confidence of both the kids and the dogs grow by the week.

By the end of the course the families had become good friends – round each other's homes, holding barbecues, even talk of holidays together.

Those dogs did so well on the course and became outstanding family pets. What a fantastic example of what owning a dog should all be about.

CHAPTER 3

Looking out of the Window

I had had sinus problems for as long as I could remember – certainly for 20 years, back to university, where my whole head used to swell up ready to explode in one particular week of November every year! It was meant to be a 'reading week', time to catch up on all the reading and study you should have done, but for me it was just a week of pain.

Certainly for the last ten years, head pain had been fairly constant. At its worst it was like a vice attached across the bridge of the nose and right over the top of the skull and then tightened … and then tightened. It wasn't always like that – sometimes it was just a dull, heavy ache. It was like carrying a brick around in your head. Some days, of course, were worse than others – particularly days requiring a lot of concentration, like long drives or days when I was delivering stand-up training at work. A whole day of that and I would be in great discomfort. At least, though, I had begun to recognise the onset and take Ibuprofen. Often, though, this had no effect at all and I had in any case always been brought up not to take tablets unless I really, really needed to, so I didn't tend to bother.

I had tried all of those tablets where the TV adverts seemed to describe exactly how I was feeling with graphic, great big, red throbbing heads and huge arrows pointing to the areas of pain and congestion. No effect – or at least only sometimes. A good old-fashioned pharmacist suggested steam treatment – sitting over a bowl of boiling water with a towel over my head.

Sometimes that would help, but not often.

One day, blowing my nose I noticed what looked like a small carrier bag hanging out – quite disgusting! My first instinct was to want to vomit. Then I became intrigued and began to poke and prod it, as you do. At the same time I had been having flu-like symptoms and had not been able to control my temperature for a week or more.

I didn't see my usual doctor. I saw the senior partner. He had a reputation as a 'pull yourself together' type and spoke in a deep public school accent – totally incongruous in the area he served. He didn't even ask me what the problem was. He only had to look at me. 'My goodness!' he said, seeming to enjoy every moment, 'I've never seen one that size!'

It was a nasal polyp. Apparently I needed to see a consultant and that should be possible in about six months' time. Oh, and I had a nasty infection that he could deal with.

Seven days later, though, courtesy of the private medical cover provided by my employer which I had never used, I was in a plush waiting room, sipping café latte and reading a complimentary newspaper. I wasn't once hit on the head by a plastic car hurled at his mother by a bored and bawling Damian, Dwain or Jason. No sign, either, of the social club of regulars you normally encounter in a doctor's waiting room.

Another seven days and I was in a private hospital having a veritable garden of polyps removed from both nostrils. The consultant had been very entertained by the doctor's letter about the 'enormous polyp' which, he said, reminded him of the 'Enormous Turnip' story which he was reading to his children. A terrible image had come into my head of a whole line of masked and gowned medical staff, stretching down the corridor, pulling each other with the consultant at the front trying to pull the polyp out of my nasal cavity.

The op itself was clearly much less spectacular. I walked

down to the theatre, flashing attractive paper pants through the gap at the back of my gown. I knew no-one here but suddenly recognised one of the nurses. Her name was Dawn and I had helped her train her two Dalmatians. Lovely dogs and excellent owners.

The next thing I knew I was coming round in the recovery room, gibbering and talking rubbish. 'There we are, then, Peter. That's it. We'll get one of the nurses to take you back down to your room.' These were the words of a kindly, matronly nurse who was bringing me back round.

I suddenly panicked, feeling very much alone. 'Can Dawn come and get me, please? Please can you ask Dawn to come and get me?'

I was acting like a 7-year-old. Quite pathetic and pretty embarrassing afterwards when I thought about it … If you are a woman reading this, no doubt you won't be surprised.

Needless to say, the nursing and care was excellent – except for the fact that I woke up in the night without the noise of oxygen bubbling through water and had to press the buzzer to get my oxygen replaced. This seemed to be done by Ramona from *Cold Feet* as I remember.

The hospital was, first and foremost, an orthopaedic one with lots of much greater operations than mine being performed – hip replacements and the like. Despite this, I appeared to be quite a novelty. I had cotton wool plugs stuffed up my nose, which felt as though it was the size of a small planet. Even so, blood had spilled all down the front of my gown and I had been fitted with a pad to catch the bleeding, which hung under my nose and was attached to my ears at both sides. A most bizarre-looking thing! It put me in mind of something a Victorian chap might wear while he powdered his moustache or something.

The next day consisted largely of sitting around, watching

the TV. I was too groggy to read and, according to my wife Alison, was still spouting quite a lot of rubbish. The consultant came, declared himself pleased and got the nurse to bring a cup of ice cubes. I was to suck on these and hold them against the roof of my mouth until it ached. He had a strange expression on his face when he told me that he would leave the nurse to remove the wadding in my nose. Well, I can tell you, I have never known anything like it. The inside of my nose had been scraped, had bled and attached itself to this wadding. This wadding was then pulled out. It was so condensed that the pack of about two inches was pulled and pulled until about four feet in length had come out! Now I understood what the knowing look was about … and there was another nostril to go. To be honest I nearly passed out, but it was soon done.

So, home it was, wearing my rather dashing nose bib.

I slept most of the day. In fact, I reacted quite badly to the anaesthetic and was fairly light-headed and other-worldly for the best part of a weekend. So, the next day I didn't feel like doing much. Tom's challenge, though, was very much on my mind, so I decided to see what types of dog I could see just by sitting in the front window all day.

This is easier said than done. I remember I used to have a section on one of the courses I used to run which helped people to identify whether they were 'Type A' personalities or 'Type B'. Basically, Type A cannot sit still and are on the go all the time. Type B at its most extreme is so laid-back it is horizontal. The point of this is that true Type As have a much greater risk of suffering a heart attack. One of the things the course suggested for 'Type As' was to force themselves to do nothing for a whole day. Just sit there. Well, I'm certainly no true Type A – I'm a bit of both as most people are, but just sitting all day is pretty difficult.

Another thing I found is how obsessive you can become. In your mind you always fear that what happens in the Kit Kat commercial – or is it Penguin? – will happen. You'll look away or pop to the loo or something and the most unusual dogs in the world will go by on roller skates or something. Look back and there will be another Labrador!

Now, where I've lived in the past I would probably have seen a dozen dogs a day – probably the same six dogs twice. That's not true now, though. I live on the edge of town, on a small new development. It's a close and I'm right at the end, looking outwards onto a field of wild grass and flowers which is only cut from time to time. To the left are a farmer's fields usually full of sheep, other than when they escape and come to graze on our front garden.

The 'wild' field is crossed by a couple of footpaths which continue under an underpass and then form a loop of around half a mile around a stream, a couple of ponds and landscaped areas. This is paradise not just for dog walkers, but pram pushers and trike-trundlers.

Although it is much maligned, I actually like living in a 'new' town. There are literally miles of footpaths which criss-cross the town and link the park areas without going anywhere near roads. Sure, you wouldn't really want to walk these paths at night without a dog, but everywhere else I have lived has meant walking down busy roads and streets with narrow pavements and other dogs behind gates waiting to mug you as you go past. We've even got dog poo bins on this walk, which are regularly emptied. It's a shame, though, that not everyone picks up after their dog.

In fact, while we're at it –

10 things I hate about the world of dogs:

1 People who don't clear up after their dogs.

2 Vets and others who use the dog's name with the owner's surname. 'Buster Smith?'
3 Leggings in the world of dogs – women who wear them seem to do this in directly inverse proportion to their suitability to do so. Oh my God, some of the sights, especially when they start running with their dogs!
4 People who choose dogs that are completely incompatible with their lifestyles and circumstances.
5 The Dangerous Dogs Act.
6 Dog food in bright colours and silly shapes like hearts. (Dogs are, after all, largely colour-blind and certainly don't mind what shape their food is. Those marketing people are just playing the foolhardy.)
7 Town Councils who complain about irresponsible dog ownership and then don't let dog trainers use their venues to teach people about responsible dog ownership.
8 Choke/check chains.
9 Dog snobs and dog know-it-alls.
10 People who smoke in non-smoking dog showing venues and hold their cigarette out of sight at dog-eye height.

I could go on … in fact, while we're thinking about dog poo and lowering the tone a little, one of the things I found fascinating from my sickroom window was watching toileting behaviour from dogs and their owners. Admittedly, the toileting was exclusively by the dogs on this occasion, but the owners do of course play a huge role in this. My informal survey suggests that only about one third of owners pick up after their dogs – even though there are actually bright red, conveniently placed poo bins in this area.

The normal response from the owner seems to be to pretend that they haven't noticed what their dog is doing. This is achieved by staring into the distance, as though contemplating the meaning of life. This appears to be made much easier by smoking a cigarette at the same time. Others are quite brazen and stare you out if you look at them while their dog is doing its business, just daring you to say anything.

Perhaps the oddest behaviour, though, is from those who go up to their dog's latest offering and *pretend* to pick it up. This is for the benefit of those watching from a distance. It's clearly a guilt trip of major proportions. Perhaps they are all Catholics?

As you now know, dog shite everywhere is one of my pet hates – as it is with a huge proportion of the rest of the population. Just have a guess at how much dog turd is produced in the UK each and every day? One thousand tonnes! You don't have to be a genius to work out that that is 365,000 tonnes per annum. Of course there are well-documented health risks to this – although not everyone accepts the research and risks really are minimal – especially of passing on worms and even a remote chance of blindness, particularly to children.

Of more everyday concern, though, is the magnetic relationship between dog turds and shoes – especially kids' shoes. Given the complicated tread patterns of your average £90 Nikes or whatever, this can necessitate a good hour or more with a matchstick and the unmistakable aroma of *turd du jour*.

Now, people often comment (depending on the circles you mix in) that dog turds used to be hard and white when they were kids. 'Where have all the hard white turds gone?' they ask. I think a lot of this has to do with the role of bones, which used to form a big part of dogs' diets but which no longer do so. Bones lead to that sort of poo. Don't worry, though, you can still get it if you know where to look for it. You need to find a follower of the BARF diet (Bones and Raw Food), which is being taken up by some real dog enthusiasts. Their dogs are fed on raw meaty bones and foods such as raw (definitely not cooked) entire chicken wings, bones and all. Once or twice a week they get a 'gloop' of eggs, spinach and other elements to balance their diets. You can play football with their turds.

These days, though, few dogs eat that way. It's a bit like the computer adage 'Garbage in, Garbage out' really. The cheaper, poorer foods often result in a pile of wet, sticky slop. This is particularly true of tinned foods, which can be 70 or 80% water.

A good-quality dried food can result in mess which is a joy to pick up! The best foods maintain one protein source, so the dog's stomach is settled, and uses good-quality ingredients like brown rice to fill. They also use top-quality meat – indeed it is strongly rumoured that one premium pet food manufacturer sells its chicken carcasses on, when they have taken what they want, for mechanical stripping of meat for use in human fast food!

Other cheaper foods use whatever is available to provide the 'meat and other animal derivatives' element of their food – feathers, beaks, eyes, feet: anything from different animals – and then add colourants so the food appeals to us, even making it into different little shapes, again for our benefit rather than that of the dogs. Some of this is what is most likely to result in the sloppy, semi-liquid pile of stinking gloop that young Charlie paddles through on his way home from school.

Meanwhile, it is said that one top pet food manufacturer has a team working on achieving 'a firm kickable stool' – and I don't mean what they're sitting on in their labs. Just imagine the scene when the kids grow up to that inquisitive stage and ask at the tea table, 'what do you do at work, Daddy?' 'Well, it's time I told you, son … it's like this …'

It's true to say that to the philistine, one dog laying a turd is probably like any other, but I would like to suggest otherwise.

Here are some of the styles you can expect to see, now that you have had your eyes opened and been alerted to the possibilities.

First, The Wanderer. This dog's patron saint is the singer Dion who produced a song of the same name. Indeed it includes the line 'he goes around, around, around, around around', and that's what this dog does. Not content to leave his deposit in one pile, he feels the need to spread his offering over as great a distance as possible, and sets off on a route march while neither standing nor sitting but assuming a curious position somewhere between the two.

Next, The Exhibitionist. This dog will always seek out the place which most raises his (and your) personal profile. You can walk him up and down for ten minutes outside the vet's surgery to no avail, because he's still going to squat in a crowded waiting room. You can walk him for miles in the countryside but he'll wait until you're in a long queue at the car park ticket machine before emptying his bowels. Our Jake, who is very much this brand of poo merchant, used to like to wait until the much disliked neighbours were having their tea outside on a warm summer's evening before going down the garden and making eye contact through the chain-link fence while delivering his message. Bless him.

On everyday walks, the tactic will be to wait until people come the other way, no matter how remote the area, before letting rip.

Our next dog is The Strainer. Pooing seems to come as a great surprise to him. It is almost as though there is a mismatch between his ambitions and his anal orifice. Painful to watch, this one. The legs go as far apart as possible and the dog assumes a deep squat. The tongue is pushed as far forward as possible and the eyes bulge, with the whites around the edge quite bloodshot. To watch the dog's face is to watch torture – muscles tightening and relaxing until the whole back half of the dog begins to move up and down rhythmically, while the tongue comes out even further than you ever thought possible. Not a pretty sight.

Next, The Perfectionist. This is no mere biological function for this dog, but an experience to be savoured in every aspect. If a job's worth doing then it's worth doing well, as it were. Sniffing may begin several minutes before the act is committed, searching for the perfect location. The ground cover has to be just right and of the right texture. It shouldn't be too dry, nor too damp. Wind direction has to be considered and the body will be angled accordingly, like a weather vane. Proximity of other dogs' deposits – their age, colour and bouquet – needs to be added into the equation. This is a high point of the day and to be savoured with nothing left to chance. If only he could read, he would probably enjoy a good book to make the most of the experience.

The Gourmet is a different type of dog altogether. He really sees the laying of a turd primarily as an opportunity to recycle some protein. No sooner has he dropped his offering than he will try to eat it, presumably preferring his meals warm. On the other hand, the cold buffet, left by other dogs, sheep, cats or foxes is equally delicious. Don't let him kiss you when he comes back to you. Or if you do, don't do tongues.

The Scooter is to be dealt with, with some compassion. Having offered up his gift in probably a fairly unremarkable way, his specialism really kicks in afterwards. This is to sit tight to the ground and propel himself forwards using his two front paws. If dogs had an Olympics this would no doubt be one of the top events, as great speed can be achieved. Carpet is the ideal surface as opposed to grass or other outdoor floor coverings. Canine research suggests that light beige, as supplied in most new homes, is just perfect.

In reality, the dog may be having trouble emptying his anal glands (two small sacs by the anus which should be encouraged to empty and secrete a very smelly substance by the passing of a firm, fibrous stool). If he keeps doing it, then Fido should be off to see the vet.

The Scooter can be at one and the same time The Plumber – so called because his backside is like a tap, producing a smelly sloppy mess rather than a solid poo. This poor dog will probably leave a sticky trail and, as a groomer, I dread seeming the state of the fur at the rear end.

The Businessman sees this bodily function simply as a transaction to be completed with as little fuss and use of resources as possible. Regular in his habits, his transaction is stress-free and completed no doubt in accordance with his Gantt chart and the calendar function of his personal organiser. A great dog to have, though – a pleasure to do business with!

Last, but by no means least, we have The Wallflower. He puts me in mind of Reginald Molehusband from the public information films of my childhood in that he is perfect at reversing. Wanting nothing more than to merge into the background, he will reverse into any hedge or undergrowth and make his deposit as inconspicuous as possible. He will avoid eye contact at all costs while doing so – well you do, don't you?

Back to dog-spotting in the more conventional sense (if there is one) I have to say that I found the results of my research at the window quite surprising. There were definite peaks in activity, between 7 and 8 in the morning, around lunchtime and then from about 5.30 until 7. What a range of dogs, though! There were the normal dogs – the ubiquitous

Labrador in yellow, black and chocolate together with the golden retriever. Both Springer and cocker spaniels were popular. The German shepherds came out when the owners thought they wouldn't meet anyone else. I saw a beagle, a bearded collie, a Staffie, two Rough collies (à la Lassie), a couple of Yorkshire terriers and a pair of Jack Russell terriers.

A Dalmatian was out jogging with his owner, who seemed to have a laugh and a word for everyone. Very sociable, like his dog. In fact this dog once came up to one of mine while he was squatting to evacuate his bowels. 'I don't know,' said the jogger in a thick Brummie accent, 'you can't even have a shit in peace, eh, mate?' And off he went with Pongo (I suspect) behind him.

I really saw very few crossbreeds or mongrels. Very few indeed. How things change. Everyone had crossbreeds and mongrels when I was a kid. Two out of three of mine now are mongrels.

I saw one or two dogs that did surprise me, though. The Husky would have surprised me but for the fact that I saw it every day – quite an impressive and impeccably behaved beastie. In fact, the first time I saw it, I had stopped the car to ask the owner what it was. I was pretty sure it was a Husky, but it could just about have been a Malamute. When he told me what it was, I said, 'Well, you don't see many of those around.'

In reply, he told me a Husky-handler's joke: 'Yeah, he replied, they're like London buses. You don't see one for ages and then 14 come along together!' (14 being the size of a sled dog team).

I hadn't seen the Newfoundland before, a huge, shaggy black dog with webbed toes capable of pulling in fishermens' nets in icy waters. Although the day was only mild he was clearly suffering in the heat. Even so, I had seen many

'Newfies' before, although none to qualify since I had been completing my spotter's guide.

The real surprise for me was a dog that I rarely see – a Large Münsterlander, a black and white dog from Germany with a wavy coat. In some ways it looked like a *Drentsche Patrijshond*, which I already knew could be my Achilles heel in completing my task. I needed to be sure that it was a Münsterlander and rushed (as much as I could) to fiddle with the bushes in the front garden so I could just strike up a confirming conversation with the owner as he went past.

People with unusual dogs are nearly always delighted when someone recognises their dog's breed and this man was no exception. Even when the person asking seems to be wearing a Victorian moustache bath.

I had a similar experience a few weeks later when walking in Leamington Spa town centre, where I work. Many of the Guide Dog for the Blind puppies are trained there and you get used to them walking the streets. They are generally the well-known guide dog type, with occasional German shepherd dogs and the odd Border collie. I had also once seen a curly-coated retriever. I make a point of never bothering these dogs or their handlers when they are out working.

I did make one exception, though, and this was when I was waiting to cross the road at a pelican crossing and a huge hairy dog sat down next to me. 'Wow!' I thought to myself, 'a Leonberger!' I was really shocked when I looked up and saw that he was a guide dog in training. I just had to confirm that it was indeed one of these large German dogs and asked the handler. The girl's face positively lit up: 'You're the first person who's ever got that right. Most think it's a crossbreed or a German shepherd.'

In fact the dog was created in the 1800s by crossing the Newfoundland, the Landseer, the Saint Bernard and the

Pyrenees mountain dog. (Yes, just close your eyes and imagine!)

We crossed the road and walked a few minutes together. These dogs have a reputation as gentle giants and I was very curious to hear how he was getting on. Apparently he was doing really well but was expensive to keep and, crucially, was really too big to get on and off buses. I really hope he made the grade. Still, as they weigh up to 110 lb, you can see the problem.

So, there was a good range of dogs walking past the window. To these I could add the other dogs that live in the close: a bulldog (accompanied, just like Morgan, by a wide selection of bulldog memorabilia and statuary in the window and garden), a French bulldog, an Irish red setter, another cocker spaniel and a Labrador–like crossbreed. There may be others that never venture out …

There is really a huge variety here – much, much greater than there would have been, say, 20 years ago. This is partly due to the success of campaigns to encourage neutering and round up stray dogs. When I was a child in Walsall there were always gangs of dogs roaming loose. Sometimes you would encounter these dogs on their own. Nearly always, the leader of the gang was a German shepherd (or Alsatian, as we used to call them then). The big boss where we lived was a big male German shepherd called Smokey. No-one knew who he belonged to. As a child, though, you used to cross the street if he was heading down the pavement towards you. A lot of these dogs used to go 'home' at nights and be left to roam during the day. One thing was for certain: much of the local dog population had been sired by Smokey. It was not common to neuter males or females back then, and Smokey certainly used to put it about a bit.

Now it is really rare for me to see a dog roaming – and certainly never a pack of them. There is even a waiting list for crossbreed or mongrel puppies in some areas. The other feature at work is, though, I believe the 'designer label' syndrome which seems to be an even greater feature of modern life (how many little toddlers do you see in £80 'branded' trainers, for example?) A dog used to be a companion and friend or alternatively a worker, first and foremost. Now, more and more they are a fashion statement or status symbol. According to the Kennel Club, who register all pedigree dogs, the top 20 breeds registered in 2003 were:

1 Retriever (Labrador)
2 German Shepherd Dog
3 Cocker Spaniel
4 English Springer Spaniel
5 Staffordshire Bull Terrier
6 Golden Retriever
7 Cavalier King Charles Spaniel
8 West Highland White Terrier
9 Boxer
10 Border Terrier
11 Rottweiler
12 Yorkshire Terrier
13 Lhaso Apso
14 Shih tzu
15 Doberman
16 Weimaraner
17 Bull Terrier
18 Miniature Schnauzer
19 Bulldog
20 Dalmatian

Back in 1949, the top 9 registrations were as follows:

1 Cocker Spaniel
2 Alsatian (GSD)
3 Wire-haired Fox Terrier
4 Scottish terrier
5 Corgi
6 Cairn Terrier
7 Golden Retriever
8 Bulldog
9 Irish Setter

There is not a lot of overlap, is there? Noticeably, for the most part, the 1949 consists of smaller dogs. There is also a majority of dogs with (at least theoretically) a working function.

What does this mean – if anything?

It may suggest that people were much more sensible about the size and nature of the dogs they could accommodate back then. My heart sinks sometimes when I go for a home visit and meet a Doberman in a small flat without even a garden (of course, the owner may take the dog out for long walks several times a day, but this isn't usually the case and isn't the same anyway).

Perhaps it is saying, too, that dogs were much more functional then, often kept with a specific job of work to do. I suppose it would have been a luxury to have 'pets' just after the war, after all.

Now, many people take dogs with highly developed working instincts and try to keep them as family pets, often without offering any stimulation for them. A Border collie or working sheepdog is a classic example of this. So many are bought cheaply from a litter of working farm dogs, only to chase children and joggers, to nip or to become destructive or depressed through lack of activity and stimulation. Some of the most distressing cases are dogs which go 'stir crazy' and begin to chase their tails endlessly, day after day, scratch at themselves until they bleed or chase shadows quite manically. Some end up just sitting and staring into corners.

What is really needed is advice *before* buying a dog. So often, potential problems are apparent once a puppy has been bought and advice sought, but it's just too late.

Fortunately, there are many exceptions to this, where what would in theory be a potentially disastrous combination of dog and owner in fact turns out really successful, because of the approach taken by the owner, their commitment and the chemistry between the pair.

As a group of dogs, terriers are very much on the decline. Just compare the 1949 list with 2003. Even at dog shows, there seems to be fewer and fewer terriers being entered. They certainly don't seem to be fashionable, or 'designer'-style dogs. They don't have the immediate macho presence of some of the guarding breeds (except perhaps the bull terriers). Maybe all the adverse publicity about Pitbulls has worked against terriers in general. Certainly, though, they seem to have been left behind to some extent in the trend towards larger and more fashionable dogs. Terriers were after all never the glamour dogs but originally the dogs of the working classes. This is a shame though, in my eyes, as they are some of the nicest all-round dogs I meet.

The relationship between owner and dog has certainly changed over the years. The dog is no longer generally living and sleeping outside. He or she has moved into the house – part of a multi-million-pound industry for food, toys and equipment. They are living much longer as a result of better nutrition and health care and really have become one of the family. Nowhere is this better illustrated than in the names we give our pets. When I was a child, dogs were always called Rex or King, even Rover. There was an occasional Spike and perhaps a Spot. Don't forget Smokey, of course.

These days, we have very complete data on dogs' names provided by pet insurance companies. The names we give our pets are now, broadly speaking, human ones. There is a tendency to mirror current trends in children's names. Many dog trainers will, in fact, tell you that they suspect dogs are becoming surrogate children in some cases. Not that there is anything wrong with it (as long as the relationship built is adult-human to dog and not adult-human to human-child). I certainly get a disproportionate number of young couples and newly-weds at my classes. Perhaps they are trying out their parenting skills? It is interesting that in 2003, no fewer than 13 of the top 20 dogs' names appeared in the top 20 baby names!

Here are the top 20 dogs names in 2003 according to Norwich Union:

1 Molly
2 Max
3 Charlie
4 Holly
5 Jack
6 Ben
7 Jake
8 Rosie
9 Buster
10 Meg (Megan)
11 Oscar
12 Lucy
13 Sam
14 Jess
15 Alfie
16 Millie
17 Sophie

18 Harry
19 Oliver
20 Benjamin

It's quite possible that dogs are now being treated more and more like little people. Some even have clothes, their own bedrooms and so on. It won't surprise you to know that the United States is well ahead of us in this 'pet fetishism'. The UK pet food and care market was worth £2.3 billion in 2003, whilst in the United States people spent $35 billion, which is more than was spent on children's toys. Some things which are available, like full body clothing and $400 dog beds with real linen sheets seem pretty obscene to me.

At the same time, one trend tends to point in the opposite direction, and that is the tendency towards cat ownership away from dog ownership.

This is quite a recent phenomenon. Going back to 1998, 23.4% of UK households owned a dog, compared with 21.4% owning cats. In May 2002, the BBC announced that 'Britons prefer cats to dogs' and claimed that 'man's best friend is now his cat'. They quoted figures from the Cats Protection League suggesting that there were 7.5 million cats kept in households throughout the UK, compared with 6.1 million dogs. The research further stated that the increase in cats had been from a base point of 4.9m in 1979.

Of course, the figures do not necessarily conflict with those above. It may be that people tend to own more cats per household than dogs.

Whatever the detail is, it does seem that there is a tendency towards cat ownership.

It could be argued that this is inevitable in the context of changes in lifestyle – more families where both partners go out to work, busier lives etc. You could also see all this as part of a move towards life becoming centred on the self. Seeking minimum inconvenience, not wanting to invest time and effort into another creature, nor feel responsibility for it.

High on the list of reasons for liking cats is their affectionate nature (?!), their independence and their cleanliness (in other words they dump in other people's gardens, not yours!) Many other cat owners added to this that they preferred cats because they were 'low maintenance' and the owners liked the fact that they didn't have to exercise them. It's a shame, but if that is how people feel, then as a dog-lover I'd rather they had a cat!

Just to put the record straight, I suppose I should come clean and say that I actually like cats a lot, too. It has to be said more as individual animals than as a concept, but I do really enjoy their company. I suspect that these two creatures simply appeal to different parts of our personalities and it may just depend on which part is dominant.

Whatever the situation with cats, there's no doubt that we are still failing our dogs – definitely man's best friend – in a big way. In 2002, there were still over 110,000 stray dogs in the UK, with over 10,000 put to sleep. What a terrible indictment of an animal-loving nation.

Worse still, of course, is the number of dogs that are neglected, starved, beaten or abused without being left to stray. The good news is that under the proposed Animal Welfare Bill, the RSPCA will have significantly enhanced powers to deal with suspected cruelty rather than having to return up to 25 times to a household to prove it.

Oh, and if you're thinking 'well, they're only animals,' here's one final sobering thought for you. There is a strongly proven link between abuse of animals and violence to children and others. People who do one tend to commit the other …

CHAPTER 4

Show Dogs and Dog Shows

By this stage some would say that it was all getting a bit obsessive.

When I got home, the first thing I would say to Alison was, 'Any messages?' If, as I hoped, there had been a new potential dog-training customer, my inevitable question was, 'What type of dog was it?' Almost as inevitable was the answer: 'I don't know, I didn't ask,' or (worse), 'I can't remember,' or (worse still), 'I'm not sure, I think it was some kind of spaniel.' Although good natured, the exchanges that followed containing accusations of inefficiency, lack of support or disinterest would be met with a threat of 'removal of (unpaid) secretarial services' or worse.

If I did know the breed of dog was one that I needed to 'spot', or if I didn't know what breed of dog the potential customer had got, the nature of my phone calls was beginning to change. If they did have a dog I 'needed' they could perhaps have detected a degree of desperation in my voice when I was talking to them. I'd be telling them how much I would like their dog in my class, offering times completely at their convenience for their home visit – even the sacrosanct Friday evening (quality, uninterrupted time together) – or ludicrously early or late for shift workers.

For someone whose core values include fairness and professionalism some worrying things were beginning to happen – including the manipulation of waiting-lists so that the risk of losing 'needed' dogs was minimised. What was happening?

Out and about, I had begun to engage people in conversation if I thought that their dog could be one of the breeds I needed. I would scan the park whilst walking the dogs to see what was out there. If there was a chance, any chance, that I could see a dog I wanted I would feel my stomach tighten and hear myself saying, 'get yourself over there!'

Perhaps most disturbing was my new – but fortunately only occasional – habit of stopping my car and going up to likely-looking dogs and striking up conversation with their ever-so-slightly-alarmed owners. Tom in particular would disown me when I did this, sliding down in the passenger seat and refusing to join me. Still, as far as I was concerned, it was all his fault in the first place!

My best 'catch' through this method was a Large Münsterlander. I really did have a strong suspicion that the tall, black and white, almost spaniel-like dog was one of these fairly rare dogs, but even so I nearly kissed the poor man out innocently walking his dog when he confirmed it.

By this stage of my quest, Crufts was coming up pretty soon. This was going to be a time for tactics. The rules of my challenge said I could only count five breeds at Crufts, even though I would probably see most of those on the list in my *Dog Spotter's Guide.* I say *most*, because some of those on the list are not breeds recognised by the Kennel Club so, generally, they wouldn't be at Crufts – even at the Discover Dog exhibit where individuals and families could go and meet most breeds 'live', talk to owners and breeders and make more informed puppy-buying choices. Once I had decided what five I was counting I was not allowed to change breeds in retrospect – so the thing was, which ones to choose? What was I most likely to see and not see elsewhere?

I scanned the list many times in the run-up to Crufts. Should I go for the Anatolian Karabash, the Komondor, the Kuvasz, the Estrela mountain dog, the Puli, the Vallhud, the Griffon Brabancon, Griffin Bruxellois, the Chinese crested dog, Norwegian Buhund, the Sloughi, Australian cattle dog … not to mention, of course, the *Drentsche Patrijshond*? I would just have to decide.

Dog shows are an interesting subject in themselves. I'm talking here specifically about breed shows, rather than shows held for agility or obedience competitions.

The first ever recorded dog show was held in the unlikely location of Newcastle upon Tyne Town Hall on 28th and 29th June 1859. I say *unlikely* because the judging of dogs for breed, a sort of beauty parade, seems to me to be a bit of a 'Southern Jessie' concept as opposed to judging for working ability. Perhaps that's just my prejudice coming through.

Picture the scene, then, on a warm June day in Newcastle in 1859. A very smoky hall filled predominantly with men, their pride and joy with them on a lead. This show was just for pointers and setters and there were only around sixty dogs of each breed. There were three judges in each breed. One of the judges choosing best setter was entering his dog in the pointer class and one of the judges choosing best pointer was entering his setter under the pointer-owning judge in the setter classes. Now, out of the sixty dogs in each class, I will give you one guess as to who won each. Yes, you've got it! The judge owning the setter gave Best Pointer to the dog owned by the setter judge, who in turn gave Best Setter to the dog owned by the pointer judge! Some people would say that little has changed over the last 150 years.

At the time, the show was deemed a great success and the man who had suggested the first show, Mr. R. Brailsford, got together with others to organise a show for 'sporting dogs' in

Birmingham later in the same year. This led to the formation of the oldest dog show society in the world, still going strong, the Birmingham Dog Show Society.

The following years saw the number of dog shows multiplying, as did the scandals and irregular goings-on which surrounded them. As is often the case, it was this kind of scandal and bad behaviour which led to the formation of a 'regulatory body' – in this case the Kennel Club – to make and apply rules and take control of the dog-showing scene. Central to this process was a certain Mr Sewallis Evelyn Shirley, who saw his idea come to fruition in early 1873. He became the first Chairman of the Kennel Club, a position he held for 26 years before becoming the first President for five years until his sudden death. The Kennel Club's first show took place in June 1873 at the Crystal Palace in London. From these fairly humble beginnings, a monster was created with knock-on effects all around the world.

There is a real hierarchy of dog shows today. Starting at the bottom there are the 'Companion Dog Shows', known until recently as 'Exemption Shows', because dogs not registered with the Kennel Club can take part (i.e. crossbreeds, mongrels and 'purebred' dogs without pedigree papers). Permission to hold such a show is still given by the Kennel Club and generally only a small number – up to 4 – 'pedigree' classes can be held as part of the show. Other classes can then be held for crossbreeds, for example, and for novelty classes such as 'prettiest bitch', 'best condition', 'dog the judge would most like to take home' and so on.

First and foremost, these are fun events, often part of village fêtes and other summer events or held to raise money from entry fees for a specific charity or charities.

'Serious' dog showers wouldn't be seen dead at these events, and yet they are probably the most enjoyable way of being involved in dog-showing. Combined with an ice cream for you and one for your dog and a relaxing time sitting in the sun, they can be great fun.

I took my little crossbreed Molly to literally hundreds of shows over a two- or three-year period. It became quite addictive and we were at a show most weekends in the summer. She did ever so well and we got a wall full of rosettes – and donated a lot to charity. She even won through to 'Scrufts', a sort of crossbreed equivalent to Crufts (on a *much* smaller scale), then organised by the RSPCA, and travelled down to the final in Ascot as the winner of the RSPCA's Coventry and District Show. We didn't get anywhere in the final, but that wasn't the point.

The next steps 'up' from the Companion Dog Shows are the Limited and Open shows. Limited shows are (as is suggested by their name) limited to members of a particular society, or limited perhaps to people from a specific geographical area. Often, these are quite small-scale affairs designed to give something back to the Society's own members. Sometimes they are evening shows rather than the lengthier daytime shows held normally at weekends.

Commonly, there will only be one or two judges at a limited show, so they will be perhaps judging a wide range of breeds. There is often only one ring where the show takes place, rather than multiple rings with different classes running in each. Generally, classes will be 'mixed', in other words not breed-specific. So there may be classes for 'Gundogs' or 'Any Variety Non-Sporting' and so on rather than classes for 'Cocker Spaniels'.

I am the Treasurer of a Canine Society and our Limit Show may typically see around 80-100 dogs taking part in thirty or forty classes (obviously many dogs enter into more than one class).

Our show runs from around 10 a.m. until perhaps 4 p.m., although there are typically a couple of hours before the start and after the end laying everything out, moving tables and chairs, sweeping up and tidying.

Next up the hierarchy is the 'Open Show', which is now open to all and not limited to members of the organising society. These shows are now getting to be quite big events, staged at large halls, agricultural showgrounds and the like. Showing is getting more serious now. There may well be eight or nine rings running consecutively. Judging is now of individual breeds with the less numerically popular breeds being judged in 'Any Variety' classes or 'Any Variety Not Separately Classified' classes. Some judges will only judge one breed, whilst others will judge two or three breeds.

By this stage, we're not just bundling all dogs of a breed together, but separating them by criteria, such as age.

So, typically, there may be five or six classes for a breed (many more at some shows) consisting, for example, of:

Puppy (aged 6-12 months on the day of the show)

Junior (aged 6-18 months on the day of the show)

Novice (dogs that have not won a challenge certificate or 3 or more first prizes at open shows)

Post Graduate (dogs that have not won a challenge certificate or five or more first prizes at Championship shows)

Open (all dogs of the breed)

Dogs that win these classes (unless they are beaten in other classes in which they are entered) then compete against each other for Best of Breed.

The next stage is that all of these Best of Breed winners compete against each other for 'Best in Group'.

All dog breeds are organised into one of seven 'groups', these being:

Hounds
Terriers
Toy
Working
Pastoral
Gundog, and
Utility
(Utility really sweeps up all those that don't fit elsewhere.)

So, the Best of Breed for each breed in the Group will now compete against each other for Best in Group. This then gives us seven dogs who compete against each other for the coveted Best in Show award.

To give us a size of this, the type of show I'm involved in organising has around 250 classes with around 700 dogs competing, with perhaps around 1100 entries.

Such a show is quite a major undertaking for a small committee of volunteers who have to find venues, judges, stewards, catering, car parking, buckets, rubbish bags, chairs, tables, insurance, first aid etc. Planning for the next show starts as soon as this one finishes – just like painting the Forth Bridge.

Choosing and getting hold of judges is perhaps the hardest task. They should not have judged in the area in the last 12 months. They have to be on judge lists held by the appropriate breed club. They also have to be able to attract a decent entry – or the bills simply can't be paid. No finance, no club, now shows! Some judges are simply not popular – sometimes on account of appalling interpersonal skills, or a reputation for bias or incompetence.

Things are not that straightforward, either. Judges tend to have strong preferences for a 'type' of dog. Reading this, you're probably thinking 'a dog is a dog'. Certainly one German shepherd looks much like another? Well, don't try telling an enthusiast that.

There are schisms in many breeds – the 'continental' type of German shepherd as opposed to the 'British' type. The 'British' Border collie as opposed to the Australian/New Zealand type. People know that if a judge is known to favour one type, then there's no point in entering under that judge if your dog is of another type.

At the top of the 'canine tree' is the Championship Show. Now, the price of entering a class rockets from perhaps £3/£4 to £18/£20.

The Championship Show is basically an Open show, but one where Kennel Club Challenge Certificates (often known as CCs or tickets) are on offer. If your dog wins three of these under three different judges then you can add the much sought after 'Champion' title to its name.

While we're thinking of names, it's probably worth mentioning here that breed show dogs have a normal 'pet' name and a full registered name. So, my Border collie is Stan but his full registered name (registered at the Kennel Club of course!) is Meadoways Desert Storm. Meadoways is the 'affix' of the breeder, so their dogs will always start Meadoways. Desert Storm is simply the individual name for the puppy, where one theme will often be applied to a litter. My brother's dog Henry was one of eight bloodhounds given names beginning with H behind the kennel name (and incidentally the litter appeared on *Blue Peter* because they were all liver and tan in colour – a genetic unlikelihood of enormous proportions.)

Of course, no one ever uses these registered names in the normal course of events. The 'affixes', though, are very carefully protected and must be registered with the Kennel Club. For obvious reasons, you could not use the affix of a top kennel to sell or breed from just any old dog!

I always remember being bored rigid watching *The Horse of the Year Show* on TV as a kid, thinking how ludicrous it was to watch Ted Edgar riding Sanyo Music Centre or whatever. Now, I'm part of an equally bizarre world.

At this level, competition is keen and the requirements for those acting as judges more onerous.

For some Championship Shows such as Crufts, special entry requirements are imposed – in order to control the number and standard of dogs entering. Otherwise, the show is open to all registered pedigree dogs.

So, Crufts is in reality simply a Championship Show. However, it is unique in that it is the only show actually run by the Kennel Club. All others are shows run by individual Societies, which obtain licences to do so from the Kennel Club and have to abide by a thousand and one rules and regulations in the running both of the show and indeed of the club. Crufts, though, does hold a really special place in people's hearts and it is undoubtedly the one people want to win. Technically, this may only be another 'Best in Show', but the winner is normally thought of and referred to as 'Supreme Champion'.

For Crufts, the additional entry qualifications are based on successes in other Championship shows. The specific qualification requirements are set out each year, but commonly involve finishing 1st, 2nd or 3rd in a class at a Championship Show. Obviously, it is much easier to qualify with a dog of a breed where there are comparatively few around.

10 things I love about dog shows:

1 The strong 'doggy' smell

When you walk into a show there is a really strong smell of

dogginess. I am probably one in a million, even amongst dog fans, in loving this smell.

2 The huge variety of dogs on show
Just wander around and 'fill your boots'. So many fantastic animals in one place.

3 The hypnotic effect of spectating
If you're not showing, but merely spectating, watching a whole breed in a big show through all its classes is like watching the world in slow motion.

4 Second-guessing the judges
It's great fun (for me at least) to watch a breed being judged and try to second-guess the judge as you see what he or she is judging. You can often see the size, the shape, the type or colour the judge prefers. Of course, you're at a huge disadvantage as you can't feel the dog in the way the judge does, but it's fun all the same.

5 People-watching
The dog world brings together a huge variety of people. There are a fair number of eccentrics – in mannerisms and in dress. There are people who seem to dress twenty years out of date, those who look like they are going out for evening dinner, men in kilts, the lot. There's always something to watch.

6 Raffles
Dog show raffles are great for winning other people's unwanted Christmas presents and indeed donating your own. There is some fantastic 'tat' in these raffles which is always good fun.

7 Outdoor shows
There is little better than sitting in the sun with the smell of the grass, with a cup or tea or an ice cream watching a beautiful array of dogs. Companion dog shows are particularly brilliant for this – you can then share the day and your ice cream with your own dogs.

8 Any class with puppies in it
Fantastic to watch, not only because they're great to look at, but because they are often pretty naughty and more fun to watch – taking a bit of the sting out of the seriousness. Apparently, puppies bring out the maternal/paternal in us. Some breeds have even been developed over the years to mimic baby features.

9 Winning
At whatever level of show, it is one of the very best feelings you can have, even to win your class. It's to do with someone else recognising just how fantastic your dog is. Watching the reactions of others – especially those who are new to dog-showing, or, even better, in fun shows – is a real joy. The looks are a mixture of disbelief, joy, amazement and embarrassment.

10 The atmosphere at fun (companion) shows
Just people enjoying themselves with their dogs, not really knowing or worrying about what they're doing. Having fun, enjoying the day and raising a bit of money for charity.

10 things I hate about dog shows:

1 Hanging around
If you are showing, you want to get there in good time. You

then find that the judge of the previous breed is working at a snail's pace, leaving you hanging around, getting more and more nervous or frustrated (or both).

2 Facilities
Often there is either very little space, with rings crammed in and no room to move, or else you are in some freezing cold agricultural shed with all the facilities of a Russian Gulag.

3 Smoking
There's something about dog-showing people which makes them blind and deaf where 'no smoking' information is concerned. As well as being disgusting, this is particularly stupid where people stand around with the cigarettes at dog-eye level, especially in a tight venue.

4 'Judging the wrong end of the lead'
This is a common concern and lament you will hear in the world of dog-showing and involves being influenced or even biased in favour of a well-known breeder or handler. The judge is either conscious that that handler could well be judging his dogs in the future or (less cynically) sees a successful breeder and therefore presumes the dog they have is better than the others.

There are many cliques and 'mafias' at work in the dog show world. Many factions and in-crowds. To be honest, it makes national and local politics seem very open, honest and above board.

This low-level corruption is probably the biggest danger to the future of the hobby. So many people I know have taken it up, only to get out quite quickly again.

5 'Show Dogs in Transit' car stickers
What am I supposed to do? Was I going to drive recklessly and crash into the back of this particular estate car until I was pulled back from the brink by the words on the sticker?

6 Penny-pinching
Just try selling anything at dog shows. There are a lot of moths in wallets! (Perhaps I'm biased here as I do operate as Treasurer.) You will never see as many flasks and plastic bags of sandwiches as you do at dog shows. Everything is brought from home. This is generally because 'everything is so expensive'. And yet, for about £10, someone enters three classes in an Open Show and probably has a full day out …

7 'Jobsworths'
You don't get many jokes and smiles from officials at dog shows. The Secretary's desk is always a good barometer. If you've ordered a catalogue, require other information or need to book in, you have to go to the Secretary's table on arrival. So often you are met with impatience ('didn't you see the sign by the door?' with a subliminal 'don't bother me'), or by being ignored, or by frostiness. It makes me want to rush off to the good old High Street, which suddenly becomes a paragon of everything customer-focused.

8 Dogs looking miserable
I don't believe that people start showing their dogs with the intention of making them miserable. Many dogs no doubt enjoy it, buy most don't enjoy it like they enjoy agility, obedience, heelwork to music or even just chasing a ball. I used to stand by and watch Border collies, for example, the ultimate canine athlete, restrained in a cage waiting for their class. When they came out they looked joyless and sub-

dued. The more subdued the dog, the better the performance often seemed to be – I suppose if walking round the ring for a few minutes is the highlight of your day then you'll enjoy it well enough …

9 Moaning and whinging
This seems to be almost as big a hobby at dog shows as showing dogs itself. Moaning about the judge, the venue, the catalogue, the application of the rules, someone else's dog (especially), someone else's clothes, the cost of tea and coffee, the draught, the heat, the light, the order of judging etc.

10 Guarding seats
Germans with deckchairs, the butt of so many jokes, have nothing on dog-show people in the 'reserving territory' stakes. Seats are guarded jealously, even though they will be left unoccupied for 90% of the time. Try to move something so you can sit down and you are swooped down upon viciously like a little rodent under the claws of a bird of prey.

Crufts nowadays is a huge enterprise, five full halls at the National Exhibition Centre in Birmingham. Its roots, though, lie back in the late 19th Century.

Originally, the Crufts dog show was not anything to do with the Kennel Club. It was the work – and the dream – of one man by the name (perhaps unsurprisingly) of Cruft: Charles Cruft.

Cruft was born in 1852, the son of a jeweller, a trade in which he showed little interest. On leaving Birkbeck College in 1876, Cruft joined a certain James Spratt in his newly-formed business of selling dog cakes, based in Holborn, London. Spratt had recently returned from America where he had enjoyed some success in his new venture and he was looking to expand his business, taking Cruft on as an office boy.

Charles Cruft clearly showed true flair and the spirit of a salesman, for he was promoted to that position very quickly and travelled the country selling Spratt's dog cakes to kennels, large estates, breeders and owners. So successful was he, that he was next sent to make his (and Spratt's) mark on the Continent.

Cruft impressed the world of dogs in France and he was asked to organise the canine elements of the Paris Exhibition in 1878. This was a great success and showed his prowess in this area. Later, in 1886 he took on the management of the Allied Terrier Club Show in London. For the time, this was quite a large show with 600 dogs entered, and again was a great success.

Most significant for the future of showing dogs, though, was Charles Cruft's booking in 1891 of the Royal Agricultural Hall in Islington for a show bearing his own name. This was the beginning of Crufts dog shows.

All this time, Cruft was still employed by Spratt's, building his career and rising to the heady position of General Manager of the company. He negotiated with his employer the right to take time off to run his shows.

Cruft's shows were fairly spectacular by the standards of the day. He invited many breeds from continental Europe and this must have been really very strange and exotic for the visitors at that time, who would previously have seen just the good old British dogs. At that time, of course, there were no quarantine restrictions.

Right up to his death in 1938, Cruft worked tirelessly for dogs. He was an incredibly successful PR man on dogs' behalf, but also made a good living out of it.

The Cruft family enterprise lasted just one year after

Charles's death, with this huge undertaking being taken over by his widow. There followed a three-year gap before, in 1942, Mrs Cruft came to an arrangement with the Kennel Club whereby the Crufts name was perpetuated, but the organisation of the show was taken over by the Kennel Club.

It was six years before the Kennel Club ran its first Crufts show in 1948. The chosen venue, Olympia in Kensington, was used for the next 30 years, by the end of which the growing number of exhibitors and traders meant that the show had simply outgrown the facilities available. The new venue was again in London, this time in Earls Court. Twelve years later the show moved to its current venue, the NEC near Birmingham. Space was the primary issue, as were easy transport links, car parking and even air travel.

These days, Crufts is a huge event. In 2005, there were 21241 dogs entered in 23523 classes. The size of groups was as follows:

Terrier	2247
Hound	2979
Toy	2529
Utility	2755
Gundog	4909
Working	2797
Pastoral	3025

This is just on the 'breed' side of things. In addition there were the agility dogs, obedience dogs and all the other dogs there for displays or, for example, as Discover Dogs exhibits. There were some 375 trade exhibitors, many with more than one stand – ranging from small stalls to huge hospitality suites and selling a huge variety of goods. You can buy everything 'doggy' there – from the sublime to the ridiculous. There are representatives from all the dog food companies, trying to convince us that their food is the best. The animal charities are there, as are suppliers of grooming, agility and just about every other type of equipment. The various newspapers and magazines from the dog world are well represented, as are training associations, insurers and general 'pet shop'-type stalls. Stranger, though, are the stalls that sell jewellery and clothing for dogs to wear, doggy perfumes such as 'Calvin K9', ramps to get dogs into cars, cross-stitch pictures of dogs, little statues and so on. For serious collectors there is art, antique books, dog stamps and cigarette cards from all over the world. It's difficult to think of anything you couldn't get for dogs or about dogs at Crufts.

All this compares to perhaps 30 or 40 very business-like stalls even at Championship shows and maybe 10 or so at Open shows.

The amount of goods being carried around is phenomenal. Some shoppers can hardly move and some of the walkways are the last place you would want to be if you were even slightly claustrophobic.

In fact, at busy times, moving round Crufts is a nightmare. You move forward just a few inches at a time. I always get there really early for my shopping time and leave the busy hours to everyone else. There were, after all, over 120,000 visitors to the show in 2005.

If you're in the world of dogs, it's a great place to find new equipment, meet people, ask questions and learn about everything new.

On the other hand, for many, Crufts now is just too commercialised, with the dogs marginalised while the shopping extravaganza goes on.

These days you hear so many languages as you walk around – it is a huge international event, especially since the introduction of the Pet Passport scheme which has meant so many foreign exhibitors bringing their dogs to Crufts relatively easily. It's certainly having a pretty deep effect on the actual show outcomes, too, with many non-British dogs winning through to the later stages – often much to the discomfort of British exhibitors.

In comparison with dog shows elsewhere in the world, Crufts is huge. The most famous dog show in America, the Westminster Dog Show (dating back to 1876) held at Madison Square Gardens, is limited to just 2,500. Crufts is easily the biggest dog show on earth – something where Britain is still leading the world – and there are not many things you can say that about any more.

I always try to get to Crufts for three out of the four days. Perhaps one of the days will be spent helping out on a stand in some way. A further day will be given over to looking at new products and books and finding out what's new in the world of dogs. A final day is devoted completely to watching two or three breeds from start to finish, and then spending the evening at the 'Best in Show' event – three or four hours of events, group judging and demonstrations with the high point being the final judging of overall 'Best In Show'. It's a great day out with a really exciting climax.

There are some interesting things going on in the world of dog shows in general. Many Canine Societies are losing money and amalgamating as costs – especially of venues – can make it increasingly difficult to make ends meet. The Kennel Club has also imposed limits on how many shows of the different types any Society can run. This is not least because so many Open Shows were taking place that there were very few competitors in some. I have even travelled quite a distance to attend a show, only to find that I was the only exhibitor and automatic winner of my class. By making sure there are fewer shows, the aim is to increase competition and standards at those that do run.

Another trend is a further example of what seems to be happening in life in general, this being a quest for instant success. Instead of campaigning a dog through the various levels of show, many people are now entering their dogs – no matter how mediocre – in Championship Shows to see if they can get instant success. There is nothing to stop them doing this and nor should there be. It's a little like the first time buyers you meet these days who want a dream home straight away, full of brand-new furniture (oh, and a new car outside, too). Gone are the days of working up the property ladder and begging, borrowing and stealing your first furniture. God, I'm beginning to sound old now, aren't I?

There is no doubt that one of the most controversial elements of dog-showing today is the judging. The Kennel Club is trying to professionalise – or at least regularise – judging through a series of seminars and other activities. These sessions cover anatomy, conformation and movement and then specific points about individual breeds. Apparently, in these seminars, it was initially amazing just how little judges had known about all of this.

Just image a Premier League football referee officiating without a lot of practical experience, many assessments, practical and written examinations. Looking back nearly ten years to a course I studied, I made the following suggestions.

Judges should be subject to:

- laid-down experience requirements.
- progression through different 'levels' of show, with formal assessment at each stage.
- random assessment by observers on a continuous basis with feedback to the judge in question.
- a formal education programme for judges and would-be

judges covering anatomy, construction, basic genetics, grooming, practical interpretation of standards, working with stewards etc.

- continuing professional development: a requirement for all judges to attend a set-down minimum number of hours of educational training, reading etc., with a log kept of activity.
- special judges' seminars to be run by the Kennel Club to share experience among UK colleagues as well as illustrating best practice from abroad.

This is, after all, no more than people in other walks of life have to do. The good news is that over the last ten years this is exactly the direction that the Kennel Club has taken. (Nothing to do with me, though, I'm afraid to say.)

Judges generally have to be breeders and progress through judging lists run by the breed clubs. The top judges are those authorised to award Kennel Club Challenge Certificates in a particular breed.

Many of these judges are very self-important. They swagger around the ring, being quite off-hand with both exhibitors and their stewards (who keep the ring running for them by making sure everyone is there and in the right place). My best guess is that this behaviour compensates for a lack of power or success in other areas of their life. Many of the older lady judges appear to shop at the same pre-war ladies' outfitters, in nice tweedy suits and sensible shoes. A slight limp seems to be another important part of the ensemble.

Some of the male judges, on the other hand, are clearly colour-blind, wearing wonderful combinations of maroon jacket with browny-orange trousers, for example. Maybe a yellow handkerchief in the top pocket to finish off. I have seen many patent leather shoes in these men's wardrobes – sometimes of quite striking colours such as sky blue. The trousers and jackets explain to me why some traders find it profitable to advertise those 'polyester slacks' at £10.99 in the Sunday magazines. You know, the ones modelled by the ex-civil servant who use 'Just for Men' or 'Grecian 2000' by the bucket-load.

Occasionally, of course, there will be slim young women in trouser suits or a man who is far from smart, looking rather like a vagrant who slept under a bush the night before. We mustn't forget, either, the often well-turned-out gay judges (of whom there are a fair number) whom many people accuse of offering prizes predominantly to other gay men.

There can be quite a lot of thought going into a handler's attire. For example, you shouldn't wear black trousers if you have a dark-coloured dog – how is the judge to see the outline of the dog against your legs? A tie may have to be clipped to a shirt so that it doesn't dangle over the dog and spook him. Some frown upon short skirts and low necklines for women as the bending and stretching involved in stacking the dog (putting it into show position) can reveal too much. Killjoys, that's what I say.

For some, the judging is just one great ego-trip. There is more posing than in the local amateur dramatics production. For others, judging is power rather than ego. Perhaps a chance to further their own careers by awarding prizes to fellow judges' dogs. Let me recount a true story.

When Stan was a puppy I took him to many, many shows. At those shows, we met largely the same dogs and competed against them week after week. Some dogs always beat Stan. Stan always beat some others. Around the margins, one or two would sometimes finish above another while the next week the positions would be reversed. This, of course, is quite normal, as judges will have different views.

Stan beat one particular dog week in, week out. That dog generally finished in fifth or sixth place if it was placed at all. Then, one week the breeder handled the dog. This was a top, highly influential breeder. Normally, a judge would not know who had bred any particular dog (although they would have a pretty good idea, especially as they could have been watching or competing against it the week before).

Now, the breeder was handling the dog. She could not physically move particularly easily and so did not get the dog moving any better than usual. Suddenly, though, a dog which had finished quite lowly for weeks when handled by an unknown (but very experienced) dog person, shot to the top and won the class when handled by a well-known 'face' in the dog world. Strange, that.

Of course, everyone has reasons for their dog not winning and there is a lot of bitterness around. Even so, these things seem to be happening all too often and in my own experience they are all too common.

A little while ago, I had to choose three judges to compare and contrast for a course I was undertaking. I went to the Ladies Kennel Association show at the NEC (if you want to see dogs rather than going shopping, the big Championship shows are a better bet than Crufts). I chose my judges more or less at random. One, Mike Stockman, is a very well known and respected judge. The two others were just 'everyday' judges.

The different was marked. Mike Stockman was relaxed in the ring, talked a lot to his steward about how he wanted the ring organised and was pleasant and open with the exhibitors. He gave the impression that he really knew what he was doing. He would give a dog a second chance if something went wrong.

The lady judging the chow-chows was appropriately

dressed in her judging uniform of tweed twin-set with pearls. She really looked like she didn't want to be there, other than for the kudos. She inspired no confidence in the dogs or the exhibitors. Everything was very tentative but at the same time rushed. Overall, you got the impression that she wanted to be out of there as soon as possible. There was little clarity in what was expected of anyone in the ring. Instructions had to be repeated. There was little communication with the ring stewards and altogether it was pretty painful to watch.

The third judge I observed was what I would call a 'peacock'. For this judge, this was all about him – not the exhibitors, not the dogs, but him. You could picture him not showing an entry ticket but demanding of the security guard, 'Don't you know who I am?' I think 'strut' is the only word to describe his movement. Examination of the dogs was slow, almost painful, with an aloof rather than professional air. There was little eye contact with the exhibitors, certainly no smiles or facial gestures of any kind.

Having examined the dogs he had the exhibitors move them in the normal way. Then he would change the order in which they were standing and then have them move again. This sometimes happened several times before a decision was made.

In a bright, yellowy-beige corduroy jacket, patent shoes and light-blue trousers, this show was clearly one big ego-trip for him. He really must have believed that people had come to see him, with his theatrical gestures and long deliberations. Laurence Olivier eat your heart out!

So, what is a judge actually doing? I think it can be quite mystifying for people who don't know what's going on.

What a judge is actually doing is comparing each dog to the 'breed standard' which exists for any and every Kennel Club breed. This standard is, in effect, a blueprint for the breed. It represents the outcome of many years of wrangling between various breed clubs, Kennel Club Committees and others. You will remember a little about these breed standards from the discussions on health problems earlier in the book.

Each breed standard sets out the information under the following headings:

- General appearance
- Characteristics
- Temperament
- Head and Skill
- Eyes
- Ears
- Mouth
- Neck
- Forequarters
- Body
- Hindquarters
- Feet
- Tail
- Gait/movement
- Coat
- Colour
- Faults

Oh, and there is a special note for all the breeds, stating:
'Male animals should have two apparently normal testicles fully descended into the scrotum.'

So there. That's why you see the judge giving the dog a little squeeze in that particular region as the dog either glazes over or gives the judge 'the look', depending on its temperament.

Joking apart, I discovered Stan's testicular cancer really early by doing this. He had the operation and made a full recovery.

So, the judge has a blueprint, but this is not science. It is very much open to interpretation, of course. Hence the difference in results. It can't be assessed by computer. Much of the joy and frustration of dog-showing, I suppose, lies in the interpretation of standards by judges rather than technical precision. For this reason, the KC does not accompany breed standards with photos and hence avoids tying in a breed to a particular visual image.

You will remember some of the issues raised in an earlier chapter around breed standards calling for a 'large skull' or 'large, round' eyes and the tendency to interpret this as 'large skull must be better' or we should breed for 'larger, rounder eyes'. This has undoubtedly worked to individual animals' detriment.

Some strange statements appear in these standards, too, particularly in the categories of 'general appearance', 'characteristics' and 'temperament'! For example, an Australian cattle dog's temperament is meant to be 'alert, intelligent, watchful, courageous, trustworthy, devoted to its work'. How can that possibly be assessed in the ring? Perhaps the judge should have a one-to-one interview with the dog, asking him if he's getting enough out of his work and whether he's considered an alternative career?

The Neapolitan mastiff is to be 'devoted and loyal guard of owner and property'. Let's hope we don't find that out in the ring.

So, the judge will normally watch all the dogs come into the ring. He or she will then generally walk along the line of dogs forming initial impressions. Each dog will then be called forward one at a time for the all-important hands-on inspection. First and foremost, this is about anatomy. For example, the 'Body' description for the Irish setter states in the Kennel Club breed standard.

'Chest as deep as possible, rather narrow in front. Ribs well sprung leaving plenty of lung room and carried well back to muscular loins, slightly arched. From straight topline gently sloping downwards from withers.'

It might be possible to see some of this, but much can only be judged by feeling the actual anatomy of the dog.

After the inspection, the judge will normally ask the handler to move the dog, perhaps in a triangle so s/he can observe the dog's movement from the back, the side and the front. It is often while the dog is moving that its skeleton and structure becomes most apparent. Elbows might point inwards or flay outwards showing that they're not close to the body, for example. Movement is the practical demonstration of the body structure.

Once this process is complete, the judge will often pull out a few dogs for a further inspection and will be making his/her mind up about a final line-up. S/he may well move a couple of dogs side by side to compare them. S/he will also go up and down the line, looking at facial expressions and perhaps trying to get the dog's attention with a toy or a titbit to see whether the dog is alert and how it looks when it is.

Finally, the decision is made. The judge is comparing each of the dogs to his or her own view of the standard, and deciding which comes closest (at least this is the theory, with no notice being taken of who is showing the dog or any other irrelevancies).

My own experience is very, very limited – only at the 'fun' end, the Companion Dog Show (although you wouldn't know that some of these folks were doing it for 'fun').

I have judged the fun classes, which really *are* fun – like prettiest bitch, waggiest tail, best six legs (dog plus owner) etc. – and the 'breed' classes for crossbreeds and mongels (I used to be Secretary for the national Crossbreed and Mongrel Club).

This level is nerve-racking enough for me. Enough pressure, thank you. I don't think I would ever want to judge at a more 'serious' level than that.

I have to say that I really enjoyed it and felt very comfortable with what I was doing. Some people took it all very seriously, and I tried to make sure that they went away feeling that they had been dealt with courteously, fairly, consistently and that they had had a good opportunity to shine with their dog. For others, this was just a lovely day out, raising a bit of money for charity and enjoying time with their four-legged friend. They needed to be able to enjoy themselves and not get too serious about it all.

Some of these classes are huge – with perhaps fifty or sixty dogs. Trying to remember the ones you liked by the end is a huge challenge in itself. All this whilst trying to look cool, authoritative and in control! In practice, I had to cut the numbers down because I just couldn't juggle all that information mentally.

Even at this level, though, I experienced some 'sledging' (to borrow the term from the cricket) from some of the owners.

I got there early to sort out the ring, decide where I wanted to stand so the sun wouldn't be in my eyes, where I wanted the dogs to move and so on. Sitting behind the ring rope right by the judge's table was a very heavy middle-aged man, with untidy long hair, a beard and glasses. He reminded me immediately of Jim Royle (Ricky Tomlinson) in *The Royle Family*. By his side was a German shepherd-type dog. At first glance it looked to be perhaps 8 or 9 years old. It lay there very contentedly.

From the moment I put the papers down this man started. 'Hope we have as good a day as we did yesterday.'

'Oh, you had a good day, did you?' I reply, trying to be pleasant and not too stand-offish.

'Oh yes, swept the board at Coventry yesterday, he did,' replied Ricky T (strangely, though, in a Midlands accent) pointing at his dog. 'Placed in every class he entered, he was – won most of them.'

'Good for you, it's great when that happens, isn't it?' I replied heartily.

'Oh yes, judge really knew what he was doing,' says Ricky. This went on throughout the show. He spoke loudly, as though to himself, but only when I was around. I was just about to judge the dog in the best condition when I hear from the side, 'What did that judge say to you yesterday, boy? Never seen a dog in better condition! Couldn't believe it, could he, boy? Put you first easily, didn't he? I'll never forget that look on his face …'

I think it would be fair to say that 'Ricky T' was trying to influence the decision-making.

I would be getting a competitor to move around the ring and would hear, 'look at the state of the rear end of that!' or some other comment.

He left it to a friend (who seemed to appear occasionally from nowhere) to do the actual showing of his dog, presumably so that he himself could focus on giving the ringside commentary.

Strangely – or perhaps not – his dog did not live up to its billing. Its movement was quite terrible and its condition left a lot to be desired. The dog's coat was full of scurf and the skin had sore patches. It seemed a nice enough dog, but was never really going to win any prizes.

It came as no surprise, then, that the tone of the comments offered in my earshot changed as the afternoon went on: 'Some people don't know a good dog when they see one. Must be friends with that bloke who just won,' and so on.

I look back with great amusement. At the time, though, I

have to say that I didn't feel inclined to be swayed by Ricky T and his tactics.

All in all, the world of dog-showing is becoming quite a serious place to be. At the highest level we seem to be following the US model and using more and more professional handlers, in theory to bring out the best in our dogs. Meanwhile in 2004, a Doberman bitch, favourite for its class, was allegedly drugged by a jealous rival and had to be withdrawn from its class. Let's hope this is not a sign of things to come.

What's more, thefts of dogs, not just at shows, but among the dog population at large, also seem to be on the increase. Such dogs are often used for breeding and then simply abandoned.

Still, dog-showing is by and large a fairly low-key event with little fear of loss of life or limb. In many shows it is friendly and relaxed. It seems that the atmosphere varies from breed to breed, too. I spent some time with bloodhound exhibitors who appeared friendly, welcoming and helpful. They seemed quite supportive of each other, with lots of laughs and smiles as the day went by.

It doesn't always seem this way at Crufts, though. Nor indeed at much smaller shows. I spent some time around the Border collie show world and found it populated by many miserable and unfriendly people. There was very little welcoming for newcomers. Lots of factions, cliques and groupings. If looks could kill, then probably two-thirds of all exhibitors would be dead by the end of the show. This isn't competition in the best sense of the word. There is bitterness, moaning and whinging. If it made me that miserable I wouldn't do it (well I don't anymore). Of course you meet some lovely people. These are the rare few who see the world more in shades of grey than in black and white. People who won't look down their noses at you or your dog. People who build relationships with a wide group of people rather than factions.

One thing I have to say is that there are some really bad losers in dog-showing. Talk about JFK, Elvis, Jimi Hendrix, the Princess of Wales: there are no conspiracy theories that match up to the conspiracy theory surrounding why their dog has lost. Clearly the judge is corrupt or incompetent. 'How could *that* (pointing at the winner like there's a bad smell under the nose) possibly beat my dog?' 'They're clearly trying to do me down as they're scared of the competition' etc. Losing with grace and dignity might happen at some of the bigger shows, but there isn't even a pretence some of the time – not even the look of the 'smiling assassin'.

There are certainly some characters in dog-showing. In fact, some aspects of the wonderful *Best in Show* film seem so accurate. People have all sorts of habits, traditions and mannerisms. It's a very colourful and varied world.

You will have guessed by now that there are some real schisms in the world of dogs. One of the biggest is probably the 'docking' debate. This is one which rumbles on and on. It is also one which seems to make the blood boil.

In the past, docking was generally done by breeders. However, in 1991, the Government amended the Veterinary Surgeons' Act to prevent unqualified people from docking tails, leaving it in the hands of the vets. A further important development came in November 1992 when the Council of the Royal College of Veterinary Surgeons ruled that docking should only take place for therapeutic reasons or for the purpose of preventing disease. Otherwise, they said, docking would be unethical.

Subsequently, disciplinary proceedings found that a vet had the right to make his own clinical judgement about docking, and quite a few do continue to dock.

There are active campaigning groups on both sides of the argument – on one hand there is the Council of Docked Breeds (CDB), on the other the RSPCA and other animal welfare organisations.

The CDB and others who advocate docking put forward three main arguments:

- Docking prevents tail damage to working breeds (e.g. Spaniels).
- Leaving the tail on can be unhygienic, causing 'flystrike' and other hygiene problems where dogs have profuse soft coats which may gather faeces and urine.
- Traditions – maintaining traditional breed standards.

Those against docking put forward, to my mind, much stronger arguments. They claim:

- Docking is an unnecessary mutilation, rather like the clipping of dogs' ears, which has been banned in Britain since 1903.
- It is cruel and can be painful.
- It can effect a dog's ability to communicate with other dogs and humans. A tail is not only wagged to show that a dog is happy. There is a lot in the particular carriage of a tail.
- It offers no advantage to the vast majority of dogs who are docked and were never going to 'work'. It is performed purely as a cosmetic operation for the owner's satisfaction.

The 'pro' arguments do strike me as odd. We don't normally amputate to avoid what *might* happen, do we? And we tend to work on hygiene and keep our animals clean rather than wait for them to become infested with maggots. Tradition is a strange argument to use, too. After all, dog fighting was 'traditional' too, once, but it is barbaric and cruel and was banned. So, tradition alone doesn't seem to be a very good justification for amputation.

Just recently I have begun to see a lot more of the traditionally docked dogs with tails in the pet environment. That has to be good news, even though the buyers have often had to pay up-front for their puppies as the breeder didn't want to risk being left with unsaleable, undocked puppies.

In the world of show dogs, though, docked dogs still predominate. You do see undocked dogs, but if one succeeds it tends to be quite noteworthy.

Things are getting better, though slowly. Just a couple of years ago I was standing talking to a friend with an undocked cocker spaniel when a couple of evil old biddies came over and said, 'Oh, that looks like it could be quite a nice dog! What breed is it?'

Of course they knew what it was. Their point was that it was not a 'proper' cocker spaniel but some sort of freak with a tail. It really upset my friend. She was soon over it and we sat down over a cup of tea fantasising what we would do with the tails they no doubt docked from their own dogs!

The European Convention for the Protection of Pet Animals does call for a ban on docking. It does, however, permit the now famously 'leaky' exceptions, in particular 'if a vet considers non-curative procedures necessary either for veterinary medical reasons or for the benefit of any particular animal.' Furthermore, individual nations can choose to reserve their position on docking and not adopt that part of the Convention.

Docking is not the only issue that causes schisms in the dog world, though. Dog folk can argue about anything – quite bitterly in fact, with effortless ease.

One such issue is around Border collies, those fantastic canine athletes and herding dogs par excellence. To 99% of the population, the term 'Border collie' refers to the wonderful (normally) black and white dogs which appear, for example, on *One Man and His Dog*, herding sheep through gates and into pens.

Technically, though, these are more likely to be 'working sheepdogs', the term 'Border collie' referring only to those registered with the Kennel Club (mostly commonly as 'breed'/'show' dogs).

In fact, despite their popularity and the fact that they are one of the few breeds that almost anyone could recognise, Border collies as a 'breed' have only been recognised since 1976. Challenge Certificates (to create Champions) only became available in 1981!

Recognition of this breed for 'show' purposes was hugely controversial. Many with working sheepdogs predicted the end of the world as we know it. The argument was, and is, that breeding dogs for particular appearance characteristics would work completely to the detriment of the working skills and abilities of the breed. A farmer who wants a good working dog cares little about many of the superficial characteristics rewarded in the show ring. The best dogs would be bred together, weaknesses in one line being complemented by strengths in another.

You can see why they would be concerned after what happened to other breeds. Some people expect to see the development of two quite different dogs over time.

The use of a dog of the collie type dates back probably to Celtic times. It would have been refined for top working characteristics with no interest in appearance (unless this enhanced those working abilities). As sizes of herds and flocks increased, so did the need to involve specialist canine help.

It was probably the Romans, though, who first developed a bespoke sheep dog. One of the main geographical areas where these dogs were used was in the borders between modern-day Scotland and England.

Moving forward hundreds of years, after generations of breeding for the best working traits and culling those that didn't match up to the task, working shepherds began to compete, in however friendly a fashion, to see whose dog was the best – and sheep dog 'trials' were born.

Trialling, as it became more organised, in effect identified the best future breeding stock, to the extent that the modern breed can be traced back to very few dogs. Indeed, many of the dogs known as Border collies today date back to one particular dog, called Hemp. In fact, this is so well established that I notice his breeding is a case study in Tom's genetic textbook in science at school.

Hemp – also known as Old Hemp – was born in September 1893 and died 8 years later. In that lifetime he laid down the future of the breed. Hemp's breeder, Adam Telfer, is revered in the breed. Both Hemp's mother and father (sire and dam) were from a long line of Northumberland collies. He was famous for working naturally and quietly, causing an organically respectful reaction from the sheep he was working. Many of his puppies worked in the same way and were hugely popular with shepherds.

Hemp became an immensely respected and busy study dog. Not a bad life!

Old Hemp became an international Supreme Champion sheepdog, as did many of his progeny over many generations.

In 1906, sheep dog trialling and the world of sheep dogs in general took a huge step forward with the founding of the International Sheep Dog Society (ISDS). Since then the ISDS has developed the stud book and breed records for working sheep dogs. The ISDS remains the governing body for working sheep dogs and is concerned solely with the breed's ability

to do the job it was initially bred to do. The objectives of the ISDS are:
'… the breeding, training and improvement of the working sheep dog; this to secure the better management of stock by improving the shepherd's dog.'

They run the main national and international sheep dog trials, produce a magazine, register dogs and hold all the breed and pedigree information which someone looking to breed and build on particular working traits would need. They also promote eye-testing in the breed.

ISDS-registered dogs must have a sire and dam registered in the ISDS stud book and have passed defined eye tests. Exceptionally, older dogs can be registered on merit on the basis of the working abilities.

As you can perhaps imagine, it took literally years of negotiation between the ISDS and the Kennel Club before the Border collie could become a recognised registered breed in 1976. Breed standards had to be drawn up.

As a Border collie owner and exhibitor I must say that I often feel looked down upon by owners of other breeds. It is a recent 'breed' with a strong working history. Sometimes you feel as though you are showing a 'mongrel' (not that there's anything wrong with that).

On the other hand, those concerned with the working sheep dog see the Border collie as a real threat – diluting the gene pool on the basis of looks alone, losing potentially all of the attributes which make the dog such a fantastic worker.

The duality of background of the breed is reflected in the unusual circumstances around making a Border collie into a 'Champion'. The normal rules do not apply. Three Challenge Certificates make a Border collie into a 'Show Champion' and not a full 'Champion'. Only once these Show Champions have passed some working tests organised by the Kennel Club and the International Sheep Dog Society is the Border collie given the full title of Champion.

Even within the show Border collie scene there are schisms. These occur particularly between breeders of the smaller, 'prettier' Australian and New Zealand-type, for example, and those who support the rangier 'British look'.

Supporters of the former consider 'British' dogs 'crude', while those of the latter say that the Southern Hemisphere dogs couldn't do a day's work and are beginning to look more and more like Shetland sheepdogs.

How those that work their dogs must despair. They don't care about markings or predominantly white faces, for example, which would preclude a dog from the show world. They are, of course, very concerned with the dog's 'eye' – it is the main way a Border collie will control sheep. The strength and nature of the stare will be all important. Some shepherds prefer lighter eyes, others darker. They have no interest in show standards, though.

In places, on the web and elsewhere, there is a lot of derogatory comment about 'show' collies. It almost makes you feel guilty for owning one.

I loved showing my dog, Stan, though. I used to subscribe to a now defunct international magazine called the *Sheppherde's Dogge*. This was devoted to all things Border collie. They had a sort of 'Readers' Dogs' (rather than Readers' Wives) feature where you could get, if you were very lucky, a picture of your dog and a pen portrait in this international magazine. I couldn't believe it when I opened my airmail envelope one day to find a picture of my Stan on the back page. I was so proud! I ran upstairs and almost threw the magazine at Alison, saying, 'Quick, look at page 9!'

Alison went quiet, looking intently at the picture and then said the immortal words, 'You could have shut the back door

– you can see our tumble dryer in the background.' That, Ladies and Gentlemen, is a fair summary of the difference between the sexes.

Stan didn't have a hugely successful show career. He was a big lad, right up to the upper limits in size when the fashion, under the influence of Australia and New Zealand, was to be smaller. He used to get overexcited in the ring, too. He'd had enough of standing around by the time he got to move in the ring. He was ready for the off! Not one of the subdued caged collies, but a bit larger than life. (When he had more chance to get involved and less hanging around he did well – for example winning through round after round of a handling competition.)

His worst fault, though, was that he used to 'fly' his tail. He would hold it up like a flag (something I love seeing when he's leading the way 100 yards ahead in the Forest of Dean). Apparently he shouldn't do this. When a dog is 'working' and 'concentrating' his tail would be down. There's no doubt about that. I just don't think Stan saw the show ring that way. There were no sheep and very little to 'work' or 'concentrate' about!

I was given all sorts of advice about this – including hitting his tail with a stick every time it flew in practice. You can probably imagine what I said to that. This was just one 'tip' I was given though, which included blue-tacking a dog's ears to get the right ear carriages. This from a bloke whose ears made Prince Charles's look minimalist and attractive …

So, not just at Crufts but at any dog show there are all these undercurrents just below the calm surface. If you want some entertainment, just watch the body language and facial expressions of some of the losers.

Having said all this, it's the exception which proves the rule, of course. I have just helped to run an Open Show for several hundred dogs and people. The weather was beautiful and the whole show took place outside. People and dogs just relaxed in the sun or in the shade of a tree. People had picnics and watched lazily as the show proceeded. The sunshine and relaxed tone set a great atmosphere. There were fantastic dogs to sit and admire, no pressure of space and people genuinely seemed to be having a great time. There were very few complaints about anything, quite the contrary. Compliments flooded in and, quite unusually, quite a crowd stayed on right until the end instead of going as soon as their dog was bounced out. Many of the judges stayed, too – chatting and swapping views and opinions.

There was such a feel-good factor – the warmth and sunshine set the whole mood and atmosphere. This was what I had been missing about dog shows.

Crufts, then, is just a (very) big dog show. The ultimate prize. A mixture of supportive fellow-feeling and bitterness. Just about like any other hobby, interest, sporting activity or work environment actually.

So, there I was, filling myself up with the sights, sounds and smells of Crufts, but all the time with a really uncomfortable feeling inside. I'm sure you've all had it. There's something on your mind, something worrying or bothering you, but you can't think what. And then, every now and then, it would surface – which dogs was I going to choose? Would I regret it? Would Tom smirk if we came upon one of my choices away from Crufts just a week later? Of course he would!

So my final five choices, after much deliberation and heart-searching and even an attempt at applying pseudo-science and probability theory to it, were:

1 The Anatolian Shepherd Dog

This is a big dog. It is a 'shepherd' dog in the sense of

guarding the flock rather than herding. Its origins date back to the Middle Ages. It weighs between 41 and 64 kg and can be up to 32 inches in height. It is strong willed and independent, able to protect sheep against wolves and bears. Quite a dog to look at and be near. Tick!

2 The Norwegian Buhund (*Bu* meaning 'stall' or 'shed')
A smaller dog at 24-26 kg and just about 18 inches in height. It is a multi-purpose dog – very lively and an excellent herder. At the same time it is a good farm guard and companion. It has been around in Norway since early times and is increasingly visible all over the world. The one I met, Finn, was extremely cheeky. Tick!

3 Estrela Mountain Dog
The Estrela mountain dog originates in the Estrela Mountains of Portugal. It is of the mastiff type, which for those of you who don't know, means DON'T MESS. It both herds and defends flocks, for example against wolves. In many ways it is a very ordinary dog to look at, almost looking like a large crossbreed. It has a thick double coat to give protection against cold weather, and thick legs with plenty of bone. It weighs up to 50 kg and can reach 29 inches in height. It is descended from Asiatic mastiffs and is related to the Spanish mastiff. It is, again, a lot of dog. Tick!

4 Chinese Crested Dog
This is one strange-looking dog. It you didn't know, you would probably think that the dog was ill or diseased. Its body is devoid of hair, except around the head and ears, lower legs and feet and the tail. Although known as the Chinese crested dog, many believe that this breed originated in Africa like other hairless dogs and subsequently travelled to Asia.

This breed is for use solely as a companion and needs protection from heat and cold. They are not easy to breed. Often, coated dogs are produced instead of the hairless variety and these are called 'powderpuffs'.

The dogs only weigh between 2 and 5.5 kg, with a maximum height of 13 inches. Quite different from the Anatolian Shepherd.

I tried to like the dog I met. He was certainly friendly. I didn't really like seeing and touching bare skin. Very weird. Tick!

And number 5 was …

5 The Swedish *Vallhund*

This little dog, also known as the Swedish cattle dog, or the *Vasgotaspets*, is all dog in a smallish package – just 12-14 inches in height and weighing a maximum of 15 kg.

When I first met Harry he put me very much in mind of a corgi, except that I thought the grey-brown coat looked a little more interesting. His owners told me that both the *Vallhund* and Corgi probably originated with the low basset dogs on mainland Europe. It was even suggested that Vikings returning from Wales took some 'corgis' back to Sweden and originated the *Vallhund* back there.

These dogs are heelers: brave little dogs that will get in amongst the feet of cattle and nip them to move the animals along. They also make fantastic ratters and good guards. My kind of dog! Tick!

Well that was it now, my five choices. Would I live to regret them? And no sign of a Dutch partridge dog anywhere, even at the largest dog show in the world …

In our traditional manner, we spent the afternoon watching a breed that we really didn't know much about – Alison and Tom chose the Bedlington Terriers. At the end of the judging, there was one of Tom's ominous silences. I always know there's something brewing when that happens. A question formed on his lips: 'Dad, do you think there are many Bedlington Terriers in Bedlington?'

CHAPTER 5

Are There Many Bedlington Terriers in Bedlington?

It would be some months before we could travel up to Bedlington in Northumberland to see if we could see any Bedlington terriers there. One thing about terriers is that many of them are named after a geographical area, sometimes really quite small and specific. They would have been the result of localised breeding in times when people did little travelling, least of all the working classes who tended to own these types of dog.

Myself, I was brought up in Staffordshire before some quango or other decided that my home town should now be part of the glamourless and grey West Midlands. I knew that it was certainly true that Staffordshire was full of Staffordshire bull terriers and I was really curious to see if Bedlington was the same. Well, not if Bedlington was full of Staffies, but you get the point.

My Granddad had owned a Staffie, as did many of the people in the back-to-back terraced houses with yards in that area. These dogs were a great source of pride, of course. To this day, attending Staffie Breed Shows and Ringcraft Classes is quite a different experience from anything else in the world of dogs. Generally in dog-showing, dogs are moved around a hall to show them off to their best advantage and are then shown in profile to the judge. It can be quite a graceful and athletic affair with big free-moving dogs like an Afghan hound, a setter or a collie. None of this for the Staffie fans, though. I was once asked to judge a handling competition in the Black Country and was surprised to arrive at a smoky pub, rather than the usual church or village hall. There were tables around the edge with various tattooed gents (and indeed ladies) standing with a pint and a cigarette in one hand and a beautiful shining-coated Staffie on a lead in the other. These dogs were not going to move any more than they had to and were presented to the judge head-on – giving me a full-on view of that 'don't mess with me ' expression, which nevertheless to me looks more like a broad smile than anything else.

I couldn't help thinking that there was something marvellously antiquated about the scene. It was like paintings and photos from 100 years earlier of working people's dog shows, but minus the hats.

I was really struck by the Staffie owners, who were good-humoured and enthusiastic, not tense, miserable and sour-faced like so many others who follow the hobby.

Anyway, Tom could equally have chosen Manchester or Sealyham, or even the West Highlands for this part of the challenge, I suppose, but fate had decided on Bedlington.

In the time we had watched them being judged at Crufts I had become quite taken with what I had always regarded as a funny-looking little dog (it's the one that looks like a lamb) and had never really taken that seriously. They seemed to be full of character and pretty feisty, though. But would there be any walking the streets of Bedlington? And where exactly was Bedlington anyway?

Our first venture into Bedlington was very much a virtual one. Into the internet search engine we went with 'Bedlington' and, ignoring for the time being all the references to Bedlington terriers, we were directed to the town's very own website (**www.bedlington.co.uk**). What a treat that turned out to be! I love the internet and although it was very much under construction and quite small, it turned out to be a lovely little site.

It opens quite gratuitously with a pleasant but dull picture of a tree-lined avenue, but this home page offers you access to some exciting (?) features plus a promise of a lot more to come as the website is developed. I haven't been back since, but really hope it's lived up to its promise. There are at least three top features which make it worthwhile clicking onto the site. The first one is accessed straight from the home page and it is called 'Traffic-Calming Zone – The Movie'. This does exactly what it says on the tin, as it were, and allows you to see traffic-calming in action in Bedlington – well worth seeing and typical of the humour of those who put the site together.

The second 'top' feature, accessed by clicking on a lovely picture of none other than a Bedlington terrier, is the Bedlington quiz, 'Can you call yourself a Bedlingtonian?' The quiz takes you through twenty questions about your knowledge of local history, geography and so on and tells you whether you are right or wrong as you go.

The first time I did the quiz I scored 7 out of 20 with no knowledge of the area. Three months later this had improved to 11 out of 20 – a pretty impressive increase, I'm sure you'll agree, especially if I justify the increase in percentage terms, which I fully intend to do of course. This is still unsurprisingly short of the standard required to call myself a Bedlingtonian. The website suggests that living there for ten years might pull up the standard of my performance sufficiently!

The third feature worth mentioning comes under the 'Entertainment' section. This is a plain simple game where the aim is to 'mash' the Bedlington terrier's head with a 'miggity

miggity ball-pen hammer' to score points. The animated terrier heads appear out of the 'ground' anywhere on the screen and you operate the ball-pen hammer to try to knock them on their head back underground. A bit cruel, perhaps, but it is only fun. I scored a measly 12 out of 100. I'm sure I could much improve on this. Please don't worry though, animal lovers: a message does come up at the end to assure you that no Bedlingtons were harmed in the making of this game.

So, not a bad start to Bedlington. There's not an awful lot of useful information yet, but a real tongue-in-cheek sense of humour to it all which is a lot more than can be said for most town websites.

Bedlington can be found in Northumberland about 12 miles north of Newcastle. The 2001 census gives a population figure of just over 14,000, almost exactly ten times the population recorded in the census of 1422. So, it's a pretty small town which has generally grown quite steadily other than the period 1861 to 1871 when the population leapt from 8,328 to 13,494. It then continued to rise over the next 30 years to a peak of 18,766, with a huge decline to 6,413 in 1911 and then a return to steady growth to today's figure.

Be honest now, how many of you had mental graphs in your head, plotting population growth when you read that last paragraph? Go on, admit it. Well, the most anal amongst you are now going to be a little disappointed as I have to break it to you that the figures above may not always be like-for-like as there were changes in administrative boundaries between censuses.

Not unexpectedly, some of the fluctuations in population can be attributed to the town's industrial fortunes. Bedlington Colliery opened in 1838 and closed in 1971. By the 1890s, almost 1,500 men were employed there, peaking at 3,661 in the 1950s. Now that industry is gone from the town. It seems a poignant symbol of post-industrial Britain, that one of the old open-cast areas has been landscaped and become an 18-hole golf course.

Just like the mining industry, the iron industry has also come and gone in Bedlington. Be honest, did you know that the world's first malleable railway track was produced in Bedlington? Be honest, did you care? Although it's easy to be facetious, a bendable and flexible rail track was a huge step forward, revolutionising transport. Not only was track produced in Bedlington but important locomotives, too.

First records of an iron works in the Bedlington area date back to 1736 – to be precise to 10th December 1736, when a lease was signed to acquire land for this purpose. This began a long and very productive association between the town and the industry of over 130 years. Bedlington really was the perfect place for an iron works. There was a readily available supply of wood for the charcoal smelting required to produce pig iron. When coke was substituted for charcoal following on from Abraham Darby's work in the Midlands, Bedlington was well placed because of its mining industry. Added to this the river Blyth provided the essential water power needed. With a port just two miles away to ship the production onwards, the location was perfect. In fact, iron was even found amongst the shale and coal excavated in the area – an added bonus.

It was nail-making which dominated in the early years, but general iron work then began to grow in significance. By the time the works went through one of its many changes of ownership in 1782 it was producing 500 tons of rod irons and hoops in a year. A strong association with the nearby port of Blyth developed and the Bedlington Iron Works became famous for heavy forgings for the shipping industry in the port and particularly for its production of anchors. Indeed by 1820 Blyth had become one of the centres for the expanding shipbuilding trade and Bedlington prospered accordingly.

The heyday of the Bedlington Iron Works was, however, still to come and was linked with that exciting period when the railways were established and expanded at a rapid rate. A deal was struck with a local pit to receive coal at a discounted rate if the ironworks built a railway on which it could be transported. The then owner, Michael Longridge, declared that malleable rails should be used instead of the short cast iron rails which had been largely used up to that time. The company's agent, John Birkenshaw, came up with the truly clever piece of all this thinking by suggesting that these rails should be 'wedge' form i.e. curved to a thinner point in the middle of their depth, keeping the same surface width for the wheels of the train but lying deeper without adding to its weight. This idea was so successful that it was patented. George Stephenson (of 'Rocket' fame) was very impressed with this and foresaw the death of cast iron railways.

If you're like me it takes quite a bit of thinking and imagination to move beyond the initial 'so what?' state. This really did revolutionise the railways, though. For example it allowed the mass production of rails by powered machinery for the first time instead of rail production being in the hands of a blacksmith. Those of you on the 07.45 from Surbiton are no doubt wishing that John Birkenshaw had come up with leaf-repelling tracks instead, but even so.

The success of the rail was such that the Stockton-Darlington Railway which we all learn about at school was built with around 80% malleable rails. This was quite an achievement, given that the railway owners had a strong interest in cast iron rails! Bedlington supplied 1200 tons of malleable iron rails for that railway.

It was not just the rails which were made in Bedlington, though. The Stephensons' first locomotive, the 'Blucher', had its axles, wheels and boilerplates made in Bedlington, as did many of this country's early locomotives. Initially, all the work was carried out in the iron works. However, in 1837 the first locomotive was built in a locomotive factory in Bedlington. This put them in direct competition with the locomotive works in Newcastle run, amongst, others by the Stephenson brothers.

The first locomotive was produced for a local railway company and was cause for great celebration. The whole of Bedlington turned out to see the locomotive hauled away by horses. Over the following 15 years over 150 locomotives were built in Bedlington, the last one to be produced being the 'Prince Albert' in 1852.

The first train out of King's Cross was pulled by a Bedlington engine, as were the first trains in both Holland and Italy. I think that's a pretty impressive achievement for such a small town.

By 1855 the locomotive factory was closing down. This was a cut-throat industry at the time and competition was fierce. Whilst the Newcastle locomotive factory was almost on top of a railway, the Bedlington factory had huge logistical problems in taking all of its production 12 miles to Newcastle on trolleys drawn by horses.

The whole of the iron industry was in decline just a few years later. Ironstone had been discovered in 1846 in North East Yorkshire. This new mineral was taking over from any other source of supply. Furnaces became bigger and more productive. Inevitably they became based around the sources of supply. By 1867, iron production in Bedlington had come to an end.

What a huge impact from such a little place, though. One, too, with worldwide implications.

One of the other ways in which Bedlington has impacted

on the world is its rearing of Daniel (later Sir Daniel) Gooch. He was born on 24th August 1816 in the town. He was not only hugely influential in the development of railways and in particular locomotives, but he also laid the first ever transatlantic cable – a huge achievement for which he was made a Baronet.

More impressively still, Bedlington gave birth on 5th January 1971 to one Jayne Middlemiss. She is one of those amazing celebrities who, seemingly devoid of any obvious talent, becomes famous for being a celebrity. Originally a nanny and then a topless/glamour model (5ft 6ins, bust 34B, waist 25, hips 35 for those of you who need to know), she has been appearing on shows for C-list celebrities like *Celebrity Love Island*, which she jointly won with an ex-manager of a boy band, and *The Games*, which showed just what a sporty type she is.

She's apparently a huge Newcastle United fan and I wonder if that was how she first developed the habit of taking her top off. Actually, she seems to have the air of a real and normal person. I'm sure she'll be relieved to hear that I quite like her, which isn't true of most of this type of celebrity. I do counsel you though, not to look Jayne up on the internet on a full stomach without applying parental controls. Oh the wonders of digital photography … boys with their toys …

In fact the boys like Jayne a lot. She has done pretty well over the years in the poll for the 100 Sexiest Women In The World run by the bloke mag, *FHM*. She came 77th in 1999, 75th in 1999 and 74th in 2000. One devoted fan on one of those oh-so-strange tribute sites interprets this performance as being one of class and real quality, contrasting it with those girls who appear high in the chart one year, never to be seen again.

When Tom and I arrived in Bedlington it was unusually

warm – the car showed 31° as an outdoor temperature. It was muggy and sticky. I presume this weather isn't the norm in the area – but then again, perhaps that's the real reason why Geordie football fans always seem to be shirtless? I thought they were just rock hard.

It looked quite a pleasant place. Whether it would on a rainy January day is another matter, I suppose. There were pleasant enough bungalows on the outskirts with a fair display of flowers. Strangely, though, it seemed to be the only place in England which didn't claim to be a 'Britain in Bloom' winner.

We parked on a very large but empty car park which seemed to be there just for the benefit of a run-down-looking Safeway and one of the shops where you can buy anything for a pound. We tried to cut through there to what we thought would be the main street, but there was no way through. The shop seemed pretty busy with people stocking up on absolute rubbish, though.

Safeway brought more success and we appeared out on a pleasant-looking shopping street, with our eyes peeled for a 'Bedler' as we had come to know it for short. It was a really clammy and warm day. We walked one way up the main street, Front Street, past a range of newsagents, bakers and chemists and then having found nothing to interest us, we turned around and walked the approximately one mile to the other end. There was nothing wrong with the place, just nothing really there at all. It had been a long time since I had passed so many closed pubs during the day. I hadn't realised that there were still places where they didn't just stay open.

There really were no places of interest. The shops didn't even seem to have any of those strange local history books or – as I had really hoped – a book about the Bedlington terrier. In fact, there seemed to be no link with the town's most famous 'son' at all. Dogs were being walked, sure enough, but no Bedlers. The normal Labrador dominated the crowd. No obvious park in the town.

After about an hour we decided that we had to take the bull by the horns, as it were, and risk embarrassment. We went straight into the vet's surgery on the main street. It was outside surgery hours and we didn't have an animal with us, so I suppose the suspicious and, frankly, alarmed look the receptionist gave us was very understandable. It was no doubt not helped by my clumsy opening: 'we're going to ask you a bit of a strange question…' No doubt thoughts of cults, perverts or, at best, desperate sales people crossed her mind. Imagine, then, the almost visible sign of relief we got when we explained what we were doing and asked if she knew of any Bedlington Terriers in Bedlington?

Interestingly, the young girl fell very quickly into professional interviewee mode. She said there weren't many but obviously 'we would love to have a lot more.'

Our chat revealed that although she'd only been there for about six months, Diane only knew of four Bedlers signed up with the practice, although none lived in Bedlington. Some of them apparently lived as far as five miles away! Two were senior citizens of 8 or 9, but the good news was that there were also a couple of puppies signed up with the practice.

Our 'isn't it a shame there weren't more around here?' chat did unearth a couple of treasures, though. Did we know that there was a pub called the 'Bedlington Terrier' in the town? We did not. Did we also know that the football club were called the Bedlington Terriers and they had a home friendly match that very evening? Indeed we did and indeed we did not.

From the disappointment of apparently not seeing a single Bedlington Terrier in Bedlington, suddenly our visit had rays of hope. We set off looking for the pub, getting lost several times along the way. People were incredibly friendly when we asked them the way – really difficult to understand though. I love accents and am generally pretty good at them. But here it sometimes seemed like a different language altogether. We'd noticed the change in accent as we moved up from York, with what we thought to be traces of the North Eastern accent beginning to appear, to our surprise, as far south as Thirsk. This was something else, though!

We eventually found the red-brick pub on one of the major roads out of the town, in what appeared to be an area largely of 1930s council houses. Like all the other pubs in Bedlington it was closed. It wasn't quaint or interesting, just a very workmanlike pub. There's nothing more to say. A few pictures of the sign, featuring our elusive hero, and off we walked back into town. People were so friendly that some of the individuals we'd asked for directions on the way to the pub were even keen to check that we had indeed found it as we passed them on the way back.

Later than evening – Bedlington is a very difficult place to pass a couple of early evening hours in unless Lidl is open late – we set off in search of the Welfare Gound, home of the mighty Bedlington Terriers. More conversations which left me feeling guilty like some sort of lazy Englishman abroad insisting that the 'foreigner' speaks my language in his home land, and we finally found the ground.

It was tucked deeply away in an area of terraces, seemingly Victorian. Perhaps some of the original housing from Bedlington's industrial past. Very neat and nicely maintained. I quite often go to smaller grounds and enthuse to Tom, 'now this is from a time when there were real football grounds,' while he rolls his eyes and starts saying things like, 'men were men, weren't they, Dad? And the football weighed two tons when it was wet …'

Anyway, this one was too small to be in my 'real football

ground' category, however much I liked it. We were delighted, though, to see the club's badge. It is a colliery head (or whatever the proper name is for the top of a mine shaft with the lift wheel), in front of which stands none other than a Bedlington terrier with a football!

Football started in Bedlington in around 1900, but the present club dates back to 1949 when it was founded under the name of Bedlington Mechanics. In the 1950s the team became Colliery Town and then Bedlington Colliery Welfare. The team was disbanded in 1962/3 only to rise from the ashes in 1965. The 70s saw the team in the even greater obscurity of local minor leagues before being re-admitted in 1980/81 to the comparative big time of the Northern Alliance League as Bedlington United. The early 90s was another period of real gloom before a relaunch as the Bedlington Terriers. Perhaps their greatest moment came in 1998/9 when they defeated Colchester United (then Football League Division 2) 4-1 in the first round of the FA Cup, before going out to another league club, Scunthorpe, in the second round. Only if, like me, you are a fan of grassroots, non-league football can you imagine how exciting this is and what an achievement it must have been. Teams like my own, playing probably at a slightly higher level, have to play through endless preliminary and qualifying rounds to get anywhere near even the minnows of Football League opposition. We're often playing in the FA Cup from August for this chance!

I think we were disappointed that the link with 'Terriers' had been so recent – but then realistically clubs have their history in local industries and trades really, don't they, not breeds of dog?

These days the Terriers, supported with their famous (?) 'woof woof, Terriers' chant, can be found in the Northern Alliance League. The friendly we watched was against local rivals Seaton Delaval Amateurs of the Northern Alliance Premier League and was a fairly non-descript game ending in a 2-1 win. Even so, I'm sure that Bedlington Terriers will be added to the mental list of results we look out for. We left that evening disappointed not to have seen a single Bedlington Terrier in Bedlington.

That was it, then. Post-industrial Bedlington. There was no obvious sign of where people would be working. I had the sense that the 'posher' bits might be dormitories for Newcastle workers. So Bedlington was now quite pleasant and quite dull. I found out later that the town has a large country park with five miles of paths, horse and nature trails, but we missed it. I also found that in 1999 the local Chamber of Commerce was successful in getting information about the town sent to Mars. Furthermore, market day in Bedlington is Thursday. Hope they told the Martians, so they don't come on a Wednesday.

Fortunately the Bedlington terrier itself is neither quiet nor dull. It is a smallish dog – about 16 inches high at the withers (at the back of the neck). It weighs typically around 8-10kg (18-23lbs). Its most striking feature is just how much (in show trim at least) it looks like a little lamb. With a soft, woolly coat, ears which are trimmed into tassles and an arched back, together with a well-developed top knot on its head, it really is unique. It has a very distinctive, sheep-like coat. It is a thick, 'linty' coat which stands out from the skin. I think we had seen most colour variations at Crufts and these include 'blue', liver or sandy.

The dog is a graceful mover, quite light in its step. It almost appears as though it's trying not to damage what it's treading on. I suppose it doesn't look much of a hardy terrier but it very much is one.

Like that of many other breeds, the history of the Bedlington terrier is far from clear. There is some sort of link with the Dandie Dinmont terrier, which is a much shorter-legged dog, though otherwise quite like our hero. Which came first though, is the question: the Bedlington or the Dandie Dimmont? There is certainly some whippet in there, too.

Terriers were very much the dogs of the 'working classes' in England – small, game, tenacious dogs who were bred and improved for their vermin-controlling prowess. It seems that the Bedlington was no exception and it was linked with the many miners in the area. As well as dealing with vermin, they were raced against each other and even against Whippets. Another group often said to have been involved in the development of the breed is the gypsy community on the nearby Rothbury Hills who successfully used the Terrier for poaching. One story is that the landowners were so impressed by the dogs in this illegal activity at their expense that they actually took them on as vermin-controllers.

Just like the football team, the breed has undergone many name changes, being variously Rothbury terrier, Northumberland terrier, Northern Counties terrier, Rodbury terrier, miner's terrier and Northumberland fox terrier.

It is generally recognised that the first dog truly known as a Bedlington terrier was a dog called Ainsley's Piper who was born in 1825. He was owned by a stonemason from Bedlington called Joseph Aynsley (or Ainsley). Piper was quite a dog, who continued to hunt fox and otter well into his old age. Many of today's dogs can be traced back to Piper. Interestingly, because the breed was recognised early (in 1873) and appeared at the earliest shows, many pedigrees are comparatively complete and can be traced back through the Kennel Club's Stud Books.

Today, like almost all other breeds, the Bedlington does not get to follow and hone those natural instincts for which it was bred, but spends its time as a companion dog – in other words a pet.

The Bedlington terrier actually features in the European

Convention as having a 'named fault' – in this case copper toxicosis. This is an inherited condition where surplus copper is not excreted from the body in the normal way. Instead it builds up in the liver and causes damage which can range from mild to fatal. Progress is being made to identify the problem gene, to the extent that a simple blood test could identify those dogs that are clear, those that are carrier and those that are affected. Most recent indications from the Bedlington Terrier Health Group (founded in 2002, perhaps another example of breeds being forced into action to avoid legislation?) are that the test is not fully reliable. Still, progress is clearly being made, which with ethical breeding could remove this significant health risk from the breed.

The only other real health issue with the Bedlington appears to be the eyes. Entropion (eyelashes growing inwards) and distichiasis (abnormal location of the eyelashes on the eyelid) are both issues which are possibly inherited. There is also an issue about abnormal tear production.

As the DNA work continues and removes the risk of copper toxicosis, which can lead to early death, it may be that the breed will grow in popularity – maybe there will even be some Bedlington terriers in Bedlingon!

I did contact the three Bedlington Terrier Breed Clubs, but only one responded. (This is actually a very good ratio for some of the self-important types in the world of dogs.) They confirmed that they had no members in the Bedlington area, which was a shame.

So, that was it. We were leaving Bedlington behind without so much as a whiff of a 'Bedler', nor indeed of Jayne Middlemiss, which would have offered some consolation.

Tom went quiet. I sensed something was brewing.

'Dad, do you think you would find more Scottish breeds at a dog show in Scotland …?'

CHAPTER 6

Clicking with Dogs

So there I was, sitting idly, browsing the internet when there was that tell-tale 'bong' as an item dropped in my email inbox. Looking at who had sent the message, I initially thought it was a reminder for my next magazine article. But surely an article wasn't due? Tempted to avoid looking in case I was wrong and had to pull my finger out and write something, I couldn't beat my curiosity and clicked on the message. I couldn't really believe what I saw – would I like to speak at a conference about Clicker Training? Not only that, but I would be on the 'bill' with a great hero of mine, probably the world's greatest authority on clicker training, Karen Pryor, author of the seminal work *Don't Shoot the Dog*. I would be following Karen at the conference (eek!) and would be followed by a second top clicker trainer, Attilla Szkukalek.

I now had two things to do urgently. First, rush to the toilet and secondly, find out where the conference was. Commonly these conferences are in the USA, as clicker training is much more mainstream there. Sometimes, the conferences are held on mainland Europe, particularly Holland, Germany or Belgium. But this one was in … Coventry! About 20 miles from home.

My disappointment lasted for seconds. This was a real honour. Kay Lawrence, this country's greatest clicker trainer and organiser of the conference, wanted mine to be a very active session, between Karen's session – primarily a lecture – and Attila's session, which would be a demonstration.

For the first of many times over the coming weeks I felt very inadequate – but I couldn't say no, could I? My subject was to be in the area of 'teaching people teaching dogs' where I had a regular feature in *Teaching Dogs* magazine. It was to be a lively, active session … for around 200 people. Still, although I didn't have a clue what I would do and was instantly dreading it, this definitely went under the 'good for the soul/it will be good for you' category and I accepted straight away. One thing I wasn't really worried about was the audience reaction, simply because, as a group, I cannot think of a more positive group of people than clicker trainers.

This may be a good time to describe what clicker training actually is. First and foremost it is just an incredibly dog-friendly, reward-based method of training based on positive reinforcement – i.e. catch the dog doing what you want and reward it. With some commonality to dolphin training – and perhaps initially rooted there so far as the method is concerned – it works by marking the behaviour you want with a 'click' produced by a little plastic box containing a metal 'tongue', which is attached at one end of the box and produces the noise as the metal strip is pressed and goes straight again. In itself, of course, the click means nothing – it has to be associated with a super, high-quality treat. This is achieved quite simply by allowing the dog to take the treat and sounding the click as it does so. After a few repeats, if the clicker is clicked the dog looks everywhere for the treat.

Having made this link, everything else is about timing. Catching the exact second when the dog does what you want to with a click – just like you were taking a camera picture of the desired behaviour and had to press the button at just the right time to catch the behaviour in a photo.

So, why use the 'clicker' at all? Well, it is an absolutely consistent reward-marker. It does not change with our mood or emotion: whether the dog has delighted us with his speed of learning or frustrated us to the point of tears, the reward marker is absolutely consistent. Consistency is vitally important. Just listen to how people praise their dogs – the range of voice tones, pitches and extensive vocabulary they use.

The clicker gives pinpoint accuracy, too. At the split second when the desired behaviour happens it can be 'caught' by the click. This is irrespective of distance, for example. If a dog sits at the bottom of the garden when you give a signal at the top, you can catch that behaviour exactly with a click. Even after the inevitable delay in getting the reward (a little piece of dried liver, for example) to the dog, he is in no doubt as to what he is getting rewarded for – it is whatever he was doing as he heard the click. Without the click, we would walk down to the dog and give it a titbit, trying to tell it that this was a reward for what it was doing fifteen seconds ago. In reality, the dog will have just looked up at the birds, barked at a cat, sniffed a flower or whatever, only to receive a reward seemingly in recompense.

The clicker really does harness a dog's mental energy and encourage a dog to 'try'. It is often said that a ten-minute clicker session is like an hour's walk in terms of the energy used up. This is great for young dogs who can't have all the exercise they need because of exercise restrictions owing to growth. It is also great for 'shaping' complex activities because it encourages the dog to have a go and try new things. If the click is withheld, a dog will begin to try other activities, which can then be clicked and rewarded. It's a fantastically rewarding way of spending time with your dog.

It is so 'empowering' for the dog that it is a method which those training most complex behaviours use. Hearing Dogs for Deaf People, Dogs For The Disabled and other groups use the clicker extensively to teach dogs to empty washing machines, bring ringing phones and so on. It would be difficult to 'force train' these activities.

What I really like about it is that it is such a positive way of engaging with the dog. It is also a very patient way. It takes away the need/desire for 'macho' control. It prevents the stress and frustration in so many other methods and calms down the overexcited (puppies in particular seem to elicit 'hyper' behaviour in owners which passes straight back to the dog – often ending in frustration and tears). Owners need to respond to hyper behaviour and attention-seeking with calmness and the clicker method really helps with this.

My whole aim in getting involved in dog-training was to help deal with the simple fact that the main cause of death in young dogs is euthanasia. I'm not too worried about people who are doing competitive sports with their dogs – they can look after themselves (even though they could often achieve more and have more fun with their dogs with the clicker). It is those people who need to build a good relationship with a family pet and get a happy well-adjusted companion for their busy family lives that most interest me: people who, if things do not work well, may feel more inclined to let go of their pet. Through ignorance, they may even cause a dog to become unsociable or even aggressive.

Anyway, I spent some time over the next few weeks pondering what my subject would be. In the end I decided upon a session looking at the different 'learning styles' of the handlers that a dog trainer would have in their class and what this would mean for the trainer. We tend to think that everyone learns as we do – if we have achieved success by sitting and listening to people drone on we tend to think others will, whereas many others will learn nothing that way and need simply to get up, have a go and learn by their mistakes.

There are four main learning styles in one particular model

and it was my aim to show how we could appeal to all four during a session so that everyone has an equal chance of learning successfully. The big question was: how was I going to do this in a fairly entertaining and interesting manner with 200 people?

This certainly kept me thinking over the next few weeks. I didn't really address it, though, until I went away on my habitual walking holiday with the dogs in my favourite place, the Forest of Dean. There you can walk for miles and for hours without even putting your dog on a lead. Out of season, you hardly even meet anyone. The peace and solitude and the feeling of being out as a pack is fantastic. It certainly allows you a lot of thinking time and space. Of course, all the brilliant ideas you have while trudging along for a few hours are long gone by the time you get back to the cottage … then you can lie awake trying to think what they were.

It was a sad time in the Forest when foot and mouth had taken hold. Instead of seeing the sheep roam freely and never being sure when you might come across them – usually having to avoid them pottering down the roads in a fairly suicidal fashion – there were none. So it was great when they came back – especially as my dogs don't chase sheep – not even the Border collie. He will run two or three paces towards them in the hope of being called back before he has to put any more wasted effort in. I remember seeing some sheep one time before he had seen or scented them. It was like the TV advert (for Penguin I think) when I called him and he turned round to look at me while ten or fifteen sheep crossed the path just behind him – almost dancing and bobbing their tongues out at him. When he looked back round they had all disappeared and he was none the wiser.

The deal in the Forest is that after a very long walk I get to read, write or most likely sleep whilst Alison does her cross-stitch and the three dogs have a deep, snoring sleep (which, incidentally, becomes a very light sleep if you walk anywhere near a food bowl or the back door leading to the paddock with play and extra walkies potential).

So, some of these afternoons were spent putting together the conference session. In the end I came up with a bit of 'theatre' using different people wearing different- coloured hats to represent the different learning styles, almost playing the part of a Greek chorus commenting on what was going on in the session. Add coloured cards for people to hold up, noises to represent the different learning styles and a couple of energisers to get people on their feet and that was it! I had chosen 'getting energy into your training' as the 'session within a session' and it was this that my four different learning-style actors would be reacting to. Choosing 'energy' as the subject enabled me to get people up and about and make things a little more interactive.

Once the session had been planned I could use the afternoons for what they were really meant for – catching up with sleep from our very busy lifestyle, reading, playing with the dogs, drinking lots of tea and, oh yes, dropping off to sleep again, synchronising my breathing to that of the dogs.

It was just two weeks later that I arrived in a huge hall at about 7.30 in the morning. I did not know who my actors would be and the organiser was not there. I began to feel a little hot and bothered. Various things were being set up around the hall, but nobody seemed to know who I was or what I was doing there.

It was a large venue – a very full-sized sports hall – and one end had been set up for a conference, so I thought I would just get on and set up. Suddenly, people appeared from every direction and I had my 'actors'. Fortunately, they were very enthusiastic and up for anything. A rehearsal went really well – one or two of them were even 'playing the audience' although there wasn't one there yet. The next hour was the worst part of the day – watching all these experienced-looking dog folk arriving and realising that I would be standing up in front of them soon. Strangely, though, once the conference was under way, I felt fine and was able to listen and concentrate fully on what Karen Pryor had to say. She spoke about the progress that clicker training had made over the last decade, not just in its use with dogs, but how the approach was being used with people, too.

It was my session next and, other than struggling with a strange headset microphone, it went really well. People were standing up as asked, impersonating bees when asked, holding up coloured cards and generally getting into the swing of things. I spent the rest of the day getting really positive feedback from lots of people. What a place the world would be if everyone had such a positive outlook. After the pretty surreal experience of having lunch with Karen Pryor, her daughter Gale and the other speaker, Attilla – who had been speaking about some fairly advanced and technical features of clicker training – the rest of the day was spent taking part in practical workshops.

Looking around the hall, there were a lot of Border collies, but fewer, for example, than at an obedience or agility show where these fantastic all-rounders predominate, to the extent that in agility there are even special ABC (Anything But Collies) classes to give others a chance. At the clicker conference there were a lot of crossbreeds, together with dogs with less of a traditional history of 'brain work', like setters and hounds.

For me, though, there was an unexpected bonus to be had by attending the conference. I had been fretting about how I was going to 'spot' one of the dogs in the challenge as it is not a Kennel Club recognised breed – in fact it's debatable whether it's a breed at all. To make things worse, it's generally associated with the other side of the world. So I was delighted when a rather plump lady leading one of the workshops started one section of her session with the words, 'I'm going to show you this with my kelpie …'

I think kelpies (often called Australian kelpies) are marvellous dogs. They are the real workers of that continent, an incredible 100,000 of them – their equivalent of our Border collie, I suppose. They work in all temperatures – extreme heat and the cold – tirelessly for hours. They are beyond energetic: they are truly driven animals, desperate for work – a nightmare as a family pet (as are many Border collies, of course). Kelpies need an almost infinite amount of exercise and to keep going all day. When working they can typically cover between 1,000 and 4,000 acres in one day!

Like Border collies, the 'eye' is all-important in the kelpie. They use the eye to control animals such as sheep. They do, though, have tougher attributes and are quite capable of getting right in and nipping when dealing with cattle if they have to.

You might expect that these dogs would excel at obedience competition, but there is no doubt that it is the Border collie that is King and Queen of the competitive obedience world rather than the kelpie. Although they share some of the working attributes of the Border collie, kelpies are not really for obedience. They do not work particularly tidily or precisely and would lose many of the points available in competitive obedience. They are a no-nonsense, roll-your-sleeves-up sort of dog. No messing. Think of no-nonsense Australians who couldn't give a 4X about anything else and you've got it!

At about 17-20 inches high and 25-45 pounds in weight,

the kelpie is not a large dog. Their body is slightly longer than it is high. It has a long and narrow head and a low-set, medium-length tail. It is double-coated, which means that it has a short, thick undercoat and a hard, straight, weather-resistant coat on the outside. This allows for temperature control. Unlike Henry Ford's famous Model T, the breed is not only available in black, but also in red. Both colours can be complemented with tan. Fawn, chocolate and blue dogs (not all at once!) are also available, but less common. This really is not a show dog, though, and it is working ability, rather than appearance, which is of interest to owners. They are easily trained, but will find things to do if they are not kept active – such as herding children, pets, cars or anything else. They are real canine workaholics.

With regard to the breed's origins, some look to the dingo for its roots. Others suggest that there is much more compelling evidence and accurate documentation which shows that the breed descends from English North Country collies. Indeed, the first mention of the name 'kelpie' can be traced back to Robert Louis Stevenson's *Kidnapped*, where he refers to a water kelpie, and so dates back to 1870.

Nowadays, there are around 500 kelpies in the UK. The cost of importing and quarantining breeding stock had made the nurture of the breed particularly impracticable and expensive, until technology allowed for the import of frozen semen from Australia, allowing for artificial insemination in Scotland. Even so, the total of 500 kelpies compares with an *annual* registration of 6,000 working sheepdogs (Border collies) in the UK at the moment.

It really did make my day to meet this pretty unusual stranger in the flesh and to chat with his owner about this really unusual, workaholic dog. It was odd, really, because I find that dogs often 'speak' to me and this one really did have a strong Australian accent and Aussie swagger: 'G'day mate!'

By this stage in my quest, I had had a fair number of setters in my dog classes and had been able to tick off both the English setter and the Irish red setter. The latter, in particular, always strikes me as a particularly glamorous dog with its deep red colour and its flowing body lines. It was probably just about the first pedigree dog I was familiar with as a kid in a world full of mongrels with the odd 'Alsatian' as the leader of a pack of stray dogs. The Irish red setter, though, belonged to the park-keeper in my local park – Palfrey Park – where I spent so much of my childhood. Unusually, the dog – Brandy – roamed loose around its domain, making friends with kids and dogs alike. It was also a very useful early warning for us that the parkie was around!

Before the conference, though, I hadn't been able to tick off the Gordon setter – a black and tan setter with roots strongly in Scotland. In fact, there were two or three at the conference. This was largely because Kay Lawrence, organiser of the conference and my mentor for a number of years, owned and bred Gordon setters. When she had first talked about using Gordon setters for clicker training in general, and particularly heelwork to music (i.e. dog dancing), she had been met with various degrees of disbelief from the Gordon setter community who offered: 'they'll never be able to do that', 'they're too excitable', 'they're just big babies who can't concentrate', and other such comments. In fact, Kay's Gordons had excelled and this had really challenged the preconceptions even of Gordon setter fans.

It was great to see the Gordons well represented and people's prejudices and beliefs about breeds being challenged so effectively.

The morning of day one was the plenary session where I delivered my session. The afternoon was a series of workshops

– covering sessions like using the clicker in Heelwork to Music, how Dogs for the Disabled use clicker training and playing games to develop your own clicker skills, especially the all-important timing.

On day two I was still being stopped by people telling me how much they had enjoyed my session and engaging me in all sorts of clicker-training problems and questions, especially about running classes.

The real point of day two, though, is the Clicker Challenge. Groups of people get together to compete against each other in training dogs to do a pretty difficult series of tasks using the clicker. At the end of the day, judges will determine who has achieved the most. People and their dogs just have so much fun doing this – that's the main point about it. At the same time, they all achieve so much.

There were some fantastic challenges on this day – 10 in all, 8 of which had to be attempted by each team. The challenges were announced at 10 a.m., giving the teams 3 hours to complete their training and demonstrate what they had achieved.

This time the challenges were:

1 'Reverse slalom'. The dog has to be taught to walk backwards through a series of slalom gates.
2 'The Gambler'. Using foam dice, the dog has to roll two sixes, using its nose. It may not paw, lift, bite or chew the dice.
3 'Simon says'. The dog has to complete 3 behaviours whilst the handler keeps their hand on its head.
4 'Body Burrowing'. The dog has to tunnel through 6 people who are down on their hands and knees.
5 'Homework'. The dog must collect various household items, such as a duster, a nail brush, a mop-head and a

feather duster and place them in a box they have carried to the spot.

6 'Hunt the duck'. This was a scent trial, where dogs had to find a 'duck', hidden under cones or markers.
7 'It's starting to rain'. The dog has to collect items from a washing-line by releasing the pegs, dropping the item and handing it to the handler.
8 'Turtles away'. Two dogs – one showing its head and the other its tail, have to negotiate a series of obstacles, moving under a protective 'shell' created by team members' bodies.
9 'Threading the needle'. Possibly my favourite. The dog has to run from one handler to the other, jumping through a hoop rolled across their path by a third handler. It therefore has to judge the speed and direction of the hoop and adjust its jump accordingly whilst running between the two handlers.
10 'Skateboard relay'. Yes, dogs skateboarding backwards and forwards in a relay.

Some of these are advanced, complicated tasks, and watching the teams happily sharing their experience and knowledge was a joy to behold, especially as people in the world of dogs are often very slow to share their skills.

Obviously, there is nothing magical about the clicker in itself. It is, to me though, symbolic of a really positive, non-aversive and non-force-based approach to dog training. It is a fantastic tool, too, in 'shaping' behaviour – i.e. building a behaviour incrementally until it becomes what you want as an end result. Going for the full-blown end result in one go would be far too much, so start off by taking a step in the right direction and rewarding that, and then ask for a little more before you reward, and so on.

What this really involves first is breaking a behaviour down into its small constituent parts and then chaining them back together. For example, thinking of teaching the dog to jump through a rolling hoop whilst running from handler to handler, it may be that you would teach a dog to jump through a stationary hoop to start with, as not all dogs will be confident doing this. It is quite likely that the dog may have to be 'lured' through the hoop, perhaps with a juicy treat taken back through the hoop to start with. Similarly, not all dogs will come back to a stranger – especially with lots of dogs and fun activity around. Then, once the dog is happy stepping through the stationary hoop from close up, you might add a little distance to approaching the hoop (many dogs will sensibly divert around an obstacle at this stage). Again it may, for example, be necessary to hold a treat through the hoop onto the dog's side to target going through the hoop itself and then pull it back through for the dog to follow.

Adding distance either side of the hoop, then speed of approach, may well all come before starting to roll the hoop. Patience and repetition with small incremental movements and rewards for getting things right, and moving slowly towards the end result are what is required. And how it all paid off at the Clicker Challenge, where the dogs and handlers did so well and were a joy to watch.

These positive training methods readily allow training of very complex tasks as well as simple ones. In fact, many of the more complex tasks are now clicker-taught, such as Heelwork to Music, and many of the major charities make extensive use of clicker training – organisations such as Dogs for the Disabled and Hearing Dogs for Deaf People.

Watching these dogs at work is truly a humbling experience. Dogs for the Disabled, for example, aims to give adults and children their independence, improved confidence and

Nice to meet you! Meeting a hero of mine - Greyfriars Bobby

The memorial at Kamp Westerbork - the rails point up towards heaven

Tourist attraction, Drenthe-style. The biggest Hunnebedde in Holland

At a village fountain in Ischia, it's live and let live between the locals and the local dogs

...and every store has its resident dog to mind the shop!

With Eva and Ot... guess what type of dogs they are......

obviously all-important companionship. As far as training goes, clicker training is used first and foremost and the dogs really enjoy the work they are given to do. Here are some of the activities the dogs (often Labradors, golden retrievers and first crosses of these breeds) are trained to do:

- Opening and closing doors
- Helping people to dress/undress (one owner points out the dog is so gentle that it has never even laddered a pair of her tights when helping her with undressing in over two years!).
- Picking up dropped items – phones, keys, crutches.
- Fetching items such as mobile phones, blankets and slippers.
- Switching lights on and off.
- Pressing buttons at road crossings.
- Bringing in milk, collecting post and mail.
- Emptying the washing machine.
- Carrying shopping baskets and lifting purses and wallets up to the shop counter.

Training begins when the dogs are around one year old, having spent their early lives getting basic obedience training and being socialised to as many sights, sounds and experiences as possible by special volunteers who act as 'puppy-walkers'.

The training itself lasts for 6 to 8 months, covering both teaching the dogs to undertake tasks and also teaching the client to work with their new assistance dog.

After residential training for the dog and its new handler at the charity's own purpose-built centre, training continues with visits to the disabled person's home to see how the dog is working in situ.

Overall costs for training are around £5,000 per dog, with the charity dependent completely on donations and sponsorship.

Watching these dogs at work can quite literally bring a tear to the eye. They really do offer such an improvement to the quality of life of their handler, not just through the obvious practical help they offer, but through the psychological benefits resulting from the independence made possible by the dog and the consequent increase in confidence.

Since the charity was founded in 1988 by Frances Hay – herself a disabled woman who wanted others to benefit from the help of a dog as she had herself – approaching 300 dogs have been trained and gone out to make such a difference to people's lives. Some of the anecdotes of fetching mobile phones to fallen people, barking to gain attention in an emergency and literally thousands of everyday examples of much appreciated help, make these dogs real canine heroes.

Hearing Dogs for Deaf People in many ways fulfils a very similar purpose to the Dogs for the Disabled, except that it focuses its work on those afflicted by what many term 'the hidden disability' – deafness. As with many other disabilities, one of the greatest consequences of deafness can be a loss of independence and of confidence. Hearing Dogs really help deaf people get on with a much more ordinary life. These dogs are specifically trained to alert their owners to everyday sounds ranging from the useful to the life-saving, such as telephones, the doorbell, an alarm clock, a baby crying or a smoke alarm.

When the Hearing Dog hears any of these, it seeks out its owner and touches them with a paw – waking them if necessary!

Image being a deaf mum who can't hear her baby crying and the increased independence having a dog like this would give you. By the same token, being alerted to a smoke alarm could literally be the difference between life and death.

This is one of my very favourite charities and I do try to raise money for them when I can. Last year, Tom and I took

Stan, our Border collie, on an organised sponsored walk for Hearing Dogs in Stratford-Upon-Avon. We walked a particularly beautiful route, also popular with cyclists. Of course, seeing the posters advertising the event, many of the cyclists and other walkers presumed we were deaf people. The good news was, though, that I found we were being treated with greater respect than usual. Instead of the shout or frantic ringing of the bell with which we're often greeted (even though it's a *foot*-path and not a *cycle* path – but that's a subject for a different time), the cyclists were trying to give us space, making sure we had seen them and generally taking care. Tom and I raised around £100 between us – not a lot, but then I hate asking for sponsorship. Even so, we got T-shirts and medals, which was great.

The history of Hearing Dogs for Deaf People is really quite recent, like Dogs for the Disabled, but very interesting. Schemes in America have been around for some time under the title of 'Hearing Ear' schemes. Then, in 1979, an American academic, Professor Lee Bustad, gave a talk at a British Small Animal Veterinary Association Symposium. In it, he described some of the training programmes being used to assist deaf people in the United States. The TV vet, writer and columnist Bruce Fogle was one of those watching Professor Bustad's talk that day and he immediately contacted the RNID – Royal National Institute for the Deaf.

Over the next couple of years Bruce Fogle and Lady Wright of the RNID carried out research and visited some of the American schemes, before a pilot scheme was devised for Britain. Some generous financial sponsorship was available but still not nearly enough for an undertaking with such ambition.

When a facility to house dogs became available in Oxfordshire this was a huge step forward, so that at Crufts in 1982 the scheme could be launched, featuring 'Favour',

Britain's first ever Hearing Dog, who was a stray rescued from one of the National Canine Defence League (now Dog Trust) rescue facilities.

In that year, the first four dogs were trained – this proving difficult in the absence of a real training facility which could be used to replicate realistic conditions. It was four years before such a centre could be established and a further four years before the 100th hearing dog was trained. Since then progress has been amazing and growth exponential (as I believe the real word is!)

It took just three years to train the next hundred dogs, so that two hundred had been trained and placed by 1993. Over the following three years not one hundred but two hundred further dogs had been trained, taking the total to 400. By 2001, the number had reached 800 and by 2004, a thousand dogs had been placed, the 1000th being Ria, a mongrel who had been found as a stray.

Along the way, Hearing Dogs had opened two more training centres and acquired a prestigious Patron in the form of HRH The Princess Royal.

Another, to my mind amazing, event which occurred in 2003 was a joint project with the Guide Dogs for the Blind Association to place Roddy, an assistance dog with a profoundly deaf and visually impaired lady from Cheshire. This was the first ever dual-purpose dog trained as both a hearing dog and guide dog. What an amazing animal!

It's easy to look at these figures and perhaps be impressed but without thinking what an individual difference having a hearing dog made to each and every one of those thousand individuals and families.

From the dog point of view, one of the things I love about this charity is its ability and desire to use mongrels, crossbreeds, rescue dogs and others who perhaps have a harder time in life. In fact, the 'average' hearing dog is a small mixed-breed dog of either gender, selected from a rescue centre or donated as an unwanted pet. How fantastic to be taken from the scrap heap and turned into a canine hero.

As you can imagine, weeks of training are needed, beginning with a socialisation programme, moving on to intensive training in recognising and reacting to a variety of sounds, lasting for around four months, and then work in the particular placement home.

Just as with Dogs for the Disabled, early training and socialisation is undertaken by unsung heroes in the form of volunteer puppy-socialisers who ensure that the dog gets off to a really good start through solid basic training.

There is no way dogs for either charity could be trained to do this work through fear and aversives. Success in any particular activity brings reward. It is fun – really all a big game taught through positive reinforcement, often using the clicker as a tool at the training stage.

Positivity is the name of the game, and if these really complex and advanced tasks can be taught to dogs, then surely we can use positive reward-based techniques to get the basics with our pets?

I had a great time at the conference. Another feast of all things doggy. I felt like I'd achieved an awful lot personally and I left the two-day clicker conference on a real high, but to be honest not with too many ticks in my dog-spotting guide from the exercise. I really needed to make some progress …

CHAPTER 7

Isle of Dogs – Italian Style

Now, I'm just a bit wary of this. The thing is, I've found the most beautiful place for a dog-lover to go on holiday. In fact, it's completely beautiful whether you love dogs or not. It's actually pretty well known already, although not a huge destination for the British. You see, I don't really want it to get any more popular than it already is …

Still, Tom has reassured me twice over. Firstly, he has quite rightly pointed out that only a tiny percentage of manuscripts submitted to publishers become books. Secondly, even if this book is published then people still have to go out and buy it. As you can imagine, this comes as a great comfort to me and I am now ready to disclose all …

Two years before the dog-spotting challenge I went on a fantastic holiday. I had been storing a magazine under my bed for a couple of years. No – not the sort you are thinking of. In fact, it was a German-language dog magazine called *Wuff*. Now this in itself may seem a little weird to you, but I am still pretty fluent in German having studied it extensively and lived in Germany for a year teaching English. Reading dog magazines was a way of combining keeping the language skills up to date with my love of dogs.

The reason I had kept this particular magazine was an article in it about an Italian island where dogs seemed to live completely in harmony with the human inhabitants. Not being one for 'sunshine' holidays, I had kept it just in case.

I hadn't tried a lazy sunshine holiday until I was into my 30s. I had always thought that I would be bored to death just lying there. I'm sure that would have been true at one time but having been persuaded to give it a go one year and gone to Menorca I found that I loved it. Just real peace, floating on my back in the pool or lazing nearby, in the sun. Lots of reading, occasional dips in the pool, bottle of wine on the terrace in the evening – lovely. A couple of years later Malta had turned out to be just as fantastically relaxing. Moscow and St. Petersburg had been quite the opposite – a real all action sightseeing spectacular in a very exciting environment. Now the sun beckoned once more and I took the opportunity to break our usual two-month cycle of indecision in choosing where to go by putting forward the idea of going to the dog island – Ischia, in the Bay of Naples (although being honest I may have forgotten to mention to Alison the bit about the dogs).

The *Wuff* article had really captured my imagination. It talked of this beautiful island in the sun where dogs roamed free during the day, causing no trouble but happily interacting with both locals and tourists. They could apparently be seen playing on the beach, dozing on pavements and in and around shops. Well-fed and healthy animals, they could often be seen out for a walk on a lead in the evening, despite the fact that they had been roaming the very same streets all day on their own. Many belonged to the local shopkeepers and spent the day dozing at the front of the shop. I couldn't wait to get there. Apparently, these dogs were just as likely to be pedigree dogs as crossbreeds.

It has to be said that the holiday did start off quite shakily. The flight was fine, but once we reached Naples Airport we had no idea of where we were going. A rather sullen chap was standing in arrivals with our name on a board. I had presumed we would head off by coach, but through gesticulation we soon found we were to follow him. We were the only ones – very strange. Stranger still when he led us through back doors, various service tunnels, past boxes of freight. I had heard that Naples was a very dangerous city and was just beginning to worry that we had been singled out for abduction. He led us to a rather nice, shiny Mercedes and loaded our luggage in the back. We were soon driving through Naples in the direction of the harbour. Obviously, everyone else on the flight had been going to Sorrento or the Amalfi Coast.

What an experience that 20-minute journey was. Foot-to-the-floor acceleration followed quickly by foot-to-the-floor braking. All this with constant application of the horn by everyone on the road. Traffic emerged and appeared from all directions. Scooterists flashed by and wove in and out without the benefit of a helmet – presumably those are for wimps. The whole effect was made much more dramatic by driving on cobbles, amplifying the noise and giving a bumpy feel to the ride. Still, our sullen driver seemed to be taking it all in his stride.

It was here that we had our first encounter with an Italian dog. It was a black Labrador, riding pillion on a scooter, totally unrestrained, ears flapping in the wind. I couldn't believe what I was seeing at first, but by the time we reached the harbour we'd seen other dogs on scooterists' laps and some enjoying a ride in the scooter's footwell!

Our cases were unloaded at the docks and the driver was off in a flurry of Italian. It was quite disconcerting being left with our cases and absolutely no idea of what we were doing. We felt sure we had to get onto a hydrofoil but had no tickets and no idea which of the four to get on.

Out of the blue a young woman in a uniform, pushing a trolley, came up to us, picked up our bags and took them to a spot in the middle of a huge open space like a car park before unloading them and trundling off without a word. I have to be honest and admit that panic was beginning to set in big time. A few minutes later, though, a pleasant man turned up, seemed to want our holiday details and told us to follow him, leaving our luggage behind unattended in the crime den of Naples. He got us our hydrofoil tickets and gestured us on to a very large, rather smelly and down-at-heel hydrofoil. Sure enough, our bags were loaded on, much to our surprise.

Half an hour later we were there – or so we thought. The hydrofoil pulled into a beautiful Mediterranean harbour, the rusty metal gangplank was put down and off we got. We got suspicious because hardly anyone else was getting off. A few people were getting on. Something felt wrong. There didn't seem to be anyone waiting for us. In fact there didn't seem to be too much there at all. Rather incongruously, there was one very smartly dressed but very bored-looking policeman there. I decided to show him my tickets to find out what to do next. The effect was quite remarkable. He must have been *very* bored. He literally sprang into action, gesturing wildly and shouting to the muscle-bound sailors who were in the process of moving the gangplank ready for departure. If looks could kill! These chaps looked full of contempt for these useless tourists. It turned out that there was one stop on the way to Ischia – a much smaller island called Procida, where we were now standing. No-one had told us …

Anyway, another half an hour later we were in our cool, spotlessly clean hotel. There seemed to be almost endless sweeping, polishing and dusting going on. This was a family-owned and run hotel housing three generations. Grandma – a rather eccentric matriarch who had to be led everywhere – was nevertheless in charge of cleaning and was clearly a formidable task-mistress.

The hotel was small and simple. The rooms had lovely, cool

stone floors and were furnished simply but effectively. There were just two floors to L'Approdo, so no lift. Everyone always smiled and said hello when they saw you. It was immediately somewhere you could feel very much at home.

The first thing to do, as ever, was to get changed and into the pool. You were not allowed to swim, though, unless you wore a swimming cap, so that was the first purchase in Italy. It was a small heart-shaped pool with twenty or thirty sunchairs around it. On the first day, there were only about ten people there – a family with a couple of kids and some older Italians. What became apparent over the next few days was that the Italian families seemed to enjoy just being together and doing things like throwing a ball to each other in the pool and splashing about. In between they lay on loungers, read and talked to each other. All the families seemed so happy, with no need for computer games, activity programmes or anything else which you almost can't imagine the average Brit family doing without. Over the week, I found this all quite humbling. The old folks really seemed to like other people's kids, too, and seemed to be permitted to strike up conversation with the families without invitation. There appeared to be a great respect and reverence for older people, which was quite touching. I found myself thinking of the Olivio advert quite a lot that week, with wiry old men seemingly in their 80s swimming length after length in the pool or arm wrestling. They would sit around for ages, men and women, in groups of half a dozen and just laugh!

This is perhaps the time to mention that we were in a real minority as British folk. There were very few Brits there and signs would be in Italian and if they were in a second language, in German. In cafés and shops we were commonly addressed automatically in German. It was handy I could speak it – English got you nowhere. There is something really quite strange carrying out a conversation with Italians in German. Very odd. I had once shared a flat in Germany with some Spanish girls, Clara and Carmen, though, and we had only been able to converse in German all year, so I was sort of used to it!

Ischia is primarily for the Italians, especially the Neapolitans who flock over from Naples in the summer, either to hotels or holiday homes. The vast majority of remaining visitors are from Germany and (as everywhere else) some of them have stayed on to run diving schools and cafés.

The Neapolitan influence is nowhere more apparent than in the food on Ischia. It really is kept simple and Neapolitan. In our hotel there was no concession to the 'euro food' which we had come across in Menorca, Malta and Tenerife – I've always thought of it as food to keep the Brits abroad happy: lots of chips, sausages, beans etc., even when lovely local food is available. There was none of this at L'Approdo, where we had pasta with light sauces and salads, or local fish, and dessert often consisted of local fresh fruit. All this was accompanied by the fantastic local wine and bottled water (with or without *gaz*). I don't think I've ever felt like I was eating more healthily. Again, the kids seemed up for it and there were no oversized Brits demanding chips and fish fingers.

To be a waiter in Ischia was obviously quite something. Unlike in England, where it often seems to be a job for 16-year-old girls on the minimum wage, in Ischia this was a career for men in their 40s and 50s. It was a top job, one which you trained for and to which you aspired. I had noticed the same in Belgium. The head waiter was Alberto, a man in his fifties, with luxuriant hair brushed back over his head and, I could not stop noticing, the hairiest ears I had ever seen. He was multi-lingual, had the memory of an elephant and was completely charming. He was dressed in evening attire, but with a white jacket to distinguish him from his colleagues. Like grandmother, he ruled his kingdom with a rod of iron behind the smile – the smiling assassin. Our only issue with him was when he gave us a choice of two main meals one day and for some reason they were both veal-based. We just won't eat veal. For some time he kept just offering us the (veal-based) alternative before finally clicking and producing the most fantastic pasta in a light Neapolitan sauce.

The days quickly took shape. A (very healthy) breakfast followed by sunbathing by the pool until early afternoon, then a siesta or walk out to the beach for some lunch, more swimming and sunbathing until 'English tea' at 4.30. The hotel had put this on especially for their British guests, bless them. Free! A pot of tea with some unfeasibly sweet Italian almond biscuits designed to go with coffee. Still, they had gone to the trouble so we made sure we had it at the poolside bar every day. The hotel was up on a cliff looking out at the bay of Casamicciola and its harbour. The poolside bar had a fantastic view of all of this, so drinking a cup of weak tea there really was no hardship.

Tea would be followed by a walk to one of the two villages of Lacco Ameno and Casamicciola itself – we were halfway between the two. Here Alison would have a glass of wine while I enjoyed an Italian beer. We would just sit there under one of the umbrellas in a shady spot watching the people on the beach – packed far too closely together for British tastes – or just people-watching. In particular, I was watching out for dog-walkers. It was quite amazing to see a large mongrel dog lying in the shade on the beach only to be joined by a black and white Dalmatian. It was just like seeing one child call for another to play. They play-bowed (front legs down, backside in the air), feinted this way then that, then chased each other round in circles, barking with joy. They would take it in turns to 'win' and pin the other down by the throat while the adversary rolled on its back in submission. The vast majority of those on the beach (where you pay for a space) were locals, chattering away in Italian while their businesses were closed for a couple of hours. They barely gave the dogs a thought. They didn't react particularly positively to the dogs while we were entranced. Neither did they react negatively. They just accepted them.

Meanwhile a few dogs were appearing out on leads for 'walkies', at this hour, almost inevitably with a middle-aged lady dressed with typical Italian chic. A few poodles and other toy dogs, primarily. This was no practical activity to blow cobwebs away, though, or to give the dogs a walk. This seemed to be a quite carefully choreographed ritual, with greetings and chats in little park squares.

There was a lot to see each day with these dogs, but I have to say I was pretty disappointed. There was so little of what I had been promised in the German magazine.

The late afternoon outing would be followed by a return to the hotel for a bit of a read and preparing for dinner in the restaurant. One of the high points was watching a cheesy Italian quiz show every night called *Azzardo*. Basically, it was a matter of betting prize money on questions. Introduced by a pretty slimy host and (like something out of the sixties) featuring girls in bikinis pointing at inanimate objects with a big grin on their faces, the only real attraction was that it was in Italian – and we didn't speak any! Fortunately, the questions and options for answers appeared in subtitles. Our challenge was to try to work out what on earth the questions were about. Mix in a bit of Latin and a smattering of other languages and we got pretty good at it. In fact, our pot stood at 75,000 euros by the time we left!

Dinner was always enjoyable and was followed by a walk

into the village and back or coffee in the poolside bar, overlooking the villages and the harbour. There is only one real road in Ischia, running around the coast of the island. This passed under our cliff-top position, too, and the driving and frequent ambulances provided constant drama and entertainment.

I couldn't wait to meet the resort rep on the second day. Unsurprisingly, she was German (well, Austrian actually). Her name was Agnette and she was a very serious person. Unfortunately, there was no chance of missing our induction as we usually would because we were the only two punters at the hotel with that particular holiday company.

I was keen, though, to ask her about the dogs and where I could find them. So, you can imagine my surprise when she knew nothing about them. Nothing at all. She even tried saying what she thought I was saying (in English) in German in case she had misunderstood. It didn't help; she knew nothing. In fact, *Wuff* is actually an Austrian publication so surely she would know. I mean, how much comes out of Austria?

Agnette went on to explain that she had in fact married a native of Ischia eight years earlier and lived there ever since but had still never heard of anything about dogs. Sure, there were dogs around, but she'd never paid them that much attention and couldn't say anywhere where they particularly gathered.

In fact, it was becoming clear that she had a number of possibilities in her mind, none of which involved there being any particular dog view of note in Ischia. She clearly thought that I was quite mad or at least highly eccentric, or maybe this was one of those examples of quirky British humour? The other possibility was that I had totally misunderstood the article, she probably thought. (I hadn't taken it with me as it made it sound such an obvious feature of the island.) The look of absolute pity she directed to Alison spoke volumes. Even if this were true, you could see her thinking, how on earth would you let this influence your choice of holiday? To me it was like going to Pisa and people asking 'what leaning tower?'

It looked like I was on my own with this one, then. Suddenly I remembered pictures of dogs drinking in a fountain while people just sat by ignoring them. That was it – 'It's a place with a big stone fountain with benches around', I tried with Agnette.

'I am not knowing zis,' she replied. 'Many villages are having fountains. There is one very near here in Lacco Ameno, but it could be anywhere. I am not noticing dogs there.'

All this with a steely expression not aided by small, metal-framed spectacles which somehow looked so out of place on this laid-back holiday island.

Oh well, we could try Lacco Ameno as it was only 15 minutes' walk away, but that was meant to be upmarket and trendy and didn't sit with my memory of the article.

The next few days were spent with the dogs firmly put out of my mind, with the exception of evening walks to Lacco Ameno for a glass of wine and a beer and, of course, a visit or two to the village fountain without success. It was here that we saw dogs playing on the beach or going for designer-clad outings, but no great number of either grouping.

Still, it had turned out to be a great holiday. It was an incredibly friendly hotel and the whole island felt so relaxed and so safe. It was really interesting to get off the beaten track of the roads near the beach and go into the normal residential streets of tiny narrow lanes with washing strung out and groups of people who had pulled their chairs out into the streets to sit and chat. The supermarkets were dirt cheap, too, in these residential areas which looked as though they had been unaltered for centuries.

Ischia itself is an island of around 45 square miles and is

volcanic in origin. The legend is that a long, long time ago when Zeus ruled the world, his subjects the Cyclopes had to sacrifice to him a whole flock of sheep every year. One year, though, spurred on by their leader, the rebellious giant Tifco, they simply refused to do this. Zeus was not pleased and he sent terrible storms and weather which destroyed all the fields and crops so that all the sheep starved to death. Tifco decided it was time to storm Olympus and overthrow Zeus. The Cyclopes clambered up on to each other's shoulders until they reached the summit. Just as they did so, Zeus disdainfully pushed the Cyclopes over into the (Tyrheuschen) sea. Where Tifco fell in the Gulf of Naples now lies the island of Ischia. Tifco broke his bones and cried with anger and pain. Venus took pity on him and turned his tears into healing thermal waters, making Ischia the renowned spa resort it is today.

It was the Greeks who first colonised Ischia in the seventh century BC for around five hundred years, during which time the island flourished. Following on from the Greeks, it was the Romans who controlled Ischia, which was known as Aeneria for the next five hundred years. During these times the island was beset by at least four volcanic eruptions, landslides, mud-slides and earthquakes. Although Romans, of course, loved thermal springs, it was probably just too risky for the nobility to establish their homes and major buildings there. In fact the Emperor Augustus managed to swap Ischia for Capri with the Neapolitan people, even though Capri had no springs and was only one-fifth its size. By the end of the 4th century, the Roman Empire was in decline and Ischia suffered the fate of its near neighbours when it was ravaged by the Visigoths.

There followed a time of great upheaval, three hundred years of invasion by one German tribe after the other until the Saracens took over the island in 813 for some 30 years, using it as a base for pirate ships. It is from this time that the modern name originates. Pope Leone III referred to it in a letter as 'Insula' (Latin for 'island'), a name which mutated over the years to Insla, Iscla, Iscia and finally Ischia. It was set free by a little fleet of ships from Sorrento and remained under the control of the Dukes of Naples for some 200 years before being ruled by the Normans for a 50-year spell.

I hope you are keeping up with all of this, as you will be tested.

It continued to be a scene of battles and disputes between the powerful families of Naples and Sicily for some time, seeing in 1228 a terrible earthquake and in 1301 a volcanic eruption which killed 700 islanders. It was five years before the survivors who had fled to Procida and the Neapolitan coast began to return. Battles for control of the island continued.

Greater stability came to Ischia when Alfonso of Aragon returned with a vengeance in the fifteenth century and founded a large colony of Spanish and Catalans who were to provide the roots of Ischian nobility. He built fortifications, established an administration and also game reserves. Alfonso died in 1458 and was succeeded by his son Ferdinando I, who had to see Ischia through heavy raids by Turkish Corsairs and conspiracies from the Barons of Naples.

There then followed a period of intrigue involving the Spanish and the French, the result of which was, as you may by now have guessed, Ischia being raided and ransacked! The pirate Barbarossa, for example, devastated the island, attacking several different areas at once. His successor, a pirate by the name of Dragut, continued to prey on Ischia, despite the building of defence towers and lookouts. The inhabitants had little with which to defend themselves and tried to repel attackers with stones, hot water and household objects.

In 1655 the island suffered troubles of a different sort when the population was ravaged by the plague, until torrential rains in the summer swept away the disease. This was known as the 'miracle of Saint Rocco'.

In 1707 the Kingdom of Naples, including the island of Ischia, passed to Austria. Thirty years later, Ischia and Naples became a Bourbon dominion. Attempts were made to drive out all of the dodgier citizens of Ischia who dominated the island, but within a few years, in 1764, Ischia was once more abandoned and left in the hands of criminals. Terrible famine followed.

In March 1799 inhabitants of Ischia followed the example of the French Revolution and put up the revolutionary symbol of the tricolour red, yellow and blue cockade. It was the English, by command of Nelson, who re-established order and the royal government one month later.

Next came Napoleon, who expelled Mary Caroline of Austria and forced her to leave Naples. A French military sector was established in Ischia, with new fortifications and cannons. This was to counter the attacks being mounted by the English and the Bourbons from Sicily. However, this was of little use and the whole Anglo-Bourbon fleet attacked and took over both Ischia and Procida in June 1809, leaving just a month later to go back to Sicily and Malta.

As if all of this were not enough, the next big event in Ischia's rich and eventful history was a terrible earthquake in 1825 when Casamicciola, this time, was devastated. Things got no better over the next ten years when a cholera epidemic followed. Finally, you'll be glad to know, it was Italian unity which brought peace and harmony to Ischia after its colourful and eventful history.

Interestingly, when I spoke to Ischians about just how Italian they felt, though, the answer was 'not very'. On the international stage, sure, they did, but when push comes to shove their real allegiance is to Naples. I suppose we forget just how complicated some Italian history has been and just how comparatively recent the concept of 'Italy' is.

We did go for a couple of excursions (although strangely there had been no hard sell this time unlike any other holiday I had been on). The first of these was a garden (which is a slight understatement) called La Mortella. Now, no way are we 'garden' people. To me, a garden is a patch of ground for dogs to play on. (My garden is just grass.) But I have to say that the Giardini La Mortella are a bit special. The only other gardens I have enjoyed as much (although very different in nature) are at Chatsworth House in Derbyshire. I don't remember every day being as warm as when we went to the Gardens. The heat and humidity were terrific – totally appropriate for what seemed to be a tropical garden of almost jungle-like lushness. The garden was established by the British composer, Sir William Walton and his wife. The house now acts as a study centre for talented young musicians, under the world's leading teachers, hosting top-level musical events which attract visitors such as our own Prince Charles.

It really is an incredible place with several fountains, architectural features and over 1,000 different plant species, many of which are delicate and rare Mediterranean and tropical plants. There is a hot house for rare orchids and different areas of the garden have different themes and features. Our own favourite was the Zen temple, where there is absolute peace and tranquillity punctuated only by the light tinkle of wind chimes. Sitting there looking out at the beautiful gardens, all is well with the world. Mind-numbing in the best sense of the word. Just moving around the gardens was incredibly draining and some good cups of 'English' tea were needed to rehydrate.

Ischia is famous for its thermal waters and spa treatments. You can go to a centre and bathe in the pools for around £70 for a day. For this you can get yourself covered in mud. My dogs do this for me much more cheaply, so we gave that a miss, although it is a hugely popular thing to do.

Our only other joint excursion was a tour of the island by coach, which was well worth doing. The tour itself is quite an experience – the one road is windy and so narrow in places it is really not intended for coaches. In fact, two cars find it difficult to pass in places, so some of the trip was truly hair-raising.

It is not, in a way, a truly beautiful island in the conventional sense. It does have a volcanic feel to it. There are some interesting things to see, though, such as houses still being used today quite literally cut into rock faces like hermits' caves. The island's main towns are Ischia Ponte and Ischia Porto, the only towns of any size on the island, and there is a large and spectacular castle – the Castle Aragonese.

To us, though, the jewel in the crown was a trendy, exclusive pedestrianised resort called St. Angelo. Here you had to be dropped at the end of the town and follow flights of steps past boutiques and designer shops down to the harbour area of yachts and boats surrounded by bars and restaurants. You felt young, rich and famous just being there. It was about the only village or town we went to in Ischia where there was no sign of dogs of any kind.

This was made up for by our coffee stop on route. The coach pulled up in the village of Fontana. This is home to the base of the path leading up Mount Epomeo, the dormant volcano, for those with the heat resistance and stamina to tackle it! Needless to say, this did not include us.

We made our way to a lovely, tree-covered patio in the village square, which was serviced from the café on the other side of the main road. Watching the waitresses dodging across the busy road with trays of cappuccino and cake was something to behold. Needless to say, the whole activity was accompanied by a cacophony of horn-blowing. Serving a coachload of people was completed with consummate efficiency, though. Rather strangely, however, whether you asked for it or not, everyone was served with a local cake delicacy on what seemed to be a sale-or-return basis!

It was one of those good times in life, sitting there with fantastic coffee and delicious cake in the warmth of midday and the brightness of Mediterranean colours. What could make it better? You guessed it: this was one of those places where the dogs roamed free and uninhibited. There were three in the café square: a big Labrador, a boxer, and a large crossbreed.

They would simply come up near the tables, find some shade and lie down. Not only did they not beg for food, but positively seemed to be offended if offered any. I managed to get a nice fuss off the Labrador, but even he was quite aloof. The other two just seemed to want to be left alone and I couldn't even get a picture with them. If too bothered, they simply moved off to another spot in the village. The water fountain was there for their convenience and they just seemed to be such a natural part of the landscape. They were well groomed, well cared for and well adjusted. They seemed happy and content with their integrated way of life. This gave me real hope for my quest, but I was sure this was not the place I was looking for.

Two days later I was lying by the pool glancing at a map of Ischia when I noticed the name of a village called Forio. This seemed to ring a bell, but I wasn't sure whether this was from the *Wuff* article or whether it was just from looking at the map earlier in the week. Anyway, I told Alison that I would be deserting her for the day, leaving her by the pool and catching the bus to Forio. Ten minutes later I was waiting by a bus stop, armed with my camera.

There was standing room only on the bus, in pretty intense

heat. I had got on with my ticket, but didn't really know what to do with it when I got on. I was just staring at the ticket uselessly when I glanced up to see three hard-looking skinheads staring at me. 'Oh great,' I thought, 'guess who stands out as the foreigner.' One of the three leaned across and gestured for me to give him the ticket. Being chicken, I gave it to him without hesitation. He took it, turned round, stamped it in a machine and handed it back with a smile.

Getting off the bus in Forio, it took me a while to get my bearings. I was down by the sea, a busy little harbour area with the main road running through. A little navigation took me into the pedestrianised or semi-pedestrianised streets with a much more laid-back atmosphere. And there they were. As I looked around I began to see dogs trotting along the pavements on their own or in twos with a sense of purpose. Or, equally commonly, lazing in the sun in front of a shop. One particularly clever collie cross had found the air conditioning 'barrier' just inside the front door of the supermarket to settle under. He was completely unfazed by people stepping over him or pushing a trolley within a few centimetres of his head.

Another turn of narrow streets brought me to the fountain I had seen pictured in the *Wuff* magazine article. It was quite a large, stone fountain. Looking old and worn and covered in places with slimy green moss, it was circled with stone benches and occasional trees for visitors and the older residents of Forio to laze under and watch the world go by. Sure enough, lapping from the fountain, standing on the broad rim which acted as yet more seating, were two old dogs.

It was fascinating to see how close they were to some of the old folk and yet with more or less no interaction between the two. There was a real sense of 'live and let live', of peace and contentment.

Trying to get the dogs' attention and call them over proved

pretty fruitless. Something was going on here. I had noticed it earlier in the holiday during the café stop on our coach trip. There seemed to be a 'deal' between the residents and their dogs. The dogs were allowed great freedom in which to live their lives as long as they kept themselves to themselves and didn't bother the residents or visitors.

Wandering around the narrow streets of Forio in the warm sunshine was pretty idyllic. There were dogs everywhere. A Border collie lay in the doorway of the butcher's shop. The tobacconist had a Doberman you had to step over. I spent a wonderful half hour sitting in a picturesque square sipping cappuccino with the travel agent's red setter lolling nearby next to the sandwich board advertising boat trips to Capri. The dogs were such an integrated part of life here.

As I sat in the square I saw stylish ladies taking their dogs for a walk on the lead, completely unmolested by the loose dogs around them. In fact, the dogs on leads had been loose half an hour earlier and would be wandering around loose again half an hour later! Even so, they appeared to love their walk.

Strolling around again after my coffee and having ventured into some of the even narrower side streets, I was passed by a young, large crossbreed trotting quite quickly with a real sense of purpose. I turned and followed the dog, curious to see what it was up to.

I had been given really strange looks by the local inhabitants as I had tried to take photos of the dogs, looks which were a mixture of curiosity and pity. What on earth was this obviously foreign chap taking pictures of dogs for? These looks were nothing, though, compared with those I got following this dog through the streets. The pace in Ischia is very much an amble, but because of the speed at which the dog was walking I looked as though I was in an Olympic speed-walking race and the sweat was pouring off my bright-red face. What an attractive picture I must have made.

Once I realised where I was heading I felt sure that our destination was the fountain, and sure enough it soon came into sight – but why the rush?

Just before we reached the small square with the fountain my target took a sharp turn to the right, down one of the streets full of cafés, newsagents and other small shops and across an empty square. Our speed was increasing and I was beginning to look like Benny Hill. Down into a side street darted the dog, a street with a couple of municipal offices, a bar and houses. I turned into the street just in time to see my quarry dart into a gift shop. Suddenly, there was the noise of barking and yapping, followed by some excited conversation in Italian, sounding like the sort of rebuke you might give to a child.

I peered into the shop. It was full of glass display-cases carrying jewellery and little glass objects. Our hero was standing particularly tall, his ears pulled back, teeth exposed in a smile with his tail erect and wagging stiffly like an overactive metronome. Attached to his nose was the bottom of a very pretty little Pomeranian bitch, wearing a beautiful pink bow. He was clearly in love!

I could not believe the good humour with which this invasion was met. A bit of jumping around or uncontrolled wagging and a lot of damage could have been done. Instead, after a few minutes our dog was gently shooed out of the shop. Off he went at his brisk trot, not looking back, heading no doubt for the fountain. Meanwhile the shop owner told me in German that the dog visited every day, always at about the same time!

Ischia was turning out to be a wonderful place. Obviously, I don't approve of leaving dogs to stray or 'latchkey' dogs, but this really wasn't what it was like in Ischia. These dogs were happy and content – well fed and healthy. It was a really positive atmosphere of 'live and let live' and integration.

I spent half a sweltering day watching the dogs on Forio go about their very fulfilling daily lives and got quite seriously lost in a maze of backstreets before finally finding my way back to the bus stop and thence to the hotel. I was soon with Alison at the poolside after a shower and a swim, a much happier man!

So, all this had been two years earlier and it now seemed to be a good way of adding to my dog-spotting list in a much more convivial way than the norm. This time we stayed in Forio itself, in another small, family-run hotel which turned out to be even lovelier than L'Approdo. This time our hotel was the Lord Byron, in the town itself. I don't think I've ever felt so relaxed and at peace as I did there. The weather was gorgeous, the pool and the backdrop fantastic. Service and food were even better than we had experienced two years earlier.

British people were no more common. The hotel was full predominantly of Germans. There was no 'towels on the deckchair' syndrome here, though. They were laughing and full of fun, excellent companions.

Dinner every night was special. Local food and wine. Beautiful flavours. Real tomatoes, which they were so proud of. Deep red and full of flavour, but not the uniform size and shape that Tesco would require. They were so scathing about the Dutch tomatoes – perfect shape but devoid of flavour. The same was true of the local apricots and peaches we feasted on for desert every night. Best of all was the unobtrusive but totally professional service from the staff. From the moment we got there everyone knew who we were, what our room number was and had remembered our preferences for what we liked to eat and drink. The Head Waiter would come and talk us through the menu every day but would also find time for a chat.

We spent long days lazing by the pool, enjoying the backdrop of sun-soaked hills, taking occasional visits to the poolside bar. Even the pretty continuous George Michael music oozing quietly in the background seemed to fit.

It turned out that as Brits we were pretty sought after. The Germans are still going through a slump after re-unification and seemingly spend next to nothing over and above their accommodation. Most of the money for that goes to the holiday companies rather than the hotels. In fact we noticed that most Germans came by long-distance coach, with the holiday airports reserved almost completely for the British. As for the French, apparently they just don't travel, preferring to stay in 'God's own country'. The upshot of this is that not just the hotels, but bars, shops and restaurants are desperate to get the British in as we have much greater disposable income. In fact, it is generally presumed that you are German, and when you are found to be British you get a much warmer welcome!

In fact, prices seemed to have shot up – according to the locals with the introduction of the euro. We kept being told that we were doing right to keep the pound.

There were other changes, too. Now, all the motor scooterists were wearing crash helmets. Presumably, this was due to some legislation actually being enforced. The roads seemed even narrower and certainly busier. There were still lengthy stand-offs between drivers to see who would give way first. In fact, to keep the feel of the island, apparently households are going to be limited to one car between them. Quite a brave move, which shows how serious the Ischians are about their tourist economy.

This brings me to the really bad news. There are now only about half as many dogs on the streets – and the locals are very sensitive about this. I'm sure that they didn't want ill-informed opinion likening them to the terrible Greek islands full of starving, scabby dogs, but this island was never like that. Nevertheless, a lot of the dogs have been taken off the streets, supposedly to a lovely centre for stray dogs in the mountains. That sounds like a worrying euphemism to me. People won't make eye contact when they talk about it.

I still saw lots of dogs by normal standards. Many of the shops continued to have their dogs outside. Not one to be added to my spotting-list, though.

When I got home I had another look at the *Wuff* article and I found that the other place to go to enjoy the company of the dogs on the island was the stylish Ischia Ponte and particularly the Via Romana which links it to Ischia Porto. Still, there was always next year … and before that, I had my annual quality-time, male-bonding, hunting-shooting-fishing week alone with Tom to look forward to.

CULTURAL INTERLUDE

10 Things to Do in Ischia

1. Sit in the sun, eat pasta and drink a bottle of one of the local wines, Pietratorcia.
2. Wander the streets of Forio on 15th June, for the festival of Saint Vito. It's a lovely atmosphere. The streets are lit simply and tastefully and there's music to listen to as you wander.
3. Lie back and think of England. Drink a pot of English tea in the warmth and humidity of the La Mortella Gardens.
4. Take lots of water with you and follow a footpath up to the top of Mount Epomeo, the island's volcano, from the village of Fontana. From the top you get marvellous views not only of the island but also across to Capri and the Bay of Naples.
5. Wander down the island's most fashionable thoroughfare, the Via Roma, take in the shops, cafés, restaurants and atmosphere.
6. Take a day trip round the island by coach. Experience some of the tight bends and streets and see the island in all its glory. Look out for the houses hewn out of the rock faces.
7. Take time to visit the pedestrianised fishing village of St. Angelo. Sit in a café and take the opportunity to feel young and beautiful amongst young and beautiful people even if, like me, you're neither.
8. Treat yourself to a pampering at one of the island's spa cen-

tres and thermal pools. It's what attracted the Romans, after all.

9 Visit the Castle Aragonese and explore some of the wonderfully complex history of the 'green island'. Watch the fishing boats come and go.

10 Sit by the fountain in Forio, eat ice cream and watch for dogs.

MUSICAL INTERLUDE

Top Ten (fairly naff) Dog Tracks:

1 'Who Let the Dogs Out?' – The Baha Men
2 'How Much is that Doggy in the Window?' – Various
3 'Puppy Love' – Donny Osmond
4 'Love me, Love my Dogs' – Pete Shelley
5 'Shoot the Dog' – George Michael
6 'I love my Dog' – Cat (!) Stevens
7 'Hound Dog' – Elvis Presley
8 'Hounds of Love' – Kate Bush
9 'Big Dog' – Rolf Harris
10 'Hungry like the Wolf' – Duran Duran

More interesting Top Ten:

1 'Dogs Are Everywhere' – Pulp
2 'The Dogs and the Horses' – Divine Comedy
3 'Dog Eat Dog' – Adam Ant
4 'Black Dog' – Led Zeppelin
5 'Diamond Dogs' – David Bowie
6 'Golden Retriever' – Super Furry Animals
7 'Black-Eyed Dog' – Nick Drake
8 'The Dogs' – Empire Dogs
9 'Essex Dogs' – Blur
10 'Old Shep' – Johnny Cash

CHAPTER 8

A Rye Look at Dogs – or What Have Dogs Ever Done For Us?

Many of you will probably have seen the Monty Python sketch in the film *The Life of Brian*. In fact in December 2004 this scene was voted 'funniest scene of all time' in a poll of 4,000 film-goers. What happens is that, in an attempt to stir up insurrection, a revolutionary called Reg asks a crowd, 'What have the Romans ever done for us?'

Someone replies, 'Well they gave us sanitation.'

'Yeah,' replies Reg, 'but apart from sanitation, what have the Romans ever done for us?'

Someone else shouts, 'Well they've given us medicine.'

Reg then says, 'OK, but apart from sanitation and medicine, what have the Romans ever done for us?' He is still determined to run them down. This goes on through a long list of really positive contributions from the Romans to civilisation, until he ends up saying, 'All right, but apart from sanitation, medicine, education, wine, public order, irrigation, roads, a fresh water system and public health, what have the Romans ever done for us?'

I sometimes feel that dogs are like the Romans in that sketch. They have done so much for us and give us so much in so many ways, and yet the detractors are still shouting, 'But what have dogs ever done for us?'

This was the sort of conversation that we were having when

Tom and I travelled down for one of our 'just Dad and Tom' holidays – you know, male-bonding (huntin', shootin', fishin' and all that, although we never actually did any of these things).

Originally, these holidays had been under canvas in a small tent, cooking on a gas ring. Then had come camp beds. Then the need for a fridge, so we could keep food. More space, so Tom could take more toys and we could take more stuff, so we could stay longer. In the end, we were in full board in chalets, in deluxe caravans, lodges or cottages. Of course, it was nothing to do with getting soft.

This time, unusually, we were travelling southeast to a little place near Rye in Sussex. I say *unusually* because over the years we'd been west, to Wales several times and to Shropshire, east to Norfolk, Lincolnshire and Nottingham, north to Yorkshire and northwest to Chester. Up until now I had resisted the temptation of going anywhere southeast, where I had lived and worked for a few years.

Travelling down, I remembered why I had found this temptation easy to resist. London is easy: get on a train, get off, use buses or the tube and see lots of interesting things. Best still, get on a train and get out again.

In my first job in London, I had an idle moment and worked out that if I could do all my commuting in one solid stretch and if I worked at the same place for the rest of my working days, I would spend 14.5 solid years on the train!

The roads were worse. As we travelled around the M25 everyone was out for themselves – just to get one car's length further on. This was a pattern which stuck throughout the week: really miserable people being really miserable to everyone else on the road and making them, well … really miserable.

Apparently, every second counts and is a matter of life and

death. Set off 5 minutes earlier and chill out, that's what I say. I don't even drive slowly, but I can't say I relished being able to read the frame-maker's name on the driver behind's sunglasses as he was driving so close.

We were both pretty tense when we got to Winchelsea, the village where we were staying. We missed the entrance to our caravan park as it had a different company's name from the one we had booked through. So we drove a little along the front and parked. Everywhere we looked there were huge signs telling us this was a crime blackspot, to keep all our valuables safe and help keep crime to a minimum. Very reassuring.

Along with the rundown nature of everything around, this wasn't a very good start. Things got worse when we got to the site and couldn't even park. There were London cabs everywhere. We had obviously chanced upon the cabbies' little place in the sun.

I was told we could park by the caravan just to unload but then had to move the car back to the car park. When I pointed out that there was no space at all in the car park, I was told it was because it was a Bank Holiday weekend. I didn't see how that helped with the car park and just didn't bother moving my car. Nothing terrible happened.

It was while we were going back to the car that it happened. We saw our first dog and quite unbelievably it was … a Bedlington terrier! We'd travelled hundreds of miles to see one in Bedlington with no success, but it was the first dog we saw in Sussex. We stopped and spoke to a massive Eliza Doolittle sound-alike, who was (just about) clothed in shorts and a sun top. She had the loveliest little girl with her. I wondered if she would end up the same size as her mum and how that happens. In fact, looking round, the campsite was full of huge adults and, generally, their huge offspring. As the week went by and we watched them grazing on chips, burgers and cakes, washed down with buckets of Coke and lager, it became pretty clear why they were so huge. Of course, getting off their massive backsides from time to time could have helped, too.

Anyway, both mother and daughter were really pleased we were asking about their dog. Apparently, hardly anyone knew it was a Bedlington terrier. He was a two-year-old boy called Teddy. A friendly little chap, very alert, watching everything and everyone around him, never relaxing.

We had a lovely chat before I excused myself, suddenly fearful that my interest in her dog could be misconstrued as a clumsy chat-up line … I was out of there.

We saw Teddy many times over the next few days. He certainly got some walks around that campsite. You couldn't help but smile, seeing the relationship between that little girl and her dog.

Because we only needed two bedrooms rather than three we were assigned a disabled-friendly caravan. This was fine, except that it was next door to the little outdoor pool and the truly dreadful 'Lobster Pot' Club where all the 'fun' went down day and night. Talk about noisy. The general aim seemed to be to get as drunk as possible as early in the day as possible and then get even more drunk later in the day while consuming as many chips as the human body would allow. All this washed down with some cockles, mussels or other dodgy bits of seafood.

It was literally impossible to hear the radio or TV in our caravan because of the volume of music from outside.

In all honesty, this didn't matter too much as we were out most of the time. We were so busy, too, that even the music going on into the early hours didn't stop us from being tired enough to sleep. What was odd, though, was the kids – aged between 10 and 16 who, whilst Mum and Dad did the karaoke or took part in the pass-the-cucumber competition, roamed as little gangs, hiding behind caravans getting drunk (even the 10-year-olds), smoking, swearing, fighting and God knows what else. I found it all pretty depressing, to be honest.

A night-time highpoint came when one large caravan had to be moved – presumably to another site. It was obviously anchored in to the concrete in some way. So at 2 a.m. we were treated to a large crane lorry, pneumatic drills and chiselling for an hour while this was being done. I was too tired and incredulous to do anything about it.

Strangely, though, the holiday was excellent despite all of this and we really did have a laugh about the campsite. Not as much as we did the next year, though, when despite all our detailed feedback about it being like an inner-city council estate, we received a letter saying that they were glad we'd enjoyed our stay so much and inviting us back again!

It did turn out to be an excellent base for travelling around. It was only a short journey to Rye, which proved to be a fantastic old town with a real atmosphere. It was also, for some reason, a very popular place with dog-lovers, which helped me in my spotting quest. What was becoming frustrating by this stage, though, was the regularity with which we would see the same breeds.

Rye itself was a beautiful town, full of history and interest. There were also a few old book shops where I could add to my collection of old dog books and Tom could get hold of old copies of *Beano* and *Dandy* annuals and old football books.

It's a small town, home to only around 5,000 people, but it's very atmospheric. There are many timbered buildings, cobbled streets and narrow secret passageways. It enjoyed a heyday as a smugglers' den and you can see why.

For such a small town, it has enjoyed quite an important place in history linked with the so-called 'Cinque Ports' of the South Coast, stretching across Sussex and Kent.

The first thing that strikes you when you arrive in this famous sea town is a lack of sea. The sea is in fact now about two miles away as it has retreated. Back in Norman days Rye had been almost surrounded by water.

In those days, Rye was a part of the Manor of Ramersie, which was given to the Abbey of Fécamp in Normandy by Ethelred the Unready in return for their shelter when he had been forced to flee the Danes in 1014.

It was over two hundred years before Rye was returned to the English Crown, at the time of Henry III. Even then, an island area still known as Rye Foreign remained in French control until the Reformation.

Forty years after it was returned to English hands, what was known as The Great Storm took place, in 1287. This storm submerged Winchelsea so that it was eventually rebuilt on higher ground. Equally dramatically it caused the course of the River Rother to change from Romney to Rye. Rye prospered. It became a successful port, providing ships for the British fleet for several hundred years.

As it prospered, it soon became apparent that Rye had strategic importance, too. Fortifications were built in the fourteenth century to protect the town and some sections, such as the Landgate and the Castle (the Ypres Tower) remain to this day.

In around 1050, Edward the Confessor had agreed the formation of the Confederation of the Cinque Ports. (Cinque here is pronounced 'sink'.) The original towns forming these ports were Hasings, Romney, Hythe, Dover and Sandwich. Over the next century the demands made on the original five ports were beyond what they could meet. At this time, the 'ancient towns' of Rye and Winchelsea joined the confederation, which became the 'Cinque Ports and two Ancient Towns'.

The status of a 'Cinque Port' gave these towns freedom from taxes and customs duties and the right to hold their own courts of law. The Portsmen were allowed to judge and punish their own criminals. They could levy tolls. In return, the towns had to offer the Crown a safe harbour for its ships, together with a certain number of ships and sailors for 15 days' free service per year.

Given this degree of freedom the Cinque Ports prospered. They became rich, influential, powerful and difficult to control.

Of course, geography made these ports very vulnerable and both the French (regularly) and the Spanish (rarely) attacked the ports, and one such attack from the French took place in 1377. This was one of the low points of Rye history and saw most of the town burnt down. Even the bells from the main church, St. Mary's, were stolen and taken back to France.

To say that the people of Rye and nearby Winchelsea (where I was staying with Tom) were upset is a gross understatement. It was less than a year before they repaid the compliment to the French by raiding the French coast and returning not only with their bells, but a lot more loot in addition.

For my part, though, the most evocative period in Rye history is the 18th century. Rye, at that time, was a pretty dangerous place, financed as much by smuggling as by legitimate trade. The buildings and narrow passageways proved perfect for these illegal purposes, with lots of cellars and vaults in which to hide the contraband. Rather conveniently, many of these sites were said to be 'haunted', which no doubt helped to deter the curious.

Modern day Rye is largely unspoilt. It is still dominated by 'the Citadel' in the centre, built around the Church of St. Mary the Virgin. Mermaid Street is a sight to behold, as is the famous Mermaid Inn itself. The street has some superb buildings with equally fantastic names. There is 'The House Opposite', 'The House within the seat' and 'The House with Two Front Doors', just to name a few.

There's a really relaxing charm to Rye. It feels quite arty and sophisticated. Its unique history has created an almost Bohemian atmosphere. It was just four or five miles away from our holiday camp at Winchelsea Beach, yet it could have been in a different world.

Although the campsite was a huge disappointment, the caravan itself was great. Location-wise, it proved to be a really good base. Easy, for example, to feed Tom's margherita pizza addiction in various spots in nearby Rye! We visited some great places during the day, too. There was Hastings – possibly in the running for Britain's most declining and depressing town, but interesting to see – and nearby Battle, a stark contrast just a few miles away. Battle is a lovely place and the English Heritage Battle of Hastings site was one of the best we'd ever been to. So much to see and so evocative. Further along the coast from Hastings we visited Brighton (which was absolutely heaving with tourists) and Eastbourne (where you could get a really good feeling of what it would be like when you had died and passed over to the other side). Canterbury, although not on our doorstep, made a fantastic day out, as did the much smaller Pevensey with its wonderful castle and tiny courthouse, where I took a picture of Tom in the dock and in the cells. That felt good.

This holiday really did turn out to be a very fertile dog-spotting ground. It seemed that lots of people took their dogs with them. I suppose it's that sort of holiday area, really.

As you know, we had spotted a Bedlington terrier as soon as we got there. There were many other dogs at the caravan site, but really only repeats of breeds we'd seen many times before.

Rye at the weekend proved to be a very successful hunting ground, though. Almost on arrival we spotted a very well dressed elderly couple with a long-coated Chihuahua in tow. Well, not really in tow. It was trotting – almost strutting – over the cobbles as though it were the biggest dog in town and every other person and dog were there only on sufferance. Having read all about the Chihuahua, I couldn't help but wonder if this little dog's skull was 'appledomed' enough …

At the other end of the size-scale a large Dalmatian was enjoying a summer walk by the beautiful little marina area. He looked happy to be out and about. This walk wasn't like his original purpose of running tens of miles with a carriage but it seemed to suit him well enough today.

The same day we also saw a Rough collie, a Border collie, a boxer, a Labrador and a golden retriever. Nothing too spectacular but all useful additions to my 'collection'.

Over the next few days we added several more to my list (there was a danger that spotting dogs was beginning to take precedence over sight-seeing and enjoying the holiday). The dogs we saw included a Staffie, a Jack Russell terrier, a Border terrier, a Welsh Springer spaniel, a cocker spaniel and an English setter. Of all the dogs we spotted on this holiday, though, I was probably most pleased at the sight of a beautiful white fluffy Samoyed, a multi-purpose Russian dog, capable of pulling sledges and rounding up deer.

Whilst sitting one night, thinking over our dog-spotting and chewing over the inevitable margherita pizza, our earlier conversation was struck up again. All these dogs and all these breeds of dogs. Why do we have dogs and what have dogs ever done for us to be such a part of our lives?

The first dogs to associate with man were probably scavengers around the ancient camps. They would keep vermin down, help to keep the camp clean and act as an early warning system when intruders approached. Because of this, they were probably tolerated and even encouraged.

No doubt dogs began to be interbred for particular characteristics – such as the best guard dogs – and man's fascination for dog-breeding began. This was the beginning of a symbiotic relationship which continues to this day. Dogs began to show their value in finding, chasing and cornering prey. They became a useful addition to the hunt. And, of course, if other meat was short in supply, they provided a readily available source of food.

Later, dogs' ability to herd and drive cattle, sheep and other animals, which is just an adaptation of hunting behaviour, was developed and the dogs best at this would have been bred together to produce the best animals for this purpose.

Guards, hunters, herders, source of food. All these roles were fulfilled uniquely successfully by dogs amongst all animals. Companion was probably the latest canine role to be developed, even though it is the predominant role of the dog in many societies today.

These days, guarding takes many forms. There are thousands of guard dogs used by private security firms, for example, to guard property and people. Often German shepherd dogs or Dobermans, for example, some of these dogs are only lightly trained or even encouraged to become aggressive.

Obviously, both the army and prisons use dogs as guards – and we're glad they do. Many of the prison dogs are trained at the Prison Dog Section near Doncaster which was set up in 1967. In common with many of the pure 'guarding' dogs used by the military, these dogs are not suitable for a pet life at the end of their careers.

Even in this high-tech world, there are few deterrents as effective as a large, snarling dog running loose for lower-level security work.

Many private citizens use dogs either exclusively or partially for guarding work. Probably anyone with even the smallest dog feels more secure than they would without. This seems to meet an almost primeval human need in man.

With regard to herding and livestock management, the dog has yet to be beaten for versatility, talent and dedication. Working in any weather and covering tens of miles a day, the ubiquitous Border collie or working sheepdog is undoubtedly the canine champion of this art, at least in Britain. These dogs are an absolutely essential feature of many farmers' lives, without which they simply couldn't function. Watching dogs work is a very humbling experience. Their absolute focus and desire to work is a real lesson to us all.

I tried out a 'sheepdog experience' for my birthday, courtesy of the generosity of my colleagues at work. What an amazing day it was. We worked with different dogs, initially just keeping sheep within a circle. The dogs were ever watchful, sensitive to the slightest movement and nuance of body language. They also knew what they were doing and were very reluctant to follow commands that they knew were wrong.

Having mastered the commands of 'a-way!' and 'come by', we all attempted to move the sheep through a simple slalom, with the help of our dogs. We held a large crook to move and control the forward movement of the sheep. Well, I had expected the rather stupid, meek and mild animal so widely portrayed, but these sheep were strong-minded and forceful. It took every ounce of the dog's power – through its eye and its perfect sense of movement and timing – to keep them in order.

When we attempted the slalom I, like nearly all the other people there, wasn't up to the job. I couldn't get myself co-ordinated, couldn't stop the forward movement of the sheep, got my 'come-bys' and my 'a-ways' mixed up and generally made a pig's ear of it, despite the best efforts of my canine helper. If dogs could only talk, they'd have had something to say. To be honest, they didn't need to speak to leave me in no doubt about what they thought.

The lady running the course, Barbara, rather cleverly also runs corporate events, she told us. When you're working the sheep in the ring, the idea is that you and the dog should work as a team. If you move around, the dog will 'balance' you, looking at the way the sheep are facing, where the biggest gaps are and watching for any possible escape attempts.

Barbara told us, in her pithy Yorkshire way, of the oft-repeated Managing Director scenario. The MD of a company would often like to show the rest of his senior management team what he was made of and 'take control' of the situation. Typically, he would move round the circle and the dog would instinctively balance him on the other side by moving round accordingly. The MD would then like to show who's in control. He would tell the dog to 'down' and move round again. The dog would take no heed, would get up and balance him, covering the weaknesses he had inadvertently left. Inevitably, the MD would not accept this and would bark 'stay' at the dog. He would move round again, only for the dog to ignore him and do, instead, what he knew to be right, doing his job.

The MD then gets more and more irate. The dog is obviously not doing as he is told and this involves loss of face. After several repeats he gets to the stage of absolutely screaming the 'down' and the 'stay' at the dog. The dog finally, in effect, shrugs his shoulders and stays where he is bid. The MD begins to move around, at last a smile of victory through compliance on his face as the dog stays still (oh, such sweet victory) and the sheep … piss off through the gap that has been left!

How many times is this scene carried out in businesses up and down the UK every day?

If you would like to get a sense of the life of a modern-day working sheepdog, you can do no better than read or watch David Kennard's *Year of the Working Sheepdog*, a marvellous book/DVD showing the role of the farmer and his dog in all seasons. Seeing the dog perched in gale-force wind and rain on the North Atlantic coast of the West Country really gives you a feeling for what this work is like.

Interestingly, David Kennard's book and film production is an example of diversification where farming simply cannot make ends meet. Survival is always a struggle for many farms – especially sheep farms – but for many the foot and mouth outbreak a few years ago was the last straw. It broke my heart to see so many of these dogs rehomed or even put to sleep because they had no animals to work and they were literally going mad. They were also an expense which couldn't really be afforded with no income at all. Bred to work and ready to cover many miles a day in all weathers, they could not be re-homed as pets. What a tragedy.

Hunting is another task which dogs have performed over the years with tremendous success. Whether they 'flushed' or 'sprang' game like springer spaniels, 'indicated' game like pointers, retrieved game from land or water (like the retrievers), they have proved very adept at their tasks. Of course, there are other hunting dogs, too, such as the foxhounds used in the hunt for canny Mr Fox.

With the supposed demise of fox-hunting there is a big issue around what to do with the hound packs. Suggestions include retraining the dogs for drag-hunting, re-homing dogs as pets (very difficult), sending some dogs to hunt abroad or euthanasia. Time will tell.

Dating back to early times, dogs have been used in war. Originally, this involved creating massive, strong dogs which could take a man or a horse down. Fear-inducing, armoured mastiffs were used as part of the war machine. Dogs are still used, of course, by both the military and by police forces. We've already thought about guarding military installations, prisons and the like, but they have a much wider range of subtle uses these days.

It's true that dogs are still very effective in maintaining public order. I went to watch a football match between Düsseldorf and Bayern Munich once and I can tell you that anyone in their right minds would not mess with the police dogs there. Police and military dogs have a broader range of uses, though.

One common use is as 'sniffer dogs'. These are also used widely by Customs and Excise. They can be trained to detect drugs, currency, weapons, explosives and many other substances. There is even some talk of using dogs at school gates to identify drugs coming into schools. They are certainly used routinely at night clubs for this purpose. Other dogs are trained to search for people, either alive or dead. Yet others track fugitives and escapees.

With regard to sniffer and scenting dogs, it is perhaps not surprising that it is the gundogs, with their even greater sense of smell, which are favoured. Springer spaniels are widely used, as are Labradors and pointers, although collies are also used because of their intelligence. In fact, it is estimated that Customs and Excise dogs alone prevent the importation of £150m of contraband each year.

Another role which the dog performs for us today is that of Search and Rescue dog. It was the monks at the Monastery of the Great Bernard Pass who started all this off. The monks were often called to the assistance of travellers who were lost in the snow or even in an avalanche. In the seventeenth century, the monks began to use large dogs, St Bernards, initially as guard dogs. Over time, these animals began to accompany the monks on their rescue missions and proved invaluable guides. It was perhaps inevitable that the dogs became more adept at their task and began to show the monks where the missing people were, using their advantage of a far superior sense of smell. They could even detect people totally covered by snow.

While the average human has around 5 million scent receptors in our nasal passages, the average dog has over 200 million! Indeed, a dog's nasal folds, if unfolded flat, would make quite an impressive sight and cover the floor of your lounge. (Now don't try this at home, kids.) The dog also has a vomeronasal organ above the roof of the mouth which has the role of capturing sex scent and transferring this information to the brain. How about having one of those, guys?

The Red Cross used dogs to find injured soldiers on the battlefield in World War I and dogs were used extensively in Britain during the second World War, for example, during the blitz.

These days it takes two years as a mountain rescue volunteer before anyone can even think of handling a dog in mountain rescue conditions. Once trained, the dogs and handlers are alerted by the emergency services and this can happen 24 hours a day, 365 days a year.

The dogs find people by following scent carried in the air and, as such, search large areas very quickly. One huge advantage is that they work equally well in the dark. Even in daylight, a search and rescue dog is considered to be as effective as twenty men and can pick up a human scent from as far away as 500 metres.

There are around 90 fully-trained search and rescue dogs in the UK. In times of emergency they have helped out very successfully abroad, but are then faced with six months quarantine on return if they have been to areas outside the pet passport scheme. Army dogs, viewed as less valuable, are often simply left behind abroad for the same reason. We're not very good at repaying loyalty, we humans, are we?

Through all these functions, there are probably not many people whose lives are not impacted beneficially by a dog – whether it's directly or indirectly by catching and restraining criminals or stopping drugs from entering the country with all the social desolation that brings.

Other people have their lives improved much more acutely and directly by dogs, though. We've already heard about Hearing Dogs for Deaf People and Dogs for the Disabled but there are many more assistance dogs and dogs contributing to our physical and mental well-being, perhaps the best-known charity using dogs in Britain being Guide Dogs for the Blind.

The Guide Dog for the Blind Association was founded in Britain in 1934, although the first guide dogs in Britain were trained three years earlier. Guide dogs are in fact not a British concept, but rather a German one, dating back to the First World War, when they were first used to act as the eyes of a blinded soldier.

Ten years later, Mrs. Dorothy Eustis, a trainer of police and army dogs in Switzerland, was contacted by a blind American by the name of Morris Frank and arranged for a guide dog to be trained. The Seeing Eye organisation was then started in Switzerland and America.

It was Seeing Eye which supplied a trainer to Britain to train the first few British guide dogs in 1931. To talk about humble beginnings is perhaps an understatement. The starting point was a lock-up garage in Wallasey in Cheshire.

The charity grew slowly and steadily, with a huge break-through coming in 1960 when a breeding programme was started to ensure the availability of suitable dogs for training. This was the start of something very big – the breeding pro-gramme is now the largest breeding and training scheme in the world, so that these days, at any one time, there are around 5,000 guide dog/person partnerships in the U.K.

All this requires a staff totalling around 800. Such an enterprise is obviously expensive, with each dog costing about £10 per day to breed, train and maintain. Perhaps surprisingly this charity, together with many of the others we have talked about, receives no Government funding at all. Everything has to be funded through charitable donations.

A dog's working life is just about 7 years, after which it is re-homed to a (fortunately long) waiting-list of volunteers. Equally fortunately, there is quite a waiting-list for dogs that fail to make the grade as a guide dog.

The difference having a guide dog makes to an unsighted person must be huge. The Guide Dogs for the Blind Association often set up an experience whereby people are blindfolded and led around a variety of situations. Just how exposed and insecure it leaves you feeling cannot be overstated, so that these dogs really do give the blind person confidence and a chance to live. It is yet another humbling experience watching them work and watching the relationship between dog and handler.

There are many ways in which dogs help people in their lives and make them better. Another charity which helps in a similar way to Dogs for the Disabled is Canine Partners for Independence.

One of my favourites, though, and one which I am personally involved with is Pets As Therapy. In comparison with many others this is a relative newcomer, being founded in 1983. The main purpose of the charity is to provide therapeutic visits to hospitals, hospices, nursing homes and care homes.

Since its inception, around 18,000 dogs have been registered as PAT dogs, with 3,500 of those currently actively visiting a staggering half a million bedsides each year.

Before they can visit, dogs have to be tested. They need to have the right temperament, being calm and friendly. Obviously they must be healthy and well groomed. They must be insured and have acceptable references. The idea of the scheme is to help patients, particularly long-term patients, the old and the young, to overcome the tremendous feelings of isolation and even depression which come with illness. For some people, the PAT volunteer and the dog are the only visitors the patient gets, particularly in homes for the elderly. The dogs bring back memories of home, of happier times. The beneficial effects of these visits can even aid recovery.

I visited a home for the elderly for some years with my own registered PAT dog, Jake. To be honest, these visits were emotional roller-coaster rides, rising and falling from laughter to tears and back. In the environment of an old folks' home, many of the residents had been forced to give up their beloved pets to enter the home, and having a visit from a friendly dog was a real lift.

I used to start my visit by going into a very small TV room. There, Jake would meet Barbara, probably his favourite resident. She would never remember Jake or me from the previous week but we would reintroduce ourselves and soon be getting on famously. I would take treats for the residents to give to Jake, but Barbara never needed them. You see, she had this handbag. And from this handbag would come the most amazing array of goodies. There would often be a toffee – sometimes half eaten and rewrapped, but Jake wouldn't mind (although watching a dog eating a sticky toffee is something else!).

Sometimes, a potato would come out of Barbara's bag. Maybe a sticky jam tart. Some buttered toast. A few scraps of meat in gravy wrapped in a tissue. Given that Barbara didn't remember Jake and didn't know he was coming I always wondered what she was doing with this (presumably) contraband booty.

Barbara used to love Jake's visits and I always wished that she could remember them so that she could look forward to the next one. Meanwhile Bill, a large, balding man with thick glasses, was always in this small TV room, too. He liked a little play with Jake. I do remember one day offering Bill a treat to offer Jake but before I could say anything he'd popped the Pedigree Chum treat in his mouth and was chewing away.

Most of the residents spent their time in the day room. There was a real etiquette to be observed here. The residents always sat in the same chairs. You mustn't sit in their chairs and you mustn't block their view of the TV, even if they couldn't hear it or often didn't know what was on.

Some of the residents were really quite scared of dogs. I soon learned who they were, though, and gave them a wide berth.

Often, I would get the same stories each week. You would be talking to one of the old folks when they would suddenly seem to become abstracted and almost look into the air beyond you. You could see the animation return to the tired, blank faces as they recalled a dog from their youth. Every week I was told about one particular lady's father's dog who used to ride with him on the footplate of a train.

I really don't know if it's the case, but many residents almost appeared to be medicated into a fairly mind-numbing nothingness. So seeing a little glimmer of excitement, recognition or memory was quite emotional for me.

Jake would put up with the clumsiest treatment, all unintentional, from his visitees. Many had arthritis or other conditions which made their handling a bit heavy. Yet they loved getting their hand into his soft fur and his curls. As long as the occasional treat was handed over, Jake didn't mind.

He seemed to sense where he was and what was required of him and stayed calm and gentle whatever happened. His greatest test was ignoring the residents' budgie – a real test for my half spaniel.

One lady, Mary, seemed to have a memory which could last less than even two minutes. She would come up and greet us, asking whom we were visiting, then she would lavish some attention on Jake, ask his name and comment, 'Oh, he's a lovely tail wagger!' Having done that, she would ask the time and excuse herself, only to return about two minutes later and go through the whole routine again. On one visit this happened five times. One of the older men beckoned me over to his chair and confided in me, 'I don't know what she's doing here, she's daft.'

Even in a well-run home there was so little to interest or stimulate the residents. I really wasn't that surprised if they chose to switch off mentally.

Perhaps the most dramatic incident I remember, though, occurred out of the blue in the day room. I took Jake up to a frail, grey-haired lady whom I had seen before to say hello. Her facial expression changed and came alive and she became highly animated. She seemed to spring out of her chair, although she was normally so frail. She grabbed me by both sides of the face, started crying and tearfully exclaimed at the top of her voice 'Oh there you are, Charlie. There you are, oh, thank God you're safe.' With that she was trying to kiss me on the lips. Fortunately, the commotion brought a member of staff who led the lady away and helped to calm her down.

I was left quite stunned by the power of emotion and the strength of memory which had come flooding out. The incident bothered me all week, so I started the next visit by going to see the officer in charge to see if they still wanted me to visit. She explained that everything was all right and that Dorothy had calmed down quite quickly after the incident.

Dorothy's niece had visited and had explained that Charlie had been Dorothy's fiancé, who had gone to war and never come back. Something about the visit had triggered all of this off in her mind.

Most visits were a lot less eventful, I'm glad to say. It was just a matter of making human and canine contact with lonely, isolated, often depressed people who had a lot in the past but very little in the future and who got a lot out of having a visitor to talk to. For so many of the residents, we were their only visitors.

It's a tragedy that so many people have to give up the one thing they love the most – their dog – to go into residential care. That is why so many of the old folks looked forward to Jake's visits. It must almost feel like the last straw to lose that final friend, the one you love so much and who is the one thing left in life which gives you a purpose. This is why the Cinnamon Trust exists. Another charity, this one has a very specific remit and that is to facilitate elderly pet owners in taking their pets with them when they go into residential care.

So dogs fill a unique place in human hearts, in folklore and mythology and in our society. They fulfil a unique range of highly specialised and enormously useful functions to make our lives more convenient, safer and more rewarding. And yet, here's a paradox. As dogs do more and more for us, they seem to be getting less and less in return.

Instead of going on the offensive, dog-owners and others in the dog world seem to be willing to become more and more apologetic for their animals and for themselves. In my own town, the council continually moans about irresponsible dog-ownership, yet doesn't allow dogs into any of its premises to run dog classes, basically because of pressure from the anti-dog brigade. The main reason appears to be that the venues are also used by children. The two are, of course, not mutually exclusive, as demonstrated in millions of households every day. There seems to be a belief that all children will end up blinded by worms or something. All it takes, of course, is careful cleaning and basic hygiene precautions.

What's really needed is a pro-dog campaign. There are lots of organisations which advocate dogs and dog-ownership, of course, but it is still exciting when a new initiative comes forward like the Kennel Club's 'Hero Dogs' campaign, which began in 2005.

The aim of the campaign is to highlight the fantastic things that dogs do for people. The winner of the award is decided by a public vote and there were six dogs in the final at Crufts.

The dog and owner partnerships in the final in this first event represent many of the functions which we've already thought of – each finalist really representing thousands of others fulfilling similar roles or performing similar feats.

The first finalist was Mandy with owner Peter Kay Wilson. He fell asleep in the lounge and a fire started. Mandy, a former trailhound who had suffered badly from neglect, including near-starvation, had previously endured severe health problems. One of the consequences of this was an allergy to smoke, yet Mandy went into the lounge and roused Peter, saving his life.

Boswell, an Italian spinione, belongs to Maelea Forrester. Maelea lost her sight at the age of four. She owned a guide dog and Boswell as a pet. When the guide dog retired he went to live with Maelea's father, along with Boswell. Life without a dog left Maelea introverted and depressed. While waiting for a new dog, a solution was found by promoting Boswell to the guide dog role!

The third dog, Endal, is already quite famous, along with his owner, Allen Parton. Allen received a serious head injury during the first Gulf War while serving in the Royal Navy. He spent a total of three years in hospital and subsequently in rehabilitation. The long-term consequences were severe – loss of 50% of his memory, confinement to a wheelchair. By his own admission, his behaviour became bizarre and he acquired serious speech difficulties. Perhaps unsurprisingly, Allen became introverted, rude, angry and full of bitterness, rejecting human contact even from family and friends. And then Endal came into his life, refusing to be put off by Allen's manner. Initially, this 'Canine Partner for Independence' failed his assessment, but the bond with Allen had become so strong that he could not let Endal go back. What Allen says about Endal is hardly understated – he simply credits his canine companion with bringing him back to life. Endal provides very practical help: taking money out of the cashpoint and washing out of the washing machine, for example. Once, when Allen fell out of his wheelchair Endal even put him in the recovery position. All this, of course, is both fantastic and remarkable, at least it is to me, but it is nothing compared with the more abstract help given by Endal to Allen. To quote Allen when he speaks of Endal, 'He never judges me, he never looks away because of my condition and his aiding of me when I am at my weakest makes us both an invincible team. I can put my hand out to my side day or night and he is always there. He has taught me to love, laugh and live again.'

What more can any one animate being do for another?

Endal has been awarded one of the highest accolades in the doggy world – the PDSA's Gold Medal. He will soon have to retire from his role as a Canine Partner but will stay with Allen as a pet. I think it would take a lot to persuade Allen to let Endal go.

The story of Bob Bainbridge and his German shepherd, Tyson, is a shorter and simpler one, but still answers the question 'what do dogs do for us?' Bob was out walking Tyson when he was attacked and knocked unconscious by five youths. The weather was very cold and the conditions icy. Tyson stayed with Bob and kept him warm, not leaving until he heard the voice of Bob's father who had come out looking for his son. Tyson went to him and led him straight back to Bob. It is a medical fact that Bob would have died but for the care offered by his dog.

Valentine is a mongrel belonging to June Beech. June is a deaf person and Valentine is her hearing dog. Over and above this, Valentine has saved lives. She saved June's husband's life when he collapsed with a suspected brain haemorrhage. Valentine went and alerted June to his plight, as she had before when June's father-in-law had suffered a stroke and collapsed in a position out of sight between a bed and a wall. On the last occasion, Valentine pulled June back when she was trying to cross a road between two parked lorries. Another lorry whizzed by where June would have been. From that time on, Valentine will only let June cross the road at pedestrian crossings.

The winner of the inaugural Kennel Club Hero Dog of the Year, though was Buster, owned and handled by Danny Morgan. Buster is a Springer spaniel and an army sniffer dog. He has served with Danny all over the world – in Northern Ireland, Kosovo and Iraq. His particular forte is sniffing out weapons and his biggest success in a distinguished army career has been discovering a massive store of weapons in Iraq, hidden in a cavity wall and intended for use in the destruction of our forces.

As well as the Kennel Club award, Buster has also received the PDSA Dickin Medal for bravery. This is a very high honour with a long and distinguished history. It is the animal equivalent of the Victoria Cross. Nothing comes higher.

It seems that there is no end to what dogs can do for us and the range of their interventions on our behalf is growing more and more by the day.

How about this new development: a dog who sniffs out early bladder cancer in humans, well before it can be diagnosed in a conventional way.

Tangle, a beautiful cocker spaniel, is one such dog, trained by Hearing Dogs for Deaf People. The project started back in 1978 when a founder member of the charity, Gillian Lacey, was alerted to a malignant melanoma on her leg by her pet Dalmatian, called Trudii. This was brought back to Gill's mind when she saw a similar story on the news in 2002. The following year saw the creation of a multi-disciplinary team of doctors and statisticians, together with dog-trainers from Hearing Dogs who trained their own pet dogs for the task. In addition to Tangle, two more cocker spaniels were involved, Biddy and Bee, together with a Labrador called Jade, a Papillon called Eliza and last but by no means least, a mongrel called Toddy.

In the following year, 2004, an article published in the *British Medical Journal* confirms that the dogs had been trained to detect bladder cancer 'by olfactory means' – basically by smell. Originally, the plan had been to work with skin cancer, but as urine samples were much easier to get hold of than skin samples, the project was focused on bladder cancer. I remember that this caused worldwide interest and I had heard about it on Radio 5 Live as I drove home. I was pretty overwhelmed and had to pull over as I was quite choked up with emotion. Just imagine how you would feel if your dog could do that!

Of course, to reach this stage there had to be very strict

clinical and experimental conditions, so that any evidence was scientifically sound.

The most amazing part of the story for me, though, was when the dogs, after a period of great accuracy, started indicating one of the negative samples as positive. Initially spirits fell amongst the team. Try as they might, the dogs could not be dissuaded from indicating this sample as positive. Eventually, doctors decided to call the patient back in for further tests, only to find that there was a type of bladder cancer in one of the kidneys. Because it was found so early, it was possible to treat it successfully.

The hope now, as things go forward, is that dogs will be used as a non-invasive cancer detection tool.

Other 'medical alert' dogs who save lives are the Seizure Alert dogs. These dogs quite simply – or rather quite magnificently – alert their owners minutes or even hours before the onset of an epileptic fit. This time is key in allowing them to take medication, get home or to some other place of safety and prepare or make an emergency call.

Interestingly, no one can really explain how dogs can do this. Some believe that the dog is reacting to minute changes in behaviour or scent or conductivity across the skin before a seizure occurs.

No one knows how it works, but it works.

These dogs appear to be born with this ability and it does not seem that it can be trained into them. Having alerted their owner, though, the dog can be trained to take other actions like lying calmly by their side until the seizure is over. Just image how this would change your life: no longer housebound through fear and lack of confidence; given a second chance at life, just like some of the dogs involved.

Perhaps, though, the greatest thing that dogs do for us, even if one of the least remarkable, is give us companionship.

For some people they really are 'Man's (or Woman's) Best Friend'.

Some people prefer their dog to their partner. Consider this. (I'd love to attribute it to someone and give them credit but it appears in magazines and website in various formats all over the place.)

10 reasons why dogs are better than women …

- Dogs don't expect you to call when you're running late. The later you are, the more excited dogs are to see you.
- Dogs will forgive you for playing with other dogs.
- Anyone can get a good-looking dog.
- Dogs like it when you leave lots of things on the floor.
- You never have to wait for a dog – they're ready to go 24 hours a day.
- Dogs don't mind if you give their offspring away.
- Dogs don't hate their bodies.
- Dogs agree that you have to raise your voice to get your point across.
- A dog's parents never visit.
- Dogs never need to examine the relationship … and many more!

In the interests of balance and fairness and so as not to alienate female readers or enrage them to the point that their lycra leggings explode:

10 reasons why dogs are better than men …

- Dogs do not have problems expressing affection in public.
- Dogs miss you when you're gone.
- Dogs are utterly uninterested in professional sports.
- Dogs don't complain when you want to go out for a walk.
- You never wonder whether your dog is good enough for you.

- Dogs feel guilt when they've done something wrong.
- Dogs are unlikely to roll over and lose consciousness immediately following intense play.
- Dogs are willing to hold your purse in public.
- Dogs don't criticise your friends.
- You can train a dog.

So what excellent companions dogs make (indeed the posh term for a pet dog is 'companion dog').

Dogs can have the most profound effect on our lives. Owning a dog and walking it breaks down so many barriers for those who might otherwise feel lonely or isolated – or simply makes life better for those who don't have those problems. They provide an easy, neutral topic for conversation and certainly cause us to have interactions with people we would probably never speak to. Studies have shown quite simply that people walking a dog through a park enjoy a considerably greater degree of social interaction with others than those who walk without one.

Other studies have found similarly positive results. For example, it is a fact that people with pets are seen in a much more positive light in social situations than those without. Interestingly, they are never perceived negatively even by non-pet-owners, whereas the reverse is not the case.

Importantly, one piece of research showed that around one-third of pet-owners believed that having a pet helps them to make friends and meet new people. This, of course, is a self-fulfilling prophecy as, if you go out expecting to meet new people and make friends, you no doubt will. As a practical point, around 30% of dog-owners get involved in some activity and meet new people through their dog – whether it is basic training, formal obedience or anything in between.

The benefits of dog-ownership are stretched yet further

where older people are involved. Companionship is a huge factor, but the benefits of owning a dog go way beyond that. They help to counter social isolation by causing the owner to go out for walks and, in doing so, meet people. They give a reason to get up in the morning, help people to keep to regular meal times, to keep rooms warm (which they may not do for themselves alone) – in short, they can give a reason for living. Another being who is dependent on you and, of course, is always there, loving unconditionally.

When I studied to be a pet bereavement counsellor with a large charity, I was struck by just how much a pet can be a link with the past and with a loved one who may have been lost. The times shared with the pet and the loved one are anchored by the presence of the dog after the loved one's death and become a source of great comfort.

For everyone, but perhaps more so for the elderly, dogs mean exercise. It doesn't have to be walks of marathon proportions, but it helps to maintain fitness and flexibility. Indeed, a generation of kids brought up walking dogs instead of being glued to computer game consoles would be less obese, much fitter, more responsible and much more sociable.

On average, people who own dogs live longer than those who don't. Stroking a dog has been shown to slow the heartbeat and reduce the risk of a stroke. What better stress-buster than a good walk with the dog!

One study of senior citizens showed that pet-owners made 21% fewer visits to the doctor and suffered less from headaches, depression, indigestion and lack of sleep!

Similarly, children with dogs had fewer days off school and had stronger immune systems. One Scandinavian study showed that children exposed to dogs in their first year of life had lower incidences of asthma and other allergies.

And how about this? If you have a heart attack, your long-term survival rate is significantly longer if you are a pet-owner than if you aren't. So, you're less likely to suffer a heart attack and then more likely to survive one if you do have a dog.

In short, dogs play a huge role in the well-being of us humans.

Impacts on family life can be very significant, too. Dog-ownership has been shown to bring and keep families together more than ever before. It gives a neutral subject to discuss and to enjoy together and a dog causes so many more family interactions. One study found that as many as 70% of families reported an increase in happiness after getting a dog. That can't be bad.

Helping to care for a dog – under parental supervision, of course – can give children a real sense of responsibility which then impacts on all other aspects of their life. Indeed, it's not going too far to say that dog-ownership can really help with positive emotional growth and development. Studies even show that children growing up with a pet (I like to think especially a dog) develop much better both socially and academically and have a better respect for life and the environment.

This is one reason why dogs are increasingly being used to reach out to children with issues such as autism and ADD (Attention Deficit Disorder), even abused children. Some of these children find it initially easier to build relationships and bond with a dog rather than with adult humans, and it represents an important step in making their world a better one.

So, in summary, 'what have dogs ever done for us?' Well, not much really …

CHAPTER 9

Oh, them Germans!

Just imagine you have the misfortune to be a tax and debt collector in Germany in the 1870s. You have to find your way through narrow, dark alleyways and back streets, full of entryways and other hidey-holes for ruffians and crooks. When you get to your destination you have to confront people who are less than pleased to see you and probably pretty desperate. Even if they pay up, they'll probably be waiting round the next corner for you with a cudgel.

So, whatever do you do? Well, if you're of a very organised, Teutonic disposition, and your name is Herr Louis Dobermann, then you set about a carefully planned breeding programme, combining some of the attributes of the Rottweiler, the German pinscher, the Weimaraner (a large, sleek, silver hunting dog), the greyhound and the Manchester terrier.

The resultant breed bears your name. It's obedient, it's alert, it's clever. It's got 'Don't mess with Herr Louis Dobermann' written all over its face and at 25-27 inches to the shoulders and 66-88 lb in weight, you'd be foolish to ignore this advice. Nowadays, it's a hugely popular companion dog, sometimes a bit nervy and with some heart problems in the breed, but a well-trained and well-bred Dobe is a pleasure to own.

Mmm. So the breeding of a Doberman includes the Rottweiler? But, what's a Rottweiler? Well, imagine you keep cattle and other animals in Southern Germany, near Wurtenberg in the Middle Ages. Your animals are regularly stolen, or attacked by other animals. You are pretty exposed out on the roads day and night moving your stock around. What you really need is a strong droving dog to help you move your stock, who can also act as a formidable guard dog. So, if you are a citizen of Rottweil, what you do is set about breeding just such a dog, which comes to bear the name of your town – the Rottweiler. In fact, this dog's origins lie in the huge mastiff type of dogs brought into Northern Europe by the Romans, no less, for boar-hunting, guarding and droving.

This is one hell of a powerful dog and you find that you now get a lot less hassle as you go about your daily business. And why wouldn't you? After all, this dog is about the same height as the Doberman but half as heavy again with massive, powerful jaws. Because these drovers are primarily butchers, the dog actually becomes known as the *Rottweiler Metzgerhund* – the Rottweil Butcher's Dog. As you drive and sell your animals you acquire substantial sums of money in return. What better to do with it than put it in a leather purse around the dog's neck? There you go, ruffian, make my day – try taking that off me if you can!

Like the Doberman, over the years the Rottweiler comes to be regarded as a useful companion dog as well as an efficient guard and, because of its intelligence and trainability, an accomplished police dog, particularly in the land of its origin. Again, it is now a really popular dog in Britain, where any buyer has to be very careful of the temperament of the parents.

While we think of butchers and meat, what about the 'sausage dog' of our, or at least my, youth? That's another German favourite, just like sausage itself.

When I was a kid, 'sausage dog' was the only name these little dogs were known by – my Mum and Dad still call them that today. To a devotee, though, this is such a demeaning and pejorative term that your own sausage, chaps, would probably be in danger if you referred to them this way in enthusiast circles. More properly, this little chap is a dachshund – a 'badger dog' – and that gives you some insight into his true nature and character: brave, formidable – altogether a tough little sausage. They've been known to track prey for two days without a break.

Now, I don't know about you, but, having seen them handled in massive protective clothing and inch-thick gloves on wildlife programmes, I wouldn't go anywhere near a badger. The little dachshund will go down underground after him, though, and drag the badger our, whatever it's doing to him. I find them pretty strong-willed even as pets. I suppose they would have to be. Again, breeding for shows has done few favours, with a tendency to exaggerate the length of the back, leading to slipped discs and other back problems.

In fact, when you start looking into it, kennel clubs round the world generally recognise six different breeds of dachshund. There are three standard-sized ones, defined according to their coats – the smooth-haired (the one most of us think of), the long-haired (long hair but silky) and the wire-haired (a sort of spiky texture) – and then three miniature-sized sausage dogs (cocktail, maybe?) again with the three coat varieties. Fortunately, Mr Glover in his *Dog Spotting Guide* hadn't got too hung up on this and was satisfied with one of each coat-type, giving me three to get. The smooth-haired was easy to find – and get a bonus asterisk for training it, too – but the other two were harder to find.

Perhaps the best known of all the German dogs is the German shepherd dog or GSD. This really is one of the most popular dogs in the world.

Again, the creation of this breed was no accident but due

to the application of some suitably Teutonic zeal at the end of the 19th century. The breed's 'creator' was a certain Max Von Stephanitz, who set out to create the ultimate shepherd dog – shepherd not just in the sense of moving the flock but also guarding it. He and other breeders brought together herding dogs from all over southern Germany to produce the now famous breed. They look pretty wolf-like and their ancestors were probably those which caused the Romans so much concern when their scouts first reached the Rhine area.

The breed was massively successful – mastering so many diverse duties – and was used extensively by the German army in the First World War. So impressed were so many allied soldiers that they brought dogs back to their own countries, avoiding quarantine regulations on the way, and set them to work. Obviously, anything with 'German' in the title in this post-war period was to be avoided, so the dogs became known as 'Alsatians' or 'Alsatian Wolf Dogs', the former name sticking in common usage until this day.

The *Deutscher Schaferhund* is now undoubtedly the most widely used police, guarding and military dog, although it fulfils so many other roles, including guide dog and dog for the disabled.

There have been periods in the breed's history where indiscriminate breeding has produced vicious, untrustworthy dogs, motivated primarily through fear and a desire to get the first attack in as a means of defence. As I said earlier, I grew up with these dogs being the 'devil dogs' of the day in my mind, to be avoided wherever possible. Although now a highly regarded breed, capable of so much, I personally never take my eye off a German shepherd or allow myself to be distracted until I know the dog really well – and I've met some beautiful ones.

Anyway, like the Doberman and the Rottweiler, the German shepherd gave me no trouble from a spotting point of view – nor did other German breeds like the German short-haired pointer and the Weimaraner. In fact, a Weimaraner in my class refused the tiny bits of baked pig's liver which so many dogs adore as treats and would only work for Cheesy Wotsits! I've already told you about my chance meeting with a Münsterlander, which would otherwise have concerned me, so the Germans went pretty well, with a few worries about some of the dachshund varieties.

The Germans have undoubtedly made a huge contribution to the world of dogs, often in a fairly meticulous, planned way.

Above my desk, though, as I am writing this, is a lovely limited-edition print (104/500) of a picture entitled 'The Domino Effect' by Maria Heskins MA (RCA). It depicts a group of fairly stylised dogs standing and sitting outside the German Embassy, a German shepherd sitting in the doorway with its paw on a petition. The dogs outside include mastiffs, a Staffie, a bull terrier and a little toy dog, also of German origin, the Pomeranian. Some little dominoes are colliding into him. In front of him is a ball-on-a-rope-toy, only in this case the ball is a globe. 'The Domino Effect' was drawn in 2002.

So, what's all this about?

Well, it's time to put your 'imagining' head on again. This time, I want you to come with me to early 21st century Germany. Some of this isn't particularly pleasant reading, mind you. Time for a serious bit. Put yourself in these situations:

- You are a blind woman, walking through the streets with your GSD guide dog, when a young man starts kicking and screaming at your dog until he is pulled off by a passer-by.
- You are walking your dog along a city street when your bull terrier is grabbed from you by a group of strangers – you are beaten and held down while your dog is covered with petrol and set alight.

- You return to your car in a supermarket car park to find it being vandalised by four men with baseball bats because you have a bull terrier sticker in the window. When you protest you are clubbed unconscious and hospitalised.
- Your Jack Russell terrier is kicked to death because it is the same colour as a pit bull.

These are just a few real incidents from Germany as recently as 2000 and 2001, when many dog-owners only risked taking their dogs out at night. Indeed, covert filming by television crews revealed a catalogue of abuse, including being spat at and even being stoned for those dog-walkers who dared to venture out by day.

Then, in 2002, a 60-year-old man was shot 12 times at close range and killed by a neighbour who had lain in wait in a wood for him and his boxer dog. Having missed the dog, he reloaded his gun and emptied the magazine into his neighbour. He said it was because he hated dogs.

OK, probably best to take your imagining heads back off now.

The background to all of this lies in Wilhelmsburg, Hamburg, in late June 2000 when a six-year-old boy had been attacked and killed by a pit bull terrier. The owner of this dog was a known criminal and local major gangster, convicted 17 times before for robbery, GBH and dog-fighting. He had been ordered to keep his dog muzzled but no enforcement action had been taken. This dog had specifically been trained to attack humans and yet the reaction in the German media and hence in public was to focus on all dogs of bull breeds in particular, rather than to see this dog as a trained attack weapon in the hands of a madman.

Even before this attack, disquiet had been growing around Germany fuelled by tales of violent gangs breeding and training attack-dogs as the latest 'designer' weapon. Bavaria had, for example, already brought forward proposals prior to the Hamburg attack, to introduce a dog tax of £400 per year per dog for breeds such as the Staffordshire bull terrier, American Staffordshire bull terrier and the pit bull, to be combined with compulsory neutering.

What had happened in Hamburg was both terrible and tragic. In the aftermath, though, events spiralled rapidly, fed by a tabloid press which makes our own look like a bastion of serious journalism and a Government which some would say took the opportunity to deflect criticism about the dreadful economic circumstances in Germany and its own shortcomings onto an easy, common 'enemy'. Think of when we had the anti-dog hysteria over here which led to the Dangerous Dogs Act and multiply that ten-fold. The press used banner headlines accompanied by whole page pictures of snarling jaws to sensationalise and whip up a frenzy of anti-dog feeling and activity. 'Killers out of control ... who murder, threaten and tear people apart' was one headline; 'Killer fighting dogs rampaging through Germany' was another.

Rather than seeking to pacify or control the situation, the Government refused to criticise any over-reaction by the public towards dogs and their owners, saying that they had noticed only 'increased vigilance on behalf of the German public regarding these dogs.'

Of course, Germany is a Federal Nation, with each State able to enact its own laws. It became a real competition, with politicians jostling with each other to be the most anti-dog and ride the wave of popular fear and aversion towards these animals. State after State enacted draconian laws, amounting in some cases to the killing-off of whole breeds and going far beyond the provisions of even our own much maligned Dangerous Dogs Act.

The specific laws vary from State to State, leading of course to confusion and misunderstanding. Just imagine traveling from Shropshire to Staffordshire and finding that your dog was legal in one and outlawed in another … Here is a summary of one of these laws from Hamburg itself:

In common with most other States, Hamburg divides 'dangerous' dogs into three categories. The first category is for the 'Irrefutably Guilty' dogs and these are the pit bull, American Staffordshire terrier, Staffordshire bull terrier. Next comes the category of dogs 'Presumed Guilty of being dangerous, until proven otherwise', including bull mastiff, bull terrier, dogo argentino, dogue de Bordeaux, Fila Brasiliero, mastiff, mastin espagnol, Neapolitan mastiff, kangal, Caucasian owtscharka. The third category is for 'Dogs deemed dangerous by their previous behaviour'.

Can you imagine suggesting that someone was 'irrefutably guilty', just for being a member of a particular race – or even being presumed guilty until proven innocent? Just think what would happen to you! The PC Thought Police would be out to get you big-time – and quite rightly. Perhaps we could lock up all Subaru Imprezza owners as 'irrefutably guilty'?

Other States list many more breeds, or move them around. For example, a bull terrier is 'irrefutably guilty' in North Rhine Westphalia. This same State adds dogs such as Briard, Doberman, Estrela Mountain Dog, Marenna sheepdog, Pyrenean mountain dog and Rottweiler to the second category described above, bringing many more commonly-owned dogs into the provisions.

Dogs in the second category have to undertake a temperament test in most States to prove they are *not* dangerous. Dogs in the first and third categories and those in the second category who have failed the given test are all subject to the same legislation. The starting-point is that keeping these dogs is not allowed. Permission may be granted if the owner can prove a 'legitimate interest' and there is no doubt about the owner's suitability.

Where permission is granted, there are extensive conditions, including consideration of the owner's criminal record (presumably Mariah Carey would be excluded because of her criminal records) and physical capabilities. Holding liability insurance becomes compulsory, as does microchipping and neutering for the dog. The dog's death or transfer of ownership has to be registered and the owner has to display warning signs around his property. The dog must always be on a lead and muzzled in public and can not be bred from. The dog can be given no training which may result in it becoming aggressive and as the icing on the proverbial cake, the dog lives under a permanent cloud, subject to a destruction order at any time if it is deemed to present danger to life or limb of humans and animals – and that is hugely subjective.

Some of these conditions seem very sensible (e.g. a ban on training which would make a dog more dangerous, although even that is open to interpretation), but the overall aim is clearly to discourage ownership of these breeds and to see them die out.

Now, here comes the Domino Effect. Many of us may be reasonably satisfied that our dogs would be unaffected by all of this, but things have a tendency to roll and gain momentum and this could just be the start. Nordrhein Westphalien, for example, which includes major cities such as Düsseldorf, Cologne and Dortmund, extended provisions to *any dog* which 'in fully-grown status, reaches a withers height of 40 cm (15.7 inches) or alternatively, reaches a weight of at least 20 kg (44 lbs).'

This takes the legislation into a whole new area – certainly my very placid Border collie, Stan, now falls into these categories. For these dogs, the following apply:

- Compulsory registration (at the discretion of the local authority)
- Minimum age of 18 for the owner
- Proven competence in dog-ownership for the owners (examined)
- A 'clean' criminal record for owners (verified by the Police)
- Dogs to be kept on a lead at all times
- Dogs to be microchipped.
- Liability insurance

Other States go into a great deal of detail about specifications for fencing and signs to be erected. The Brandenburg edict, for example, states that you must be over 18 to walk a dog, reach certain standards of mental and physical capability and, for instance, only 3 dogs may be walked at any one time. That would be bad news for our dog-walkers and pet-sitters. This being Germany, where *Ordnung muss sein* ('there must be order'), details are given in full of requirements for collar-tags which must be worn – covering size, material, colour etc.

A maximum lead length of 2m is specified. Dogs must be muzzled in public buildings and on public transport.

There really are some very indiscriminate packages of measures being put into place in some of the German States, backed up with heavy fines and confiscation and possibly execution of dogs.

Perhaps unsurprisingly, the reaction of many to the hatred that was aroused and these draconian laws was to hand over dogs to Rescue Centres. These were then totally overwhelmed. There is an irony here in that rescue centres are not allowed to destroy healthy dogs but could not re-home many of these new 'dangerous' acquisitions. In Moenchengladbach, one rescue centre executed a number of dogs – the bodies of twelve lay in a pile on a trolley. The vets at the home had refused to undertake the task, but a State vet undertook the destruction sanctioned by the centre's director. Both faced criminal charges as a result.

Added to all of these measures were new and extensive laws governing breeding and importation of certain brands, effectively ensuring that there was no future for them in Germany.

One of the key features of the legislation centres around temperament tests. Again, these vary from one State to another. In Hessen, the Minister for the Interior appointed 30 experts to carry out tests. In addition, vets who possessed a so-called 'behaviour certificate' could also carry out the tests. The price of failure is very high for the dog – those who fail must be rehabilitated or put to sleep. The cost of the test is just over £150 at today's exchange rates – quite a sizeable tax on dog-ownership.

The tests themselves are not exactly scientific. In Hessen, the dog is observed in everyday situations, including for example walking through a children's playground. The tester's role is to attempt to threaten the dog, who should calm down as soon as the tester moves away. How truly bizarre – how do you react when you are threatened?

In Berlin, the overall criterion against which dogs are judged is that they have 'nothing in excess of the natural amount of wish to fight, attack or be aggressive to people or animals'. How on earth can this be judged?

So do the actual statistics back up the scale and nature of the State's intervention into dog-ownership in Germany? Or is it a similar major over-reaction to the one that brought us the Dangerous Dogs Act in the UK? More particularly, are these 'dangerous dogs' the most likely to bite? The statistics do not seem to make the case. Figures for the nine years up to 1997 for Nordrhein Westphalia, Germany's most populated state with 17.679 million inhabitants, show 86 attacks on people, resulting in one death, 24 severe injuries (in-patient care) and the remainder slight injuries (out-patient care).

Without scapegoating and pointing the finger at another breed, by far the greatest contributor to these figures was the German shepherd with 25 slight injuries, 5 severe injuries and the only killing of a human. Indeed it seems that if you are going to get your *Bockwurst* nibbled it is most likely to be by a breed of German origin, prompting some commentators to note that dogs of German origin have tended not to be listed by most States, although the GSD accounts for 41.9% of all attacks in this State whilst the Staffordshire bull terrier and bull terrier, for example, were not involved in one single attack in 9 years. I guess it would be pretty unpopular for the German government to give its national treasure a hard time.

Another, less accurate, source gives figures from 93 German towns over the period 1991 to 1995 and cites the number of attacks by German shepherds as 1,956, Rottweilers 542, Doberman 223 and both Staffordshire bull terrier and bull terrier at 169. Only slightly behind, at 160, is the dachshund!

Now, I don't know about you, but when I think of the police I don't tend to think, 'oh, those pinko liberals!' So it was interesting that an article from the German Police Force's own newspaper *Deutsche Polizei* shows that the police were largely against these draconian laws. They argued that gangsters would merely change their weapons of choice, even if regulations could be enforced. They attacked the hysterical headlines and tabloid coverage, seeing a sinister effort at manipulation of a nation's frustration onto a common enemy.

Furthermore, the view appeared to be that the legislation far outweighed the scale of the problem. Within a month of poor Volkan, the young boy, being killed by a dog, the police point out that six boys from different families were murdered by their fathers in the wake of divorce battles. ('Ban killer dads!')

The argument, says the article, that these laws are a way of protecting people and particularly children, does not stand up to scrutiny. In the previous year 318 children had been killed by cars and another 58,838 injured, yet there had been no moves to curb reckless drivers – nor did law-makers take away the car of a reckless driver so he could not endanger someone else with that vehicle.

The article went on to point out that the laws would be very difficult to police as well. Who could judge mixed breeds? Who was going to know about the truly dangerous fighting-dogs in the criminal sub-culture and denounce them to the authorities?

Broader points raised were the effect that this anti-dog hysteria was having on children, who would grow up with a real fear of what for many has been an only friend, the family dog. Others would see their own dogs being given up and put to sleep without ever having shown any aggression. The psychological damage and sense of injustice could be immense. The point was also raised about the strong links that have been found to exist between abuse of animals and abuse of children and protection of animals and child protection. For the State to break this link was viewed as a retrograde step.

All of this felt regrettable, frustrating and even mad, but at least it was happening at some distance from us. Things don't stay that way, though. At the end of September that year, Germany called on the European Union for a Europe-wide ban on these 'dangerous dogs'. The German State Secretary for the Interior, Hansjeorg Gerges, argued in Brussels that there should be a complete ban on the breeding, import and trade of fighting-dogs, arguing that a national ban was useless if the dogs could be imported from elsewhere.

The British argued the most strongly against this, first and foremost on the basis that it was not a matter for the EU to determine whether individual countries should ban individual breeds. This appeared to be in line with the thinking of the Commissioner responsible for these matters, Antonio Vittorini, who suggested to the Commission that these issues were best determined regionally or nationally, but not by the EU. However, this is certainly not the end of it.

The British response was, at least in part, due to fairly intensive lobbying of MEPs by dog-lovers and organisations in Britain, led quite effectively (some might say 'for once') by the Kennel Club and also Breed Groups and Councils. Certainly, a response from the Home Office in Britain to a letter from the Kennel Club was reassuring, indicating that current legislation was sufficient in Britain, stating, 'I consider that existing UK law in the form of the Dangerous Dogs Act 1991 (as amended in 1997) is adequate for both present and future control needs in this area.'

Since then, the issue continues to bubble just below the surface, with sporadic skirmishes across Europe and indeed the rest of the world as the dominoes tumble and have their knock-on effect. Now, thirty-six States in the USA have some form of Breed-Specific Legislation. The Czech Republic is planning legislation against 'dangerous dogs', as is New Zealand. Australia and Canada have begun to adopt anti-dog laws, as in Europe have France, Spain and Luxembourg. France's efforts would have been funny but for their potential consequences, containing made-up names of breeds and incorrect photographs to go with the legislation. In Germany some States have had to back down following legal action and have had to pay compensation, but still the issue refuses to go away.

Here, the call from campaigning groups is 'punish the deed, not the breed', in other words put the responsibility on to dog-owners to control, train and look after their own dogs, taking strong action against individuals as necessary, but certainly not going for bans on whole breeds.

So, it's 'them Germans' behind it all again. Always trouble! I've lived and worked in Germany myself and found so much to admire about the people, the country and the culture. I just feel so let down by them about this. As for the German breeds, I'm a huge fan. In fact we all are, as many of them number in the UK's 20 most popular dogs.

For me, this was particularly good news as they were easy to spot and cross off my list.

CHAPTER 10

Scotland the Brave

I had intended to re-try the 'Bedlington Principle' of canine research in Ireland, to look at the breeds native to those shores. (I've decided on this terminology myself to describe the situation where you travel to a place where a breed is supposed to come from, only to find that there is no sign of one. Nothing at all. Not a sausage.) I had wanted to go to the Belfast Championship Show, not least because I had never been there and was perhaps rather sickly fascinated by the promise of tours of former trouble spots. Two things conspired against me, however. Firstly, I couldn't make the dates and, secondly, I had already basically ticked off the Irish breeds such as the red setter and red and white setter, the Glen of Imaal terrier and the Irish terrier itself.

On the other hand, I was doing particularly badly with the Scottish Breeds and needed to make progress with them if I was to accomplish my task. I desperately needed to see the Scottish terrier, the Skye terrier, the Dandie Dinmont terrier and the Scottish deerhound.

Another thing which had appealed about the Irish shows is that if you travel to those you can go in a special coach, which has cages for your dogs to go with you by your side, and I really fancied that. You can even go on tour: to the Munster Circuit – four shows in as many days.

If Ireland and the special coach were not to be, though, this did give me the opportunity to try something which was new to me – using the budget, 'no frills' airlines – you know the ones, where the flight is £3.99 but then £60 in taxes and surcharges are added.

Even so, the price is fantastic. Birmingham to Edinburgh return for less than £45. That is just so much less than the train. The flight itself only takes about 40 minutes – you've just got up to height and you begin to come down to land. The train fare – for a five-hour journey – is £170 for the two of us. In fact to get to Edinburgh for 9.15 in the morning I would have had to leave at 21.58 the previous day and change at Birmingham, Crewe, Manchester and Carstairs, sitting in Manchester for 3? hours in the small hours of the morning. Mmmm, how appealing, and what a fool I was to go by plane!

It's true that the flight was early in the morning, basically ready to go as soon as planes were allowed to shatter the night's peace for nearby residents, but that was part of the adventure. The plan was to be in the centre of Edinburgh eating breakfast before 9 a.m.

The first thing that struck me at the airport was just how these cheap flights are changing things. It's putting places within easy reach of people where they never would have thought of going before. I certainly wouldn't have flown to Edinburgh for a few days. The big travellers, though, and those whose horizons had been most broadened by this cheap travel, appeared to be the stag night crews. Apparently, according to the in-flight magazine I was reading later, the average stag-nighter on one of these short excursions spends £400 plus. The group I was watching in the departure lounge had already made a brave start on this spending by lining up pint after pint of lager – and this was 5.30 in the morning. My stomach turned at the thought of it. They all wore specially printed polo shirts, with 'Dave Williams Stag' on the front with an emblem I couldn't make out (thank goodness) and (presumably) nicknames on the back like 'Nobber' and 'Long-Haired Freak'.

I was incredibly relieved to see Nobber get up and move when the Dublin flight was called. A second stag party headed off when the Palma flight was announced. Whatever happened to a local pub crawl and tying the bridegroom to a lamppost naked from the waist down with his pants on his head? Now that *was* sensible behaviour.

So, our flight was called and we got on board the 'Brummie Baby'. Have you noticed how they're giving planes names, now? A bit like trains – well locomotives, technically. Very few used to have names, just numbers, but now lots of them have names. Anyone would think I'd been a train-spotter, wouldn't they? Well, I haven't. I would just like to place on record at this point that I did not travel from Wolverhampton to Crewe with four other lads in a toilet compartment at the age of 11 because the train was so full of train-spotters going on a special day out to Crewe locomotive works. I got to sit on the sink all the way – or at least I would have if I'd been there.

Anyway, back to the 'Brummie Baby' (Baby because of the airline's name). Well I was thinking it wasn't very authentic. 'Bab' is the word more commonly used round this area as in 'How's the bab?' or 'The bab's done a wet'. Or they could have gone for a slightly more phonetic version like 'Brummoy bayboy'.

Forty-five minutes later, having been looked after by the seemingly compulsory gay steward, we were in Edinburgh airport and thanks to a really quick and cheap express bus service, using some 'wicked' bus lanes which cruised past the miles of commuter traffic, we were in the centre of Edinburgh and had dropped our luggage at our hotel just off the Royal Mile by 9 o'clock. This is hardly international jet-setting but it still amazes me how you can wake up in Birmingham and get your breakfast in Edinburgh.

This trip had a really good feel about it already. I was sure I was going to see some of the dogs I needed and my first impressions of Edinburgh (I'd only passed through once before, just as the castle and shops were closing) were extremely favourable. To be honest, we'd left nothing to chance. In fact, for that night's entertainment we'd even booked top tickets (third row from the front) for a newish musical called *Love Shack*. Now, there wasn't just a vague whiff of quality about this production – it was nothing short of a strong reek. What we're talking about here is a production starring an ex-member of Hear'Say, an ex-member of Steps and an ex-member of S Club 7, with a new song written by an ex-member of Take That. Honestly, is it possible, let alone reasonable, to ask for anything more? So, having assured ourselves of success for the trip, there was just a matter of getting the best out of the next three days and spotting some dogs. Oh, by the way this trip was for our 10th wedding anniversary and I should point out that any dog interest was of course both incidental and coincidental.

So, with a day to kill before we could get in to see *Love Shack* and having started our day with breakfast in a café, we decided to begin our explorations with a sightseeing tour by bus.

Finding breakfast, by the way, had proved to be quite interesting. Alison really wanted some toast, which doesn't seem too outlandish a request, but which wasn't available at the first three cafés we tried before giving up. Scotland is, of course, the heart disease capital of the UK – maybe even of Europe – and perhaps this was one indication why. Fry-ups or, at least, bacon rolls, were the order of the day. I was gutted. You can imagine my struggle to get down me a crusty white roll packed full of lean, juicy bacon, not too crispy and not too soggy but with the rind crisped up so it just crunched slightly as you bit into it. Horrible, shame there was no muesli.

I love those bus tours round cities. There were four different ones in Edinburgh, but one ticket allowed you to travel on any of them in a twenty-four hour period. Tom has done so many of these now that he refuses point blank to go on any more. Alison's spirit hasn't been broken yet, though, so we were soon climbing on board our first tour.

I just think they're a fantastic way of finding your bearings and getting a look at things you want to go back and look at in more detail later.

The trip took about an hour and from our vantage point on the top deck I saw a little Yorkie out for a walk (the dog, not the chocolate bar, in case any of you were struggling with surreal pictures in your head) and two frisky cross-breeds frolicking at the foot of King Arthur's Seat, the beautiful hills giving an amazingly impressive backdrop to one side of Edinburgh. King Arthur's Seat is actually a volcanic mini-mountain, accessible by a footpath up to its peak. It is around 820 feet / 250 m high. Apparently sometimes visitors just wander up in everyday clothing only to be caught out by bad weather halfway up. It was really quite a shock to me, and I have to say quite breathtaking, how the City just ends and goes up into hills. I had expected urban sprawl, but was so wrong. It was on this trip that we learned that we wouldn't be able to get into Holyrood Palace because Prince Charles had rather unhelpfully decided to be in residence. Something to do with the opening of the Scottish Assembly. Doesn't he know who pays his wages?

Just a short distance from Holyrood is indeed the Scottish Parliament building which has been a bottomless pit of public funds during its construction and which, now that it's built, still looks like it's under construction. Famous for his liberal views on modern architecture, it would be great to hear what Prince Charles thinks of his near neighbour.

Having got our bearings, it was time to decide what to see first. We decided to stay with the royal theme and go to see the Royal Yacht Britannia, which has been permanently sited in Edinburgh since 1998. It's quite a sight – 125 metres long (over 400 feet) and demands a crew of over 240 to keep it going. The good thing about this was that it gave us another guided bus trip to get there – this time out of the centre and through some of the old suburbs. Still interesting though, seeing how the city had expanded and travelling through the now quiet but once bustling dock areas. Some of the areas seemed really run down, like Newhaven, and it was obvious that no-one would be coming anywhere near them but for the siting of Britannia nearby.

Newhaven was built for James IV at a time of great naval expansion. It was James' great wish to build the largest ocean-going ship of the day, and so it was that the ship 'Great Michael' was built at Newhaven – carrying 300 sailors, 1,000 soldiers and 120 guards.

Leith docks, too, have been very important in their own time. They have a history of being used for whaling, not least by Christian Salvesen & Co, the world's biggest whaling company. In fact, that company first brought back penguins for Edinburgh Zoo, for which it is still famous.

Leith was also the site of Britain's first dry dock in 1720. The 19th century brought iron-hulled ships, though, for which the waters were not deep enough, so that a rapid decline was inevitable.

In fact, Leith was not a part of Edinburgh until 1920 when incorporation was literally forced upon it. I gathered that some people from Leith were still struggling with the concept of being part of Edinburgh.

Furthermore, going back to 1548, Leith had even been the seat of Scottish Government. At this time, it was Scotland's most important port. Mary of Guise, who governed Scotland while her daughter, Mary Queen of Scots, was too young to do so, even had the town fortified, feeling threatened as she did at the time of such anti-Catholic feeling. It was only two years, though, before these fortifications were taken down by victorious protestants.

Much more recently it provided the setting and filming location for the powerful film *Trainspotting* and some of the area seemed as dark and threatening as the film itself.

You access the yacht via Ocean Terminal, a shopping centre with restaurants, a cinema etc., making it the biggest shopping area in Edinburgh. This had clearly been a very run-down area before. Now it has lively shops, bus services and new housing springing up. Quite an example of urban regeneration. It shows just how important a decision like siting Britannia in Edinburgh can be to an area and yet, if you're like me, the decision at the time was probably met with a yawn.

One thing that did strike me on the bus tour around the centre and particularly out to Britannia, though, was just how few dogs I saw, given such a large population. To be fair, I don't suppose you see that many dogs in a city centre anywhere. Still a disappointment.

I wasn't really sure what to expect from seeing Britannia. I don't have any real interest in the royal family, to be honest. It really was worth it, though. For one thing, you don't get to go around many ships, so that in itself was interesting. What I definitely liked most was the slightly run-down 'shabby chic' of the yacht. It didn't strike me as particularly grand. Some of the ornaments were really gaudy. One room was like a lounge in a country home with an incongruous chintzy suite and an electric coal-effect fire – all floating out at sea. The telephones and intercom system in the rooms looked like something from the Stone Age.

The bedrooms, all singles until a double bed was put in for a royal honeymoon, did show the personality of the person whose room it was. Prince Philip's room, for example, was all dark polished wood with no frills or decoration.

It was interesting to go through the various decks and mess rooms, to hear of some of the seemingly ludicrous tradition and games of the officers and see everything get scaled down more and more until you reached a sort of cupboard where twelve of the normal ranks would sleep with the bunk of the person above them just twelve inches above their head. At times these tiny rooms would need to accommodate twelve sets of uniform for each soldier, too.

When moving round the ship, apparently, the sailors were expected to avert their eyes from the Royal Family and also the normal tradition was not to wear their caps, so that the Royals were spared the bother of having to return a salute, which they would have had to if the sailors had been 'fully dressed'. Some of this rubbish brings out the republican in me, I have to say.

Overall, the feeling was of a rather antiquated and in fact quite sad symbol of times gone by – very much of the past rather than the future.

The rest of the day was spent wandering along the Royal Mile – the road that joins Edinburgh Castle and Holyrood Castle and in fact is just over a mile. It still has a really strongly historical feel to it. The buildings are old and tall, built of a stone which has aged and blackened as time has gone by. The shops are touristy – whisky, tartan and that sort of thing. There was one gadget-type shop with a splendid name very appropriate to my quest, called 'The Mutt's Nuts'. There are bars, cafés and restaurants and various centres for ghost and other walking tours, including some time spent underground below the City Chambers, where a whole network of streets have been discovered which were once part of the old town. One Close, Mary King's Close, was sealed off in 1645 following a serious outbreak of the plague and it has recently been re-opened, filled with actors bringing the past to life and ghostly apparitions appearing in a really spooky atmosphere.

A very quick look around the Museum of Childhood was all there was time for before grabbing something to eat and hitting the highlight of our short stay, *Love Shack*! In fact it proved to be an excellent feel-good night out (except that the theatre was half empty). As far as I could see, I was one of very few males there and judging from the males I heard around me, probably the only straight one. It was a great show.

The next day brought us to our serious business (well, my serious business to be honest) – going to the Scottish Kennel Club's Championship Show, right back near the airport. An old chap told us where to catch a bus and even what time the buses ran, off the top of his head. This seemed too good to be true and Alison thought that it was a Scotsman enjoying the opportunity to take the piss out of the English. I of course am not so cynical, and his information proved to be spot-on.

Having got off at the nearest bus stop it very soon became apparent that it had never occurred to anyone to do with organising the show that anyone might arrive by public transport. You could see the site through a wire fence and see and hear many of the dogs being walked, but there was no indication of how to get in and we ended up walking for 40 minutes around uneven ground and roads with no pavements, past various locked gates, losing our tempers and getting hotter and hotter before finding our way in. Ironically, the show ground was just one wire fence away from the runway where we had landed the day before.

What a show this was. It seemed to contradict so much of

what I have already said about dog shows and dog showing, and yet reinforced other points even more.

It was a funny day weather-wise. It was bright and sunny on one hand – even sticky and muggy – and then really cold and wet on the other. This type of show takes place in large marquees and/or outside, depending on the weather. When we got there it was cold and pouring with rain. Luckily, as a member of the Scottish Kennel Club, I was able to shelter in a special pavilion where tea and coffee was provided free of charge. I could see that Alison was quietly impressed.

We sat there and planned the day – looking at the order in which each breed appeared in each of the various rings, working out how many classes there were in each breed and estimating times so that we could get around everything we wanted to see and focus on those breeds I needed to spot. Of course, none of this planning exactly paid off, but it looked like we knew what we were doing poring over the catalogue and writing notes all over it.

For all the planning over our cups of tea, though, it proved quite unnecessary as far as the deerhounds were concerned. We almost tripped over these dogs as we left the tearoom – if you can trip over an animal quite as big as this one. There were no fewer than ten of them gathered together while their owners chatted away happily. They were really placid and content all together in one little group, completely non-reactive to each other. Just one large grey mass. I don't think most people would expect this. These are large dogs, typically 76cm to the withers for males and 71cm for females. They are quite commonly mistaken for Irish wolfhounds, which are in fact a few centimetres larger and the world's tallest breed of dog. I stood there gawping at a dog called 'Pines Six Five Special to Gartlove' and just thought, 'what a massive, amazing dog!'

There were 54 deerhounds competing at the show and we were probably looking at most of them now.

The deerhound was (and some of you will have noticed a pattern emerging in the naming of dogs by now) bred to hunt deer and stag. It resembles a large, shaggy greyhound but was once known as the Royal Dog of Scotland. Quite simply, by law, no one below the rank of Earl was permitted to own one of these dogs. One strange but interesting fact is that the only payment a nobleman condemned to death might make to earn a reprieve was 'a leash of deerhounds'. So basically, if you were a dodgy Scottish Aristo it was definitely work having a leash of deerhounds up your sleeve in case you were found out.

The deerhound is quite a softy really, very much enjoying human company. At the same time, this breed can be very courageous and persistent. They have a great degree of dignity and quiet about them, and it was this that we noticed when we looked at the little pack in front of us. It is a breed which has remained remarkably consistent in appearance and temperament over time, from the period when it was a hunting favourite with Scottish chieftains in the Middle Ages.

As a breed, its decline came with the advent of hunting by gun, but also the onset of forced agriculture.

Indeed, as far back as the 1800s, there was a real danger of the breed dying out altogether. It was largely down to the hard work of two brothers, Archibald and Duncan McNeill, that the breed was saved, only to enjoy a revival when Queen Victoria acquired one.

Today, the breed is first and foremost a pet dog, but they are still expert in hunting, tracking, agility, racing and especially in chasing hares – a 'sport' where hares basically run for their lives, chased by very quick dogs who seem to get marks for causing the hare to turn and change direction. If it's not quick or agile enough it gets torn apart. Coming soon to Sky Sports (Bloodthirsty and Brutality Package).

It was some time before any of our 'chosen' breeds was going to be judged, so we mooched around watching people and dogs and seeing if I could disprove my point about the unfriendliness of show dog people and show dogs. It proved very easy actually – everyone I spoke to was friendly and helpful. For example, I wanted to clean up my confusion about the petit Brabancon and a wonderful lady cleared my confusion over different names for the same dogs here and abroad. Not only that but I got to tick off both types in my spotter guide.

We then watched the soft-coated wheaten terrier being judged from start to finish. Lovely dogs. I had a puppy of this breed, the splendidly named Frank, in my class at the time and was interested in seeing how he would develop and how big he was going to get. Not for the first time that day I was struck by how much coat colour seemed to influence judges – at least it appeared to. I found that a full-grown Frank would be about up to my knee. The dogs all seemed very good-natured with each other and with people, even in the very cramped conditions of the marquee. We happened to be standing by the most successful exhibitor of the day in the breed and it was great watching their excitement and joy grow as the day went on. Quite a vicarious thrill.

Imagine the excitement of the man I met at one of the coffee trailers later. This chap, smartly dressed in a tweed jacket and a tie, had just got Best of Breed with his Australian terrier – and this with a dog he had only decided to bring at the last minute, thinking that it didn't look up to much on the day! He explained that the dog was an import from Finland and had a tail. The judge was American and the breed isn't even recognised with a tail there. Bringing this particular bitch had, against this background, been an 'afterthought'. Winning would make the whole year or more for some of us and yet it had just landed in this chap's lap. I'd simply asked him while we were queuing if he'd had a good day and he had very modestly let all this slip. I was so envious. Such a nice chap, too.

By this time I'd drunk my coffee and convinced both myself and Alison that I wasn't really jealous, bitter and twisted, it was time for one of our breeds to be judged – the Dandie Dinmont terrier. There were not many of them all together – just twenty. I asked the lady seated next to me if this was normal for such a big show. She turned out to be very knowledgeable about the breed and even on the breed club's committee. She told me that more northerners travelled south with their dogs than southerners travelled north, so that the entries in shows in southern England were often the largest. This struck me as a bit strange for a northern breed and a bit of a shame. There were just 20 dogs and 20 entries for the breed. It did make, though, for a fairly quick and very enjoyable hour watching a breed from start to finish. Especially in the knowledgeable and fascinating company of the couple we had met. We spent the whole hour chatting away – with the exception of the few minutes when they were entering their own dog.

It turns out that as a breed, the Dandie Dinmont terrier has not been doing so well. It has in fact been included on the recent Kennel Club 'Endangered British Breeds' list, an initiative aimed at stimulating interest in and ownership of some of the endangered native breeds. There are 29 breeds on the list and they include some of my very favourite dogs. Here's the list in full:

Sealyham terrier, Skye terrier, Glen of Imaal terrier, otterhound, bloodhound, deerhound, greyhound, Gordon setter, Irish red and white setter, curly-coated retriever, Clumber spaniel, field spaniel, Irish water spaniel, miniature bull terrier, Dandie Dinmont terrier, smooth fox terrier, Irish terrier, Kerry blue terrier, Lakeland terrier, Manchester terrier, Norwich terrier, soft-coated wheaten terrier, Welsh terrier, smooth collie, Lancashire heeler, Cardigan Welsh corgi, English toy terrier and King Charles spaniel.

So there you go. I bet you wish you hadn't asked now!

There were parades of these breeds in Crufts this year, together with features in the official rather excellent programme. The Kennel Club also managed to get the BBC to feature the breeds and the scheme quite heavily in their TV coverage of the show. This, it seems to me, is a totally appropriate and very worthy use of its resources by the much criticised and much maligned Kennel Club.

You can see the problem, though. Guess how many Dandie Dinmont puppies had been registered in the 12 months before the Scottish Kennel Club show I was at? Thousands? Well, no. Hundreds? Well, no again. Eighty-one. Just eighty-one. If you compare this with golden retrievers (10,165) or even, say, pugs (2,116) you can get a feel for the nature of the problem.

In fact, my unofficial guide to the world of Dandie Dinmonts was the puppy co-ordinator for the breed, putting potential owners in touch with breeders. The situation is now simply this: bitch puppies will only be allowed to go to breeders. The breed cannot afford to have bitches taken out of breeding – obviously unless there is a medical condition or similar circumstances. So, if you or I were to enquire after a Dandie puppy, it would be males only for us – and up to an 18-month wait!

The good news is, though, that the Kennel Club campaign has been successful in stimulating interest in this breed (and presumably the others) and a lot more enquiries have come in since the campaign started.

The Dandie Dinmont itself is a hugely likeable dog, I discovered. We were both really taken by it. It has a dachshund-like long, low body with short legs. The coat is about two inches long and down the centre of the dog's back it is a mix of hard and soft hair. It is just 8 to 11 inches high (20-28 cm) and obviously quite a light dog at 18-24 lb (8-11 kg). Most appealingly it sports quite a funky hairdo, all standing upright on its head in an interesting way. In terms of character, it is not snappy or looking for a scrap. In some ways it is not a typical terrier at all, being fairly docile and easy-going. This doesn't mean, though, that it won't stand up for itself if it needs to. It's a dog that loves people of all ages and has a surprisingly loud bark, making it a good guard dog.

All sorts of theories abound about where the breed originally came from. Some point to old Scottish terriers, others to the Skye terrier. Some people say that our old friend the Bedlington is in there and others suggest a link to the otterhound. Certainly, if you think of a sawn-off otterhound you won't be far away!

They come in two coat colours only, these having the unusual names of mustard (a sort of fawny colour) and pepper (a grey colour).

I was intrigued by these terms and was keen to find out where they came from. The answer is, of course … Sir Walter Scott. In fact, the Dandie Dinmont terrier is the only breed of dog named after a fictional character, in this case a bluff, strong, brave and loyal hill farmer from the borders called, well, err … Dandie Dinmont. He appears in a novel called *Guy Mannering*, published in 1815.

One of the great joys of writing a book like this is just following wherever you are taken – whether it be to places, to people or to other things which you wouldn't otherwise have encountered. The novel *Guy Mannering* is one of these unexpected gifts. I would never have picked it up, or, if I had, I would have put it down pretty quickly. In fact, the first obstacle to be overcome was even finding it. I was amazed that shops like Waterstone's in Edinburgh didn't even stock it, despite one of the shops standing pretty close to Scott's monument. Admittedly, in their special Scottish fiction section they did have some of his novels, but little beyond *Ivanhoe* and *Rob Roy*, a copy of which has been standing untouched in a rather nice Folio Society edition on my bookshelf at home for some time. Things were even worse at the Edinburgh Castle bookshop, where I genuinely had difficulty explaining that *Guy Mannering* was the title and Walter Scott the author and not vice versa.

Anyway, it does take a bit of perserverance, to be honest, especially in getting through some of the passages in dialect. Fortunately, I do like to mix modern novels with classics, thrillers, even more avant-garde things. If you don't enjoy a good classic, though, I wouldn't recommend it. No car chases, sex or that sort of thing. Plenty of plot, though, and some pretty good characters.

One of these characters, who appears and reappears around the periphery of the story, is our Dandie Dinmont. It took me about 120 pages to find him – which in this book must have been only around 150 paragraphs. When he first meets Mr Brown, one of the main characters in the story, Dinmont admires his terrier and explains that he owns terriers too:

'I have six terriers at home, forbye other dogs. There's auld Pepper and auld Mustard, and young Pepper and young Mustard, and little Pepper and little Mustard.'

He goes on to explain how he has trained them, giving an insight into what they would have been used for.

'I had them a' regularly entered, first wi' rottens – then wi' stots or weazles – and then wi' the brocks – and they fear naething that ever came wi' a hair skin upon it.' (I hope that's clear?)

When asked why he has such a restricted range of names for his dogs, he explains.

'O, that's a fancy of my aim to mark the breed , sir – the Deuke himsell, has sent as far as Charlieshope to get ane o' Dandie Dinmont's Pepper and Mustard terriers.' And so, the use of these two words to denote the colours in the breed is actually continuing a tradition established by this fictional character after whom the breed is named.

Other passages in the book show the dogs as fearless hunters, but other than that they are hardly mentioned. I kept going, all the way to page 355, but to no avail.

Scott himself was adamant that the character of Dandie Dinmont was made up, an amalgam of various types of people he had met. However, at the time there was a farmer by the name of James Davidson who did, before the novel was written, breed terriers and name them all Mustard and Pepper. It may well be that Scott had heard this and forgotten it. He was in any case once introduced to Davidson and whilst saying that he knew nothing of the man, did admit that he was typical of the hill farmer type of the day and a real-life Dandie Dinmont.

Although the dogs featured little in the novel, it was quite a challenge and a huge reward to plough through *Guy Mannering*. I really enjoyed it and have those wonderful terriers to thank. Watch out *Rob Roy*: you could soon be dusted down and brought off the shelf …

I learned a lot more about the breed on the day. The coat is clearly of vital importance and it has been necessary to breed the dogs back to get the right coat. It is a coat which requires 'hand stripping', which is beyond the patience and ability of many pet owners. This is in effect very carefully and systematically plucking the growing hairs from the dog's coat between the thumb and the middle finger. It's painstaking and a bit tedious, but doesn't cause the dogs any discomfort or pain.

Two particular health conditions which can effect the breed are glaucoma and, in later years, Cushing's disease. Breeders are doing what they can to reduce and eliminate risks. At least the numbers in the breed are a bit more manageable than in some other breeds.

There seemed to be a really good-natured atmosphere around the ring, which was great. Even so, people were able to say who would win and who would lose, again largely on the basis of how well known or connected the breeders and exhibitors were.

The difference here is that people didn't seem too disillusioned – they would keep turning up for their genuine interest and love of the breed. Even if they know they have no chance of winning with their dog, they still go and smile and enjoy themselves. It's asking a lot of people, though, isn't it?

I was quite sad when the Dandie Dinmonts had come and gone. I was really taken with them and wouldn't rule out having one in the future (if I could get one). In fact, in no particular order, here are ten breeds I would like to own in the future:

1. Lancashire heeler
2. Manchester terrier
3. Dandie Dinmont terrier
4. Basenji
5. Miniature pinscher
6. Pug
7. Australian cattle dog
8. Norfolk terrier
9. Norwegian buhund
10. Dutch partridge dog

Anyway, next in the ring was the Scottish terrier and we were very entertained by two Geordie ladies sitting next to us eating their lunch (which seemed to be about 98% garlic) and telling us tales of their Scotties. 'Little bugger' seemed to crop up in most sentences. Certainly the implication was that these dogs were very wilful, full of naughtiness in a very humorous way and enough to drive the owners mad. Most of the 25 dogs on show (27 entries) were of the traditional black you probably imagine, although they can also be wheaten, red-brindle or black-brindle.

As a breed, these dogs are probably more popular in the US than in Britain. Of course, Jock is a key character in Disney's *Lady and the Tramp* and has helped their popularity. More important in this regard in the US, though, is Franklin D. Roosevelt's Scottie called Fala who accompanied him everywhere and became a huge part of American forklore. They are very similar in height and weight to the Dandie Dinmont, but with quite a different nature. This is a rather reserved dog, a hard dog, even aloof. Again, it makes a great guard.

It is another breed which has fun with facial hair, sporting the most fantastic beard and wonderful Dennis Healey-esque eyebrows. It has neat, pointed ears and, I think, a marvellously appealing expression. I think they look old and wise but definitely not to be messed with. They have a long, skirted coat as though they are cleaning the floor as they go. When you touch the coat it is very harsh on top, but soft below that outside layer. This is a proper terrier, built to go underground after any small mammal, including the fox. It's a little toughie.

Until the mid-19th century all terriers in Scotland that went underground after the fox were known as Scottish terriers. The Scottish terrier itself was originally known as the Aberdeen terrier, although some trace its earlier history to the Scottish Western Isles. The breed was first registered with the

Kennel Club as a distinct breed over a century ago in 1897. Of course, although brave and tough, primarily today the breed's main use is as a pet.

The dog has a tapering tail, thick at the bottom and thin at the top which is held upright. Exhibitors seem to consider this tail to be a handle and use it as the way of lifting one end of the dog onto the table for examination.

So, tough, aloof, full of character and a 'little bugger'. I do like dogs to have spirit and seem to collect 'little buggers', but whilst I enjoyed watching them, these dogs did comparatively little for me and I was ready to go and have a look at the last breed I needed at the show – the Skye terrier, another on the list of vulnerable British breeds.

On the way I saw some quite spectacular dogs being walked and exercised. One, a Finnish Spitz, was of such a deep red that I could hardly believe it. In the sun, the depth of the colour and the shine and vitality of the coat were quite stunning.

I was really keen to see the Skye terrier, not least because I was planning to find out a lot more while in Edinburgh about the most famous Skye of all time – Greyfriars Bobby. But much more of that later.

Now, there is once again a clue in the name of the breed to this dog's geographical origin – can you spot it? Yes, that's right, this terrier originated from Skye in the Hebrides. Originally it was used to track all manner of animals with anger management issues and big teeth and claws, like badgers, otters and weasels, but now it is first and foremost a pet. Again, similar in size and weight to the Dandie Dinmont and the Skye terrier, this dog has exceptionally long and straight hair, although this is naturally shorter on the dog's face. Most often seen in grey, it can also be black, cream or fawn.

It has quite a history, this dog, dating back some four hundred years, with remarkably little change over all those generations. Not as friendly as the Dandie Dinmont, nor as aloof as the Scottie, the Skye terrier fits somewhere between the two in terms of temperament. The Skye terrier is wary of strangers and tends to build strong relationships with one person rather than a group of people, but it's certainly not vicious.

I found the expression quite appealing but hard to read as the eyes are hidden behind curtains of hair. The nose is quite long and black and the ears erect and covered in hair. I was quite taken again with the Skye terrier.

We watched the Skye terriers to the end and then decided to call it a day – there was after all a lengthy yomp to the bus stop to look forward to at this public-transport-friendly venue. It's always amazingly tiring spending the day at a dog show – especially when you wander around like we do. We were just so relieved to get back to our hotel and take our shoes off.

An hour later we were leaving again in search of food when the hotel was besieged by, you guessed it, a stag party – matching rugby shirts and all. Old Mozza and Beardie and 'One Ball' and the rest seemed to be on good form and in good spirits at least.

It had been a really good day and some of the more elusive ticks had been added in my spotter's guide. We'd met some great people, had a good number of laughs, learned a lot and seen some fantastic dogs – what more could you ask?

As for whether there are more of these Scottish breeds in Scotland, it's not that easy to answer. Crufts is, after all, so much bigger than the Scottish Kennel Club Show – how can you compare? This was one subject of conversation over a wonderful Italian meal and a bottle of pinot grigio that evening.

You will, I am sure, be glad to know that I came up with a way of rationalising all of this, using percentages! So, out with the calculator and onwards! My theory is that, if the Scottish breeds are more popular in Scotland, then these breeds should form a higher percentage of the overall group entry at the Scottish KC Show than, say, at Crufts. Do you agree? Good, so here are the figures:

Percentage of hound entry taken by deerhounds:

Crufts	4.1%
Scottish KC	4.8%

Percentage of terrier entry taken by:

1 Dandie Dinmont terriers

Crufts	2.9%
Scottish KC	2.2%

2 Scottish terriers

Crufts	4.0%
Scottish KC	2.7%

3 Skye terriers

Crufts	2.2%
Scottish KC	2.6%

So, there you have it: proof which would surely even meet Tom's stringent requirements. The maths had only taken me a couple of hours, lying in bed to the accompaniment of a drunken Scottish ballad outside my window.

My quite remarkable finding was that it seems that some Scottish breeds are more popular in Scotland than elsewhere, whilst others are, well, less popular.

With a feeling of contentment and a job well done, I turned over, reached out to the light, turned it off and went off to sleep dreaming of winning a breed at a Championship Show with a little bitch that I had just popped into the car as a bit of an afterthought.

CHAPTER 11

The Dogs of Edinburgh

I woke the next day feeling refreshed and still very elated from my statistical success in neither proving nor disproving that the Scottish breeds are more popular in Scotland than elsewhere. I think the term used in Scottish Law for the level of evidence I had to offer would be 'case not proven'.

We had a good breakfast and really very good value. I'm a huge fan of the Travel Inn/Travelodge places like the one we were staying in. They have everything you want at about half the price of hotels with heavier floral covers just up the road. I always try to get into these places. After all, I only need somewhere decent to sleep. And the towels fit into your luggage easier than those from posher hotels. Our particular Travel Inn seemed to be doing a roaring trade and was full of all sorts of nationalities, including an incredibly colourful African contingent. What was most striking, though, wherever we went in Scotland, was the amazing customer service and hospitality. No cheesiness or insincerity, just genuine smiles and warmth – even in very touristy places and, even more remarkably, also from the trendy young men who are usually so surly elsewhere. You know the type: trying to hang on to reality before they finally disappear up their own whatsit. What a place Scotland is and what wonderful people.

We later found out that there was a big rugby match on at Murrayfield on this particular weekend and there wasn't a bed to be had in Edinburgh. One Belgian couple I spoke to had come by train from Glasgow only to be told that the nearest hotel they could be found was in … Glasgow.

Of course, to add to the rugby match there was the normal trade in a busy city. And this is where my thoughts about stag and hen nights just the day before at Birmingham Airport caught up with me. Trying to leave the hotel after breakfast was a nightmare as at least fifty St Trinian's schoolgirls were blocking reception, the doorways, the stairs and ramp and the street outside the hotel. What a rough lot they looked, too! For many of them, I think their school days were some way behind them. In fact some of them had quite a lot behind them, emphasised by their short gym skirts. Still, it would give the boys somewhere to stand their drinks later in the day. Although it was about 9 o'clock in the morning they seemed pretty drunk, fairly raucous and very crude. Couldn't wait till they met Nobber and his pals! Apparently, when a stag night and hen night get together it's called a shag night. I don't know why.

Anyway, I sheltered behind Alison and hurried out, all men apparently being fair game for not particularly good-natured abuse (whereas good-natured abuse I thrive on, of course!).

Outside the hotel, we turned right onto a very old Edinburgh thoroughfare called the Cowgate. I didn't remember at the time that this was one of the most important settings for the story I was trying to look at today: that of Greyfriars Bobby, a Skye terrier who famously lay on his master's grave for some fourteen years – the ultimate symbol of canine devotion.

What a strange road the Cowgate is. It feels as though it is the back of everything and the front of nothing. Even on a bright, sunny day it doesn't feel like a place you want to be. It has lots of dark doorways and entries and really narrow alleys leading off, up to the Royal Mile. Dark, high buildings flank the Cowgate. There are a couple of pubs on the road, but otherwise there is very little reason to be there and any tourists you see appear to have wandered away from where they should be. People are quite wary of anyone else on the street. If feels quite remote and rather risky.

As we walked along it, it began to fan out into a more open area. The people here were quite different from those on the Royal Mile or Princes Street. Here, there were lots of alternative folk – grungy in greatcoats. Women in black with colourful scarves tied in their hair and very pale make-up. Drunks and one or two drugged-out-looking people. We were now in Candlemaker Row and very close to the home of Greyfriars Bobby.

The first gate into the churchyard we came across was ominously locked, so we followed the road up towards the Museum of Scotland and, sure enough, found a way into Greyfriars churchyard.

It was a sunny day, but this place had quite a strange atmosphere. Stone darkened by age and grime was all the way around the yard, with very gothic statuary and carvings everywhere to be seen. The oddest thing about it, though, was the way that some of the statues and tributes were built on to the walls of the buildings which surrounded the churchyard, with windows peeping out in between. These windows, then of tenement slums, played quite a part in Greyfriars Bobby's story. 'Atmospheric' probably best sums up the churchyard. It really was quite unlike any other churchyard I'd ever been to, although I have to admit that I don't actually visit that many – well, at least not nowadays.

Following a simple sign and somehow managing to get lost first time, I found the stone which marked the final resting place of 'Auld Jock', that is to say John Gray, Bobby's master. In fact, the red granite stone was not there in Bobby's time but is a recent addition funded by the 'American Friends of Greyfriars Bobby' many years later. They were not allowed to mark Bobby's grave because he was only a dog, so they marked John Gray's instead, acknowledging him as 'master of Greyfriars Bobby'.

After a quick tour of the churchyard and all its heavy stone and statuary, I found my way back to the gate and, near it, to a little triangle of ground under a tree. Here, since it was finally permitted in 1981, is a matching red granite headstone for Bobby himself. On it is inscribed: 'Greyfriars Bobby. Died 14th January 1872, Aged 16 years. Let his loyalty and devotion be a lesson to us all.'

Of course, back then, Bobby was not allowed to be buried in a churchyard, let alone have his grave marked, and his internment was a secret, night-time affair closely following his death on 14th January 1872. A stone was originally put up but soon taken down.

On the day I visited there was a little Canadian flag stuck in the ground by the headstone – a small reminder of how much this dog's fidelity and his story has touched hearts all across the world. Indeed, it was a strange feeling – I always feel this with historical venues – to think that the events I had read about had actually played out here, under these trees, in front of these stones.

There are several versions of the story of Greyfriars Bobby and it has been re-told many times in many formats and in differing lengths. The version that is perhaps best known, though, is Eleanor Atkinson's version, published in 1912 and entitled *The Story of Greyfriars Bobby*. Not a very imaginative title, but that's not everything, is it? As they say, it 'does exactly what it says on the tin'.

Eleanor Atkinson was, in fact, an American who never visited Edinburgh in her life, which spanned from 1863 to 1942.

Her book was therefore based on some of the more fanciful accounts of the day and embellished with the sentimentality that was so much a feature of that period. There's no denying that Bobby's is a fantastic story and very moving in its own right, but as we shall see it portrays a rather idealised and sentimentalised view of life, particularly that of the poor at the time.

In Eleanor Atkinson's book, the human 'hero' is Auld Jock, who is described as 'a farm labourer' and a 'pious old shepherd'. He is a man of some considerable age, 'worn out at last by fifty winters as a shepherd on the bleak hills of Midlothian and Fife'.

In terms of his appearance, 'a grizzled, gnarled little man was Auld Jock, of tough fibre'.

In this book, Bobby is in fact the pet dog of the daughter of 'the tenant of Cauldbrae' on the Pentland Hills outside Edinburgh. Bobby hates being fussed, cuddled and cosseted and escapes at every attempt to follow Auld Jock about his work on the farm. He would accompany the old shepherd into Edinburgh on market days, when it is Jock's habit to eat at Mr Traill's 'Ye Olde Greyfriars Dining Rooms', where Auld Jock would sit by the fire and smoke his pipe. As a matter of routine, Jock heads off to Traill's when the 1 o'clock time gun is fired from the castle.

Because he is too old, Auld Jock is let go by the farmer in Eleanor Atkinson's novel and has to take lodgings in a cupboard-sized room in a slum in the Cowgate. Although Bobby is not allowed in, he is so persistent that Jock smuggles him in under his coat.

In fact Auld Jock sees Bobby as a nuisance, and several times Bobby is returned to the farm only to escape and find his way back to Edinburgh and Auld Jock once again.

When John Gray (Auld Jock) dies he is buried in Greyfriars

Churchyard, although there is no explanation of how this comes to be as he is not a parishioner and would not, in reality, therefore be buried there.

Bobby watches his master's burial but is not allowed to stay in the churchyard. He is forced to hide until the graveyard is locked so that he can lie on his master's grave.

After a couple of days Bobby is starving, and appears at Mr. Traill's, guiding the landlord to the grave, Traill previously being unaware of Auld Jock's death.

In the early days, Bobby has many difficulties to overcome, not least the displeasure of the church caretaker, who is desperate to get rid of the dog. Again, the little terrier is returned to his owner's daughter but is once more determined to escape and he tunnels out of the byre where he is left overnight.

Returning to the churchyard, Bobby has to spend his days cramped up under a fallen tombstone, hiding from everyone and anyone, biding his time until the churchyard is locked and he can take up his position once more on his master's grave.

According to Atkinson's tale, Bobby proves his worth to the caretaker, James Brown (woo! I feel good!) by catching a veritable mound of rats and mice and piling them up on his master's grave. This wins over not just the caretaker, but his wife too, who then goes on to play an important role in Bobby's future welfare.

As I have indicated, the book is very sentimentalised and one of the many sugary scenes in the book occurs when Traill offers the children of the tenement backing onto the churchyard a reward to catch Bobby and take him to his dining rooms as he has been unable to find the elusive dog. The group, of course, includes the obligatory Dickensian cripple. Not only does Traill give the children a shilling when they take Bobby to him, but he also feeds the children a feast on his linen-covered tables, encouraging them to think of it as a picnic. A whole group of dirty, scabby street urchins, sitting around a beautifully laid-out dining table. Surely a scene suitable for the stage in the West End or on Broadway? Are you reading this, Mr Lloyd Webber?

James Brown and his wife now begin to look after Bobby, who still refuses though to sleep indoors, returning every night to sleep on his master's grave as before.

In this account, little Bobby heads off to Traill's to eat every day when the time gun sounds. He has a little bark and run around and then heads back to the churchyard where he hides from visitors, except the children of the tenements overlooking the churchyard and the boys from Heriot's school, which also borders Greyfriars church. In true Dickensian fashion, Bobby becomes a particular friend of the crippled boy and indeed a great favourite with the poor children. There is a fair dose of sentimentality when the author tells us, 'Bobby was host to the disinherited children of the tenement'.

Occasionally, Bobby goes on long walks into the countryside with the Heriot schoolboys, but always returns to lie on Auld Jock's grave.

Eventually, Bobby's cover is blown and he is publicly discovered by the Church Minister, who, it turns out, has known about Bobby all along. He takes no action, however, and continues to turn a blind eye, much to Mr Brown's relief.

It is eight years later in this account that a soldier from the castle is so taken with Bobby that he offers to buy him from Traill. He wants Bobby as a castle pet or mascot, but the restaurant owner refuses and points out that Bobby is not his to sell. At the end of this chat a policeman comes in from the rain for a cup of tea and sees Traill with Bobby. The next morning he turns up to charge the restaurant owner with keeping an unlicensed dog, for which Traill is summoned before magistrates. Dogs without owners were being rounded up in Edinburgh at that time and poisoned, so it is not a good position for Bobby to be in. Traill, however, cannot accept ownership of Bobby without potentially getting a criminal record for not licensing him. In any case he is adamant that the dog is not his, and the case against him is eventually dismissed.

Whilst good news for Traill, this dismissal, however, is not good news for Bobby. Not having an owner could be a death sentence. Word gets out about this and all the children of the tenements and former Heriot pupils swing into action in heartwarming fashion, even though they are penniless and destitute themselves. Picture the scene: 'we only have three pennies to feed ourselves and our thirty-three children for the next ten weeks, but the money must go towards Bobby's licence'. No one actually says that by the way, but you get the idea. The dog becomes a rallying point for the penniless and dispossessed.

Meanwhile the case is taken to the animal-loving Lord Provost of Edinburgh who agrees that Bobby will never be happy living away from Auld Jock's grave. When he hears about the children's collection his is deeply moved, again the author making Bobby a glowing symbol of hope and togetherness. The Lord Provost thinks 'it was an incredible thing that such a flower of affection should have bloomed so sweetly in such sunless cells. And it was a new gospel, at that time, that a dog, or a horse, or a bird might have its mission in this world of making people kinder and happier.' He is moved to such an extent that he gives Bobby the freedom of the city, no less, and provides from his pocket a collar with a tag inscribed: 'Greyfriars Bobby, from the Lord Provost, 1867 licensed'. He gives the children the responsibility of looking after the dog. Mind you, it's not clear whether he pockets the money they've collected. I'd like to think he does.

It is a little while later that Bobby follows a group of soldiers on a route march, walking for miles and following them back to the castle. He has a good time playing with the soldiers and doing tricks, but they like him so much that they lock him up and won't let him go. He tries everything to escape but to no avail. Meanwhile, the poor children are beside themselves with worry and upset.

Eventually Bobby becomes so desperate that he risks life and limb by escaping the only way he can – down a sheer cliff face. Unbelievably, he survives and crawls, broken and bleeding, back to his resting-place.

Hearing this tale, the great and the good begin to visit and admire him. Atkinson creates another sickly little scene where every night, every child in the surrounding tenements opens the window and calls out goodnight to Bobby before going to sleep. Aah.

Having become such a celebrity, Bobby is visited by a 'Grand Leddy', Lady Burdett-Coutts. She is amazed at the pride that the tenement-dwellers take in their homes and surroundings. Her housemaid explains that this has been since the children have had Bobby to love and not be neglected.

Lady Burdett-Coutts can see that Bobby is very old by this stage and her mind turns to where he will be buried as this cannot be in the churchyard. She commissions a portrait by a top artist, Gowlay Steele. Controversially, she even wants Bobby buried with his master, but this is not allowed.

She is deeply impressed by Bobby and the effect he has had on those around him. She thinks to herself, 'All the endearing qualities of the dog reach their height in this loyal and lovable Highland terrier; and he seems to have brought out the best qualities of the people who have known him. Indeed, for fourteen years hundreds of disinherited children have been made kinder and happier by knowing Bobby's story and having that little dog to love.'

She manages to obtain the Council's permission to erect a memorial outside the churchyard at the start of George IV bridge. She has a drinking-fountain built, with a low-level drinking basin at dog height and a statue of Bobby on top.

Eleanor Atkinson's tale is a very uplifting one, if at times rather sickly and sentimental. It is still, though, an amazing story and is another example of 'what have dogs ever done for us?' It is a fantastic illustration of loyalty and devotion, even more astonishing for the times in which it happened.

Disney, no less, have produced a film of 'Greyfriars Bobby'. I haven't watched it – I doubt whether I could stomach it without a sick-bag. I suppose there's always Christmas.

Another version of the story is Lavinia Derwent's Young Puffin version, published in 1985 for children as *The Tale of Greyfriars Bobby*. There are many similarities with Eleanor Atkinson's story, indeed it is presumably based upon it.

In this story, Bobby is given to a farmer for his young daughter, even though the farmer himself doesn't see the use of such a dog. The story again begins in the Pentland Hills near Edinburgh. Bobby latches on to the shepherd John Gray, known as 'Auld Jock'. We learn that 'he was the best shepherd in the district, trusted with the care and rearing of collie dogs'.

Jock, though, is getting too auld for his work and is being kept on at the farm really only as a matter of kindness. He certainly doesn't take to Bobby initially and constantly tries to shoo him off until he is won over by the little terrier's spirit.

Just like in Atkinson's book, Bobby is a great escape artist, escaping regularly from his would-be mistress.

Jock enjoys nothing more than his regular visits to Edinburgh and his meal and pipe at Traill's dining rooms.

In this story, specially written for children, a lame boy plays a more prominent part. Unwelcome with the able-bodied children, Geordie becomes particularly interested in Bobby. He is highly amused by Bobby's habit of running off to Traill's for dinner when the one o'clock gun sounds. Bobby is not welcome at Traill's, but evades capture so many times that he becomes tolerated as a regular visitor.

Auld Jock is finally let go by the farmer and ends up dying in a hovel, with Bobby snuggled up against him. Bobby feasts on the rotting flesh of the putrid corpse … oh, sorry, that last bit is made up – I don't know where it came from.

Again, Bobby settles on his master's grave and is persecuted by James Brown the caretaker. Mr Traill looks after Bobby and tries to send him home to the Pentland farm, only for Greyfriars Houdini to do his stuff again.

Lame Geordie is quite a major character in Derwent's version of the story and when James Brown goes to hit the dog (no doubt in a real soulman fashion) he is saved by Geordie and the others snowballing him. In the end, James Brown has to admit defeat and Bobby spends 14 years in the churchyard becoming quite a celebrity. Every day he goes to Traill's for dinner and then returns straight to his master's grave.

So famous is Bobby that when he dies a statue is put up commemorating him.

But this isn't the end of this children's story, oh no. When you stand in the churchyard on a blowy day and the wind is whistling, 'could that be Greyfriars Bobby barking?'

With these thoughts in mind, it was time to see the statue. I turned left out of the churchyard gates and looked back the way I came, down Candlemaker Row. I couldn't see a statue anywhere.

Looking around again, there it was straight in front of me. (Alison would say that this is a very common occurrence with me, especially in relation to car keys.) Nothing too flashy about this statue. Rather nice, in fact. It stands at the end of George IV bridge and is still a water-fountain and basin. While I was admiring it and trying to take a picture, it became apparent that it still gets a lot of visitors. There were a number of foreigners and then a Scottish grandmother and grandson, listening to the whole story with wide eyes as grandma told it.

Looking back from the statue towards the gate I realised that I had in fact been standing outside a pub called Greyfriars Bobby's Bar with a Skye terrier on its sign. It looked as though it may just have seen better days, but had apparently again been one of Bobby's feeding and watering holes.

Inspired by Bobby, we set off back towards the centre, passing, just about 100 yards from Bobby's statue, the café where JK Rowling had eked out a cup of coffee on many days as she couldn't afford to heat her flat while writing *Harry Potter*. Another source of inspiration.

A little further on we passed a day centre for the homeless. Outside was a pile of *Big Issue* magazines together with a little trolley and a little Staffie-cross-type dog. Full of the warm glow left by Bobby's story and uplifted by thoughts of that special relationship between man and his best friend, I went over to put a £1 coin in the pot and take the *Big Issue*. I thought I might even give this fine animal a little stroke. Well, that's what I thought. Two seconds later my feet were about 12 inches off the ground, doing a fine impersonation of a cartoon character who has been electrocuted as I started and narrowly avoided the closing jaws of this streetwise canine. It was some minutes, and we were in fact nearly in the High Street by the time Alison stopped laughing, while I for my part was desperately looking for somewhere to indulge my need for urgent bowel movements.

Window-shopping on the way up to the Castle, imagine my surprise and delight when I saw in a shop-window a little display of books entitled *Greyfriars Bobby – the Real Story at Last* by Forbes Macgregor. Just think, Forbes was going to dish the dirt on Bobby, his sexual peccadilloes, the company he keeps (you know, a bitch in every town) and his addiction to various substances.

What a gem this book turned out to be. Not, though, for the reasons speculated on above. Indeed, this was more *The Times* than *The Sun*. Written in 1990 and since updated, published by Steve Savage, it uses contemporary newspapers, eyewitness accounts, actual photographs and historical research to tell a story 'which explodes many of the myths concerning the famous Skye terrier and his master, John Gray'.

This was fantastic and merited the time and expense of travelling to Edinburgh on its own. Unlike other versions of the story, Macgregor's book is fact-based and gives an incredibly powerful and insightful report of the Old Town of Edinburgh in those days. It gives a real sense of the danger and misery of life at that time, brings the Cowgate to life and spares us the honey-covered sentimentality of the account of the noble poor given in the other two editions.

Macgregor's account begins with the awful bad weather of 1853. Storms combine with freezing weather to cause hundreds of shipwrecks and to bring agriculture to a standstill. This is a bad time for all those who work on the land, be they gardeners or agricultural workers. The land cannot be worked; crops cannot be harvested. There is no food for the animals.

In this true account, Auld Jock is not in fact a shepherd at all, nor is he a loner, nor indeed from the Pentland Hills. It turns out he is a gardener on big estates, which now have no work for him. He has a wife and son and stands in line in the market place waiting for someone to hire him. No-one is hired.

Falling back on Edinburgh, John Gray and his family find

accommodation in a one-room hovel off a narrow alley stinking with filth and misery. The room is wretched with no furniture at all. With no work, the only option appears to be the workhouse, which is seen as a fate worse than death.

In his desperation for himself and his family, 'Auld Jock' ('Young Jock' until his father had died) decides to go for a job that nobody else wants. And so the real 'Auld Jock' is not an agricultural worker but … a police constable. Macgregor reports the following account of John Gray:

'Aged forty, five feet seven and a half inches in height, eleven stone in weight, oval face, grey eyes, sandy hair, fresh complexion, no occupation, married, Scottish.'

At the age of 40, John Gray was old for the job. The beat he was given was probably in the roughest area of Edinburgh, known as 'Hell's Kitchen'. It was our old friend, the Cowgate. His house is just off this thoroughfare – a dangerous and unruly place. Part of his package is a 'watch dog' – more of an alert than a modern-day police dog.

The work was hard and gruelling. Constables could not take shelter whatever the weather conditions, and crime and disorder was of course very high.

At night, constables had to patrol the churchyards, including Greyfriars, because it was the time of body-snatchers, who would sell the recently buried to medical schools and students. The most infamous of these were the duo of Burke and Hare. Indeed, some graveyards had little observation towers built where the wealthy would station a guard for the first few days after a relative's death, until the body was no longer of interest or use to body-snatchers.

Others depended on the watchful eye of the constables like John Gray. After his beat, Gray would return to his home at the very top of a rickety old tenement, built above stables full of rats and mice attracted by the straw. This cannot have been a good place to live, but better than the alternatives.

At one stage the Old Town had been the home of the well-to-do. As Edinburgh expanded, however, this area was left behind as the well-to-do moved to the New Town. The large homes they left behind were divided again and again until they were largely just individual rooms, inhabited by the very poor lowland Scots and particularly the Irish, for whom illegal whisky provided almost the only escape from the awful reality. Rubbish and human waste was simply thrown out of the window into the narrow streets below.

In this squalor the police – a new organisation and quite subject to ridicule – were very busy dealing with the drunk and disorderly. A policeman's lot is not a happy one and all that.

Add to these dangerous and unpleasant work conditions the incredibly unhealthy atmosphere and you have a picture of John Gray's life, brilliantly evoked by Forbes Macgregor. Edinburgh sat under an almost permanent sulphurous smoke cloud, visible for miles and giving the capital its nickname of 'Auld Reekie'. Life expectancy in this area was 26 years, with tuberculosis and typhus being the big killers.

When you consider this particular package of work and lifestyle benefits it is not hard to see why few stuck the job of being a constable for more than two years. In fact, when he died, John Gray had been exceptional in his length of service, at five years.

Nobody knows how John Grey lost his first dog, but it is a fact that he got Bobby the Skye terrier around 1856. This little dog went everywhere with him, day or night.

When off duty, Gray would sometimes go to the Coffee House in Greyfriars Place. He would also spend his time getting out of the filthy city, walking on the nearby hills (just a ten-minute walk would get you out of Edinburgh in those days, and the nearness of the country hills was still a feature which really struck me when we visited). Gray and his dog would be out in all weathers and conditions, patrolling the markets by night, for example. Indeed, the markets seem to have been Bobby's favourite area.

By October 1857, life had taken its toll on John Gray and he became too ill to work. In view of his good service he was given a small sickness allowance to live on. His condition soon worsened, however, and he fell victim to one of the commonest killers – consumption. As he was from that particular parish, he was indeed buried in Greyfriars churchyard. Macgregor points out that had he in fact been a shepherd from the Pentland Hills he would simply not have been allowed to be buried there.

The gates of the churchyard were locked and Bobby couldn't get in to his master's grave until the police did their rounds at night, at which time he was able to slip in unnoticed. There he lay on his master's grave and there is a lovely portrait modelled from life by Gowlay Steell RSA in 1867 of Bobby doing so.

Unlike in Eleanor Atkinson's version, it appears that in reality the caretaker, James Brown, gave Bobby little trouble. Although it was one of his duties to keep dogs out, it seems that he just let him be.

As we know, homes backed onto the churchyard and people's curiosity must have been aroused by the little dog. It seems that one of the residents gave him shelter on particularly stormy nights.

In time, Mrs Gray and her son (perhaps rather unsurprisingly and unimaginatively 'Young Jock') were re-housed to a better area. Try as they might, though, they just could not coax Bobby away from John Gray's grave.

Bobby simply carried on as before, often eating at what was

now Ramsay's Eating House. Without really knowing the story, when the Ramsays leave, the new owner William Peterson is happy to carry on feeding him until he, in turn, leaves just one year later, when James Currie takes over the restaurant.

In fact, the Edinburgh time gun was first set up in 1861, four years after John Gray's death. There was never any way that Gray used to go for lunch when the time gun sounded, so this is another myth promulgated in Atkinson's account.

It was a certain Sergeant Scott based at Edinburgh Castle who really taught Bobby to go to eat when the time gun sounded. He had heard about Bobby and had befriended him. People soon heard about Bobby's timekeeping and small crowds regularly formed to watch Bobby leave the churchyard and head off to the eating house when the gun boomed. Of course, the eating house was closed on Sundays, so that Bobby rather cleverly got into the habit of burying bones and meat earlier in the week to dig up on a Sunday. Given his choice of location, we can only hope that he was careful what he dug up.

It is a fact that John Traill first took over the coffee shop in 1862, renaming it 'Traill's Temperance Coffee Shop'. When he asked around, perhaps surprisingly nobody seemed to know Bobby's story. Traill of course never knew John Gray. For reasons unknown, Traill began to put the story around that Bobby's master had been an old farmer who had come to the restaurant when the time gun sounded. Although, logically, people could work out that the time gun hadn't been set up for nearly four years after Gray's death, the story still spread. As Macgregor says, this is 'responsible for the myth of Auld Jock the farmer or shepherd of extreme old age whose home was in the Pentland Hills.' The story, of course, was made much more famous by Eleanor Atkinson.

There is no doubt that Bobby's fidelity and unquestioning

devotion to his dead master struck a chord with the Victorians. The nobility and dignity of the natural creature was of huge interest and inspiration to them and Bobby would just be a perfect icon. Their sentimentality would account for Bobby's fame and the number of visitors he attracted.

It is true, too, that graveyards would have been dark and sombre places at that time, especially given the activities of the grave-robbers. Having a living, breathing animal in there would have been an uplifting symbol of hope, giving a much better atmosphere.

In Edinburgh at that time, yet another problem encountered was with stray dogs. As well as being dangerous, many of them carried disease. In an effort to encourage owners to take care of dogs, the licence fee was dropped from 12 shillings to 7 shillings. The penalty for not licensing was a huge £5 fine for defaulters.

Understandably, the procedures for proving ownership of a dog were not complex. In effect, it was enough to see a dog at a property to prove that the person there owned the dog. Bobby was seen as Traill's.

Traill refused to accept ownership of Bobby – it's not completely clear why, but the court accepts Traill's story: that the dog belongs to the deceased John Gray. This leaves Bobby in danger.

In this instance – without the moral about the nobility of the poor – the accounts coincide. The Lord Provost, Sir William Chambers, stepped in to save Bobby's bacon. His argument was that the Town Council owned the churchyard where Bobby lived and he, as Head of the Council, should therefore pay his licence fee. He committed to paying the fee for life and gave Bobby the famous collar and tag.

It was this incident which brought Bobby wider fame and recognition, the story being picked up and published in the

Inverness Courier in 1864. However, by this stage, the story was already inaccurate and embellished. In their account, they said that no-one knew who Bobby's master was. They also mentioned Sergeant Scott but stated that Bobby would not follow him beyond the end of the George IV bridge. This inaccuracy is a little strange as there were still many eye-witnesses alive at the time, and in fact details of John Gray and his profession were documented in official records.

In an odd twist to the story, the journalist concerned later claimed that he'd made the whole story up as there was so little news that day. Yet, as we know, much of the story was in fact substantiated.

Following the gift of collar and tag, Bobby became quite a celebrity. Artists came to sketch and paint him and photographers to take portrait pictures (some of which are reproduced in Macgregor's book).

Bobby was not, in fact, completely loyal to the Traills' establishment over the last few years of his life, but chose rather to spread his favours and to eat and drink at a number of local hostelries, including the bar which was to become Greyfriars Bobby's Bar outside the church gates. It may be, though, that the Traills took day-to-day responsibility for him over his last years.

The exact date of Bobby's death is known: 14th January 1872. We've already heard about his secret burial in the churchyard.

The 'Grand Leddy' of the Atkinson story in fact only heard of Bobby just before his death. This lady was indeed Baroness Angela Georgina Burdett-Coutts and she offered to erect a memorial – the one at the end of George IV bridge – after his death. The offer was accepted and the statue on the top of the fountain was unveiled on 15th November 1873.

The plaque reads:

'A tribute to the affectionate fidelity of Greyfriars Bobby. In 1858 this faithful dog followed the remains of his master to Greyfriars Churchyard and lingered near the spot until his death in 1872.'

As well as the statue and the headstones there are other mementos of Bobby to be seen. A visit to Huntley House Museum allows you to see his dinner dish as well as his famous collar and tag. Photos there help to bring the story to life. This, together with Macgregor's book, gives you a pretty good insight into the life of Greyfriars Bobby. Indeed, Macgregor's book is a marvellous, thin volume. He backs up his account with excerpts from newspaper articles and eye-witness accounts.

Having revelled in the story of Greyfriars Bobby for an hour or so, our big target for the day was Edinburgh Castle – not least because of its Dog Cemetery.

On the way, there were a couple of things we wanted to see. They are almost directly opposite each other on the immediate approach to the Castle. We wanted to see The Scotch Whisky Centre ('Experience the history and mystery of Scotch Whisky') and the Camera Obscura and World of Illusions ('where seeing is *not* believing!')

We'd been wondering what the 'no parking this Saturday from 9 am to 1 pm' signs had been up for all week and had been struck by the enhanced security everywhere. Very elegant people were standing around and very large, smart cars were everywhere. Occasionally, we caught glimpses of people in ceremonial dress. Of course, they could have been people enticing tourists to a theme bar or attraction, but rather than this it turned out to be the State opening of the Scottish Assembly, to be attended amongst others by Prince Charles (hence his refusal to allow us entrance into Holyrood Palace).

The Camera Obscura is over 150 years old. It is basically a lens operating as a sort of periscope on top of a very tall building, which projects its image down onto a large dish below. This gives really good and detailed images of sights, architecture and people. In fact, beware of scratching your backside on Princes Street as you may be causing mirth and amusement up in the Camera Obscura. Sort of very early CCTV.

The guide rotates the Victorian periscope to give a panorama of the city. Handed bits of card by the guide, you appear to be able to pick up characters off the dish and splat them back down again – without them feeling a thing: harmless fun for the voyeur within you!

Our own visit was fairly surreal as our guide was a young Spanish woman with an amazing vocabulary and command of the English language but with a very broken English accent. Most of our group were French rugby fans, so there were a lot of misunderstandings and strange expressions flying backwards and forwards. All good fun and the Camera Obscura was really worth visiting.

The actual time you spend in the darkened Camera Obscura room is probably only 20 minutes, but that is just a small part of the overall attraction. There are great 360-degree views to be had from the rooftop, with plaques explaining what you can see as far as the Forth road and rail bridges in the distance and beyond.

The other floors in the attraction make up the 'world of illusions'. Cynical though I tend to be, I have to say it was great. It's all about vision and visual reality. There's fun to be had with the usual range of squashing, stretching and manipulating mirrors – a cause of a huge amount of mirth and japes for the French rugby fans.

There are all sorts of special effects with lenses, with colour and light and quite a collection of clever 3D holograms –

although when you've seen a few, to my mind, you've seen them all.

There are some of those 'Magic Eye'-type pictures around – you know, the ones where if you stare at them you start seeing other hidden images. Except that I don't: I could spend my life there and never see them, because I don't have binocular vision. In old language – the language of my childhood – I have a 'squint'. So, I have to say these effects were rather lost on me. Presumably not as lost, though, as they would be on one man we saw there. This is apposite to our subject because the man had a dog with him – a guide dog. Now this is God's honest truth, there was a blind man going around this attraction based completely on sight and vision. Obviously, there was no way I was going to ask him what he was getting out of the experience. It really did intrigue me, though. The dog wasn't wearing anything to suggest it was in training.

There was fun to be had with a machine which morphs your image into a selection of others – the most effective being an ape-like caveman. I shall cherish the memory of Alison's morph for the rest of my life!

At the other end of technology, there's an opportunity to see 'what the butler saw' in some of those old drum machines.

Having had a good time at the Camera Obscura we paid only a short visit to the Scottish Whisky Centre. This place was clearly doing well, selling very expensive bottles of specialist Scotch to very wealthy tourists. The price of the whiskies in the shop was quite incredible.

There's a bar and restaurant as well as the extensive shop, together with a film on the making of whisky followed by a whisky-tasting and even a little 'whisky barrel ride' through a display of three hundred years of Scotch whisky history – complete with sights, sounds and smells. I noticed that even here, a collie-type dog appeared in one of the displays – looking out for smugglers, I think.

So it was off to the castle, hoping that no-one in the Camera Obscura was picking us up and splatting us down again, or making us walk up a steep hill only for us to drop off at the end. I certainly wasn't going to adjust my underwear, no matter how much the tigerskin thong was digging in.

The large courtyard area outside the castle was having a huge amount of scaffolding seating erected, ready for the famous Military Tattoo. Queues to get into the castle were long but very good-humoured. Some Canadians behind us kept us highly entertained with their wicked sense of humour. They tried everything they could to convince the young lady steward that they were in fact tour leaders who should be able to enter through the short queue reserved for them, but to no avail.

When we reached nearly the front of the queue we were behind some Japanese folks who asked the cashier rather curiously, 'Is the ghost working today?' Quite a surreal moment.

We got into the castle to be greeted by not one boom of the time gun but no less than a twenty-one-gun salute. It was a bit of a disappointment to find that this was not for us but for the opening of the Scottish Assembly in the High Street below.

There's a great audio tour to follow around the Castle. I love these: they keep you (and everyone else) moving, tell you just enough and give you the highlights. The Castle is certainly a good place to go. There is loads to see and hear about, with spectacular views. Soldiers are still stationed there, which feels odd as castles are so often just historical relics. Shocking, though, was the sight of these soldiers – infantrymen – close up. They were just kids. I know policemen famously get younger as you grow older, but this was ridiculous. They looked immaculate in their green dress-coats and tartan trousers and were enjoying chatting away to groups of girls around the castle while off duty, but when you looked into their faces they looked barely old enough to shave. Changed out of uniform into tracksuits and trainers they looked like any other teenage lads around town. Yet they had recently been in Iraq, based around Basra. What they had seen, experienced and done just shouldn't be in the mind of kids of that age.

Anyway, our main interest in going to the Castle on this occasion was to learn about the Castle's Dog Cemetery. Here, the Castle Bookshop (where you'll remember they'd never heard of Walter Scott) helped. They had a little self-published book by George Robinson all about the Dog Cemetery (although, bless him, George couldn't help including the story of Greyfriars Bobby).

There are 27 headstones in the Dog Cemetery for animals that have been of great importance to soldiers based at the Castle. There's always been a strong bond between soldiers and their mascots and companions whether at war or just at their normal base. They must give some sense of normality, of home and domesticity to men lacking all of these things.

With regard to the Dog Cemetery, it has been really hard to find out much of its history, so I am relying on George Robinson's account of the happening. Whether this is a true account, I know not! It appears, though, that it is based around real characters and dates, so it seems that it could well be a true account.

The story focuses on a 13-year-old-boy, James MacGregor, whose father is an engineer up at the Castle. Young MacGregor is fortunate in being a friend of the Commandant's family. He loves visiting them, not least because they often invite him to eat in their butler's pantry. This was no doubt quite a treat, even for an engineer's son.

One summer, during his holidays from Edinburgh High School, James MacGregor goes to visit the Commandant's family, probably in search of some extra food, but finds everyone sad and miserable. The cause of this turns out to be the death of their spaniel, Fido. This was despite the fact that, being a Colonel's dog, he had been ministered to throughout the night by an assistant army surgeon.

Without his parents' knowledge, James had previously earned a little extra money by taking a job as a coffin-liner until his mother had found out and forced him to give up this promising career. Nevertheless, this seems to have given him an entrepreneurial idea – perhaps he could tell there was no mood for free food at the Commandant's house that morning and that the only way of getting something extra to eat was to earn a little money and buy some.

Whatever was in James's mind, he offered to give Fido a good burial in a quiet, suitable place for the fee of just one sovereign, an offer which the Commandant accepted.

James sets about his task by measuring up Fido's body and then boldly instructing the regimental carpenter to build a coffin for Fido. Fido's coffin was to be in black with his details painted on the lid in white.

Probably buoyed by his success with the carpenter, James then uses the Commandant's name to have the pioneers, the regimental labourers, dig a grave in a quiet spot where the camp children used to play, situated just down below the Mons Meg Canon. Perhaps I should clarify that I don't mean that these children minced around impersonating Larry Grayson, Frankie Howerd or Graham Norton, but rather that they were children associated with the army camp.

Pushing his luck, he then requires the pioneers to attend as a burial party for Fido. Here, though, he has to overcome some wounded pride and perhaps even outrage at being asked to act as a pallbearer for a dog. James's solution is simple. To overcome these objections he simply offers each member of the funeral party a shilling, making it much easier for them to put up with the hoots of derision from fellow soldiers as they carry the little dog's coffin to his burial.

Having witnessed the funeral, one of the officers suggested that the spot where Fido was buried would make a splendid burial ground for regimental pets. The Colonel agreed and this area became the now famous 'Dog Cemetery'.

If you go to the Castle now you cannot, sadly, gain access to the Cemetery itself, but look down upon it from the battlements above. It is laid out following the Castle's crescent-shaped walls at that point, maintained beautifully.

Many, many dogs have been buried there over the years, certainly a much greater number than the 29 headstones in the cemetery. Indeed, Fido's own grave is long lost. Some of these headstones, though, give a brief but interesting insight into the dogs' lives, for example:

'In memory of Dobbler, who followed the A. and S. Highlanders for 9 years in South Africa, Ceylon, China and Scotland. Died 19 February 1892.'

George Robinson's little book includes some more detailed accounts of dogs associated with the Castle, even briefly following the military campaigns that the dogs themselves followed. Here are just a couple, the first being about Charlie of the Royal Scots.

Charlie was a little black mongrel dog who literally trotted into the lives of the Royal Scots in 1853 when they were stationed in Monmouthshire. Because his facial expression bore a certain resemblance to one of the officers in the Regiment, he was given the same name, Charlie. He began to hang around a small group of canine camp-followers and became a regular sight around the camp. It seems that he took a particular interest in the work of the camp surgeon (again, I don't mean to imply that the surgeon minced around…).

Charlie would actually sit in the room where each soldier claiming to be unfit for duty would be inspected whilst the surgeon made a decision. Having completed this he would then join the surgeon on his tours of the wards (obviously no fear of any MRSA superbug then). This quickly became the little dog's established daily routine.

Being a medical officer, Charlie probably considered himself above the other canines and remained rather aloof and independent of them. Indications are that he often used to get into dog-fights and on one occasion was so badly injured that he had to be fitted with splints!

Charlie did, in fact, have quite a distinguished military career and was at the forefront of the Royal Scots party sent to the Crimea in 1854. He travelled there via adventures in Gibraltar and Malta and then on to Turkey and Bulgaria. He would certainly have been extremely busy with his medical duties on this campaign. As you can probably imagine, conditions were terrible and dysentery and then cholera hit the soldiers, taking 26 lives amongst the Royal Scots alone.

By the end of August 1854 the Royal Scots had been called into action, landing on a beach by darkness in a torrential downpour. They formed part of a force of some 65,000 men. As they marched towards Sevastopol, Charlie accompanied the soldiers throughout. Sometimes he would go on supply runs to Balaclava, but it wasn't long before the real fighting began, ending with hand-to-hand bayonet combat. Not only did the Commanding Officer get a medal for his successful part in this campaign, but Charlie, too, received a collar and brass tag inscribed 'Royal Charlie'.

This was not, though, the end of Charlie's war. By November, things had turned against the British troops, when a hurricane ripped up their tents and shelter and carried it all off to sea. The accompanying torrents of rain left them shelterless and knee-deep in mud. It's difficult to think how the small black dog got by. There were painfully few supplies, and the presence of Charlie must have really helped keep the soldiers' spirits up. Nevertheless, things got so bad that no fewer than 8,000 soldiers were hospitalised. (Remember, this was Florence Nightingale's war.)

Charlie was still in the Crimea as part of the attack on Sevastopol in the following September, ultimately leading to the capture of a Russian fort. In the aftermath of this campaign, it appears that Charlie's medal was taken away for cleaning, but was not the only thing taken away – Charlie was, too. An enterprising soldier, thinking Charlie was a stray, captured him and sold him to an officer in another regiment for ten shillings. Fortunately, Charlie being Charlie, he escaped at the first opportunity and returned to the Royal Scots.

This wasn't the worst thing to happen to Charlie, though. He had a near-death experience, in fact, when he spent the day with eight soldiers clearing out an ammunition store. Once it was empty, one of the soldiers decided to have a smoke. Luckily, the corporal of the team and Charlie stepped outside for a moment just as the store exploded – there was so much gunpowder residue that the store was like a big bomb and seven of the eight soldiers were killed. Only Charlie and the corporal survived, blown off their feet (and paws) and in Charlie's case badly singed from nose to tail.

Eventually, Charlie made it back to England and in 1856 was present when the Royal Scots were reviewed by Queen Victoria and Prince Albert. Charlie was there, close to the Regiment's colours, perched on a tall soldier's shoulders. Rather unusually for Queen Victoria, we are told that 'we are amused'.

Even then, it's not to be a life of ease for Charlie in Aldershot. The next year he's off on his travels with the Regiment again, this time to India.

Some twenty years later, we pick up the story of Pat – Pat of the Seaforth – in 1878, in Afghanistan. He is a young, small, white dog accompanying the 72nd Duke of Albany's Own Highlanders wherever they go.

A year earlier, Little Pat had been part of a force of British soldiers sent to warn off the Russians from invading India via the Khyber Pass. After twelve months, the Afghans had had enough of the British presence and 100,000 tribesmen joined together to drive the British back.

Brigadier General Baker was ordered to defend the capital, Kabul, by marching against the tribesmen with just 1,600 men and Pat was part of this group.

Pat's group were sheltering from the intense heat in a small village waiting for the order to attack, while artillery shelled enemy positions. Perhaps unsurprisingly, the Afghans got rather pissed off with this and, all of a sudden, launched a charge at the artillery position. Probably, there was an officer somewhere protesting, 'I say, that's just not cricket.' Nevertheless, that awful Johnny Foreigner attacked.

As the charge headed towards them, the artillerymen were ordered to load up their equipment and move out, but there just wasn't time.

This scene was witnessed by a company of the 72nd Highlanders who, together with a company of Sikh infantry, went to help out.

The very first to make contact with the Afghans were a certain Lance Corporal Sellar and Pat, the little white dog. While Sellar engaged in one-to-one combat with his rifle and bayonet, Pat was seen to get stuck in by biting an Afghan tribesman's leg. Meanwhile, the Commanding Officer,

Captain Spens, was killed with a swift stroke of a broadsword. The Indian troops sent to help were forced back, together with the British, when the Afghans captured two of the artillery guns. Eventually, however, reinforcements arrived and the guns were won back.

Standing on a ridge some distance away, watching this scene through binoculars, was Major General Roberts. He had seen everything, including Pat's heroics. Both Pat and Lance Corporal Sellar were injured in action and Sellar, for his bravery, was awarded the Victoria Cross.

A couple of years later, in 1881, the 72nd, to whom Pat belonged, were amalgamated with the 78th (Ross-shire Buffs) to form the Seaforth Highlanders. Pat saw action again with this new regiment in Egypt, at the Battle of Tel-el-Kebs.

Although Pat never got a medal himself, every year his bravery was marked by attaching Lance Corporal Sellar's VC to his collar.

In 1886, the Seaforths returned to Scotland and to the base at Edinburgh Castle. Here, Pat died two yeas later. Pat's grave is in the Dog Cemetery and his life was even celebrated in an obituary in *The Scotsman.* His headstone is one of those still standing in the Cemetery and reads: 'In memory of Pat who followed the 72nd Highlanders in P [obliterated] for 10 years. Died 1888.'

As we left the Castle and headed back down the Royal Mile it became apparent that Edinburgh is a real weekend destination. I have never seen so many stag and hen parties moving from bar to bar – singing, chanting but always (at least at this stage) good-humoured. Add into the mix several thousand rugby fans there for a big match the next day and many a Scottish landlord must have thought it was his birthday.

It was interesting really, because although it was good-natured, you could sense that it would not take much for everything to kick off as people drank quite incredible quantities of alcohol.

Princes Street, the main shopping drag, was heaving on Saturday afternoon. It seems to be a magnet for young teenage girls with thongs poking above their jeans, glued to their mobile phones and proceeding in large groups blocking the whole pavement, moving at about 1 mile an hour. I just had to get out of there. Mind you, to be fair, I don't tend to hang around in any city on a Saturday afternoon, and expect this scene is replicated all over Britain every weekend.

Grabbing one last promising-looking book entitled simply *Grrreat Scottish Dogs*, we set off back to the hotel to pick up our bags and head off to the airport.

On the way back we saw probably more dogs around the lovely green spaces off Princes Street than we had around the whole city over the last two days. Outside Argos, a big black Labrador was lying in the doorway waiting for its owner, but in such a way that any customers leaving or would-be customers entering had to step right over him.

It was a popular time for walking dogs, clearly. A white dog was out in one of those 'Elizabethan collars' that vets put on to stop a dog worrying at his stitches, whilst a wonderfully frisky brown crossbreed puppy was enjoying one of its first walks. A majestic greyhound was walking through the park, doing his best to see off the attentions of a seemingly stray rough collie. An elderly couple were walking a placid Westie and a much less placid Springer spaniel down by Edinburgh Waverley Station and a guide dog was navigating Princes Street with his master much more effectively than we had a few minutes earlier.

Edinburgh had been, I think, almost the perfect short-break destination. Even so, we were quite ready to leave as the stags, hens and drinkers took over. It's probably the same cheap travel we used which makes these places such a target for these drink-fuelled binges. Shame, really.

Edinburgh had turned out to be a great doggy city. We'd seen all the Scottish breeds we'd wanted to at the show in Ingleston. As a bonus, we'd learned a lot about historic dog tales which seemed very much a part of Edinburgh – especially good old Greyfriars Bobby.

There was so much that we didn't get round to seeing, that I would definitely go again. It felt so close and easy to get there that I couldn't believe I hadn't spent time there before. Perhaps next time we'll try to get to the Edinburgh Fringe.

A couple of hours later we were on our short flight home and I got out my book of *Grrreat Scottish Dogs*, expecting to read more heart-warming sentimental stories like the tales of Rab, Fiddy and Fan I had encountered in another small volume by George Robinson. Instead, I was shocked to see that I had been taken in and it was a humorous little book with entries in verse on such famous dogs as 'The Bay City Yowlers', 'Jackie Chewart', 'Rover Coltrane' and 'Lab C. Nesibtt'.

Oh well, it was a nice change and raised a few good laughs. Much like the journey to Edinburgh itself, really.

CHAPTER 12

Spreekt u Engels?

And so, almost unbelievably and without knowing it was creeping up on me, I had reached the stage where I had spotted 146 out of the 147 breeds needed to complete my challenge. It came as no surprise, though, to see which dog was left – the Dutch partridge dog. I had never seen one of these, either before or during the challenge. To be honest, I didn't really recall ever hearing the name or seeing a picture of one.

Still, this was all that stood now between me and ultimate victory.

I had spent I don't know how many hours surfing the net looking for a Dutch partridge dog in the UK, using all of my contacts and all the sites I knew about, but to no avail. It seemed like there was only one option – to go out to Holland and find one.

When you look a little further into the Dutch partridge dog you find, in fact, that this is not a very accurate translation. It is a *Drentsche Patrijshond* in Dutch – a Drenthe rather than Dutch partridge dog. Now this might not mean much to you if, like me, you have never heard of Drenthe, but it turns out that this is a province of the Netherlands.

It seemed, therefore, right and fitting not only that I should go to Holland, but that I should also go to Drenthe. It's true that the Bedlington trip might have haunted me and that the consequences and costs of failure this time were significantly higher, but it still felt like the right thing to do.

Now, I don't know about you, but I have found that life has become a lot easier and a lot cheaper since we all hooked up to the internet. Sorting out my Drenthe trip would have been horrendously complex and horribly expensive just a few years ago – but not anymore.

Within an hour I had booked a cheap flight with an economy carrier (Thompsonfly from Coventry), paid for my airport car-parking at a discounted rate, searched for and found a tremendous deal on car hire in the Netherlands (less than half the price of other quotes) and found, virtually inspected and booked a hotel in Drenthe. I think we sometimes forget how easy life has become in this respect. All without moving my backside from the chair in the study!

The downside to all of this is just how frustrating things can become when you can't get onto the internet or those rare occasions where something is not available by that method.

Anyway, I was happy as Larry. (Does anyone know who Larry is, by the way? And why he is so happy?) There was only one thing hanging over me – always there over the few weeks before the trip, in the back of my mind at least – and that was driving abroad. I'd simply never, ever done it. In fact, for me, not driving is one of the pleasures of a holiday. Add to the driving the fact that the wheel and indeed the traffic are on the wrong side and that I hadn't got a clue where I was going and, to top all of that, arriving in rush hour, and you may get a sense of my anxiety.

An added pleasure was explaining to my colleagues in my day job exactly what I was doing and why I was going where I was. Generally, I think you would describe the look as one of bafflement. I can't think why. 'I'm going to the least known, most obscure part of Holland. Yes, Holland. I'm looking for a type of dog I've never seen. No, I don't know that I will see one there. Oh, and I'm hoping to get to a Nazi transit camp while I'm there.'

Clearly, this didn't conform to some people's idea of how to use their leisure time.

This was my first flight from one of the many small airports beginning to offer low cost international flights. I was travelling from Coventry. Primarily, Coventry is a freight airport, infamous locally for its export of live animals, sometimes allegedly in unsuitable conditions. Indeed, it hit the headlines nationally when one protester was crushed and killed by a livestock lorry.

It's a strange little place, really. It's quite a small operation, which I have to say I felt much more comfortable with than the massive international airports where you walk for miles and get shepherded from pen to pen. It is little more, really, than a couple of portakabins with seats in, a small shop and a place to buy coffee and sandwiches. I think there were about a dozen flights going out on the day I was there. Three of them were squashed into a short, fifteen-minute spell at the start of the day – presumably as soon as the night-time curfew for flights was lifted. This meant that this was as busy as the airport would get. All the seats were taken. Long, narrow rows full of very sleepy people.

There was no music, or in fact sound of any kind really, so not a particularly relaxing atmosphere. Luckily, I had a personal radio with me and could listen to music as I enjoyed my favourite pastime, people-watching.

What struck me most as I looked around the 'departure lounge' was the similarity in appearance of parents and their kids. I was captivated by the sight of one man who was spreading himself over two seats while other people sat on the floor. He was overweight, with quite a savage crew cut, a red sweaty face and big red lips. He had a really spiteful expression on his face and spent most of his time eating. His face was such that scenes from the animated film *Animal Farm* kept coming to mind – the bit where the pig transforms into a man. Little squinty eyes in a big, round, spiteful, piggy face. This chap happened to have ginger hair to finish off his look. And there, next to him was an overweight kid of 12 or 13, unable to move without heavy breathing, eating away with the same objectionable expression and … you guessed it … spreading his ample buttocks over two seats. They were chewing in time. The poor kid doesn't really have a chance, does he? And there's me worrying about dog-breeding.

Breaking this rather sombre but quite enjoyable mood, our flight was called – on time – and it was a simple matter of walking out of the portakabin, down the side of the plane's parking area (the apron?) and up the steps into the plane. This time, the plane was rather intriguingly called The Spirit of Doncaster. I pondered what that conjured up in my mind and wondered if I wanted to fly on it.

The flight itself was quite full and I was squashed between two others – my least favourite position. Still, it was a short flight and that didn't really matter. I was even wearing my special Jack Wolfskin travel shirt which 'wicks away' any perspiration, so I'm sure I was a pleasure to sit next to, even if my arms were pinned to my side to maximise action in the armpit area.

I think we must have landed just outside Brussels as it took a full quarter of an hour at a pretty good ground speed to taxi to the terminal. I have certainly never travelled that far by plane on the ground. When we got off I understood at least some of the reason for the length of journey, as we were at the very furthest point of the airport away from where we wanted to be – the rail station, taxis, shops, car hire or whatever.

It was only 8.30 in the morning and I was slightly too early to pick up my car (and subconsciously probably not in a great hurry to do so) so I spent my first 2,50 euros on a cappuccino in one of those places where you have to stand up to drink around a little stainless steel table because you are too important and/or too busy to sit down to drink. It was very soon apparent, though, that you weren't too busy to smoke while you got your caffeine fix.

Coffee is one of my few vices. I don't smoke at all or drink any amount, but I do like my coffee. So a really good cappuccino had been very much needed and I was now in far better condition to face the day.

I walked the length of Schipol to reach the car hire desk – in fact one of many car hire desks – and was soon ready to go. I decided to add the fullest possible collision damage waiver protection at extra cost. I also decided that they could fill up my tank on return as I didn't fancy driving round and round looking for a petrol station at the end of my stay so I could return it full.

To reach my car, I had to get across four lanes of chaos to a multi-storey car park. I witnessed the normal scene at airports – taxis, people being dropped off, being picked up, abandoning cars in inappropriate positions, massive buses squeezing through tiny gaps at speed and so on. It was then that reality struck me: my first driving abroad would be all this and trying to decide which lane to fight my way into without knowing which I needed. I suppose it's a bit like someone driving for the first time in Britain in a car with a wheel on the 'wrong' side and picking it up at Heathrow. 'Oh joy!' were the words that went through my mind, or something to that effect.

In the interests of economy, I had rented a 'Group A' car, that is a 'Fiat Cinquecento or similar'. I have to say that I couldn't think what would fit in the 'or similar' category. At the same time, I knew that the Fiat Cinquecento had not been made for a few years and that it had been replaced by the Fiat Seicento, so I was quietly confident that I was going to get one hundred cubic centimetres of raw power free.

In fact, there were no Group A cars at all – I don't believe they even have any – so I was upgraded to a Group B car, a rather nice, brand-new Skoda Fabia. I must admit that this was a huge relief over the next few days, on motorways roaring with fast-moving traffic. It was bad enough as it was, but being harassed by other traffic as I chugged along would not have been pleasant. I once owned a Fiat Cinquecento and believe me, I know. I kept it six weeks. That was the end of my attempts at environmentally-friendly travel. I was also really pleased to have a Skoda now, being, I like to think, a bit of an expert on Eastern European motoring. I have had my own Skoda, not one but two Ladas and even a Yugo. That one would have been OK if the Bosnian and Serbian parts had only learned to work together. Even my current 'Japanese' car was built in Hungary. In fact, if I won the lottery I'd get me a Trabant.

There was one thing I would do several times over the next few days and I would learn to cover it with a look of nonchalance but at the same time confidence in knowing exactly what I was doing. This was something I did for the first time in front of the rental people at the airport. I strode up to the car, opened the door, sat down and buckled my seat belt, only to realise that the steering wheel was on the other side of the car. Nothing uncool about that.

I was beginning to think the extra collision damage waiver had been a good choice.

I had printed my route off at home from the internet. It seemed OK, except for these first few miles, where there were any number of interchanges and sometimes you had to travel away from where you wanted to go to join another road going back your way. So imagine going to London from Sheffield, but having to remember that you had to head towards Leeds, Hull and then Lincoln or something. Of course, the point was, I was not heading to London or Amsterdam, but towards an isolated little village in the most remote part of Holland.

In any case, it took me a few minutes just to rehearse leaving the car park and watching where others went. I was already beginning to get quite a thing about which side of the road to drive on and road positioning.

I emerged into the chaos of airport traffic, my biggest problem initially being to find the right gear positions with my right rather than left hand. The traffic was too busy and the whole process of driving too unfamiliar for me to be in with any chance to start with, so I decided just to drive safely and see where I would get to. After a few minutes of lanes merging and separating, it became clear that I was heading towards The Hague, the opposite direction to where I wanted to go. I simply decided to stay cool, turn right into side roads, turn round and go the other way. This gave me my first left turn across a busy dual carriageway with oncoming traffic, but it was fine (except spluttering off in third rather than first gear).

Now I'd got a feel for the car, I decided I would just give myself more time and focus on the road numbers. Fate was against me, with major roadworks and diversions in place, actually taking me into Amsterdam itself, but I stayed resolute and found my way through. This was one of many examples where I found my knowledge of German really useful. I know no Dutch at all but seeing a traffic sign bearing the word *Omleiding* immediately triggered the German word *Umleitung* in my mind – 'diversion', rather than the name of a town.

By this stage, I was happy enough to turn the radio on. I

hadn't thought to bring a CD with me, so settled for the radio. The first song was good old Rick Astley from the 80s – 'Never gonna give you up'. Lovely to hear it after all that time.

I had about 120 miles ahead of me and, having survived the airport area and the diversions, I was beginning to feel a little more relaxed, with my Skoda cruising at 80km/hour, whatever that meant, beginning to feel comfortable in overtaking and moving lanes.

One thing which really caught me out to start with is that the inside lane appeared to become the exit lane for the next junction sometimes, so I had to do a bit of last-minute manoeuvring to avoid a no-doubt highly enjoyable visit to an alternative destination.

I have to say that 'mirror – signal – manoeuvre' didn't seem to apply at all. In fact, on busy roads and at interchanges where you have to change lanes, indicating you are going to pull out seems to bring other drivers down on you faster, and if you do move out then you are met with flashed lights and horns, even if you've given plenty of notice. It seems that the Dutch make the Brits look patient on the road.

I was just getting used to all of this when the sky went black – and I mean black. Within minutes we were in one of those storms where the wipers simply cannot move the water off your windscreen. It was then that I realised that I had no idea where the lights were. It didn't seem to be a good idea to drive in lashing rain between heavy vehicles without lights on, so I turned every knob and pressed every button, but to no avail.

So, I pulled off to find the manual and misjudged my position in relation to the kerb as I was on the other side of the car from normal and it was a rough, potholed pull-off. There was a crunching sound. Luckily, having got soaked to the skin and got into the passenger seat by mistake again, I established that is was 'just' a hubcap. Perhaps no one would notice.

After about half an hour, the rain stopped, the traffic thinned and I cruised uneventfully towards my destination. In fact, all of a sudden, I was leaving the motorways and had the narrow country lanes and towns, with roundabouts and give-way junctions to look forward to.

The countryside, though, was beautiful as the sun came out. A really vivid green, with houses and flowers punctuating the landscape.

The roads were narrow and my biggest concern was over-compensating and hitting the kerb, so I set my passenger-side mirror to look downwards so I could see I was keeping a good position.

As in every other country, the buses hurtled around these roads at speed – even bendy-buses – leaving you wondering how you passed each other without a collision. If one of the passengers had wanted a stamp licked for a letter, I could have done it as we passed each other.

Before I knew it and with a sense of great relief, I was soon entering a very attractive village. It was beautifully maintained with houses freshly painted, gardens well tended, no litter, some interesting buildings and nicely kept green spaces. This was Westerbork, in Drenthe, my destination.

I had chosen Westerbork as it was the site of one of the few internationally known features in Drenthe – a camp used in the Second World War as a transit station for Jews and others on their way to Auschwitz, Birkenau and other Nazi extermination camps.

There was no sign of anything so bleak in this well-to-do, picturesque village of flowers and bicycles.

Primarily, it seemed to be a long strip with houses and shops on both sides, together with a large number of cafés, restaurants and bars for such a small place. Try as I might, I couldn't find my hotel – which I was sure was meant to be opposite the Church – so I pulled in and parked, deciding to set off on foot to find my accommodation.

The sun was out now and this was the sort of place that gives you a sense of well-being and contentment. There was quite a bit of traffic on the narrow main road, but the cars, buses and trucks seemed happy to trundle along behind the many bicycles, which appeared to enjoy right of way.

I had walked about half a mile in each direction, to the outskirts of the village, before returning to the car to see that I had in fact parked right next to my hotel which was directly opposite the church, but which showed a different bar and restaurant name to the front. It had a large decking area to its front with chairs, tables and parasols, a sun lounge to the side and a large car park with pots of flowers. It was exactly what I have in mind when I say something is 'continental'.

I was really too early to book in, but that was no problem. The people were so friendly and seemed genuinely pleased to see me. I put my stuff in a room – clean, comfortable and adequate in every way and just about £30 per night – and headed down to the café and restaurant. This was a real bonus which I hadn't known about: I could get what I wanted to eat and drink when I wanted it.

With the trauma of my journey behind me and without a sight of any dog, let alone a Dutch partridge dog, I needed coffee and treated myself to a cappuccino. It was only about 11.30 in the morning, but I'd had my breakfast at 5.15 and was ready for something to eat as well. I had spotted *Croque Monsieur* on the menu and ordered one. The waiter was delighted that I'd already spotted what they had to offer, chatted like he'd known me all my life and left me sitting in a sun lounge looking down the pretty street and across at the church with some music playing quietly in the background. It was a good feeling.

It was still incredible to me that I had had breakfast at home, flown from Coventry to Amsterdam, hired a car and driven across Holland and was having a very early lunch in Drenthe. What an amazing world we live in.

Drenthe itself is an odd sort of place. Whilst the Netherlands is such a densely populated country, Drenthe has always been sparsely peopled, viewed by many Dutch folk as little more than a boggy wasteland. It is certainly rural in nature and has endured times of grinding poverty, even in the twentieth century.

One of its main claims to fame is the existence of dolmens (*hunnebedden*) – the megalithic tombs, particularly in the northeast of the province, which prove that there has been life in this part of the nation since the times of prehistory, dating to around 3500BC. Its landscape is a product of the last Ice Age.

The first mention of this remote area (by Dutch standards) comes in 820 when it is called Pago Treanth (district Drenthe). It is then mentioned as a 'county' in archives of the area (*Het Drents Archief*) in 1024.

It has spent most of its history under the control of the Bishops of Utrecht, before coming under the control of Charles V in the 16th century. Drenthe became a part of the Republic of the Seven United Provinces and in 1796 became a Province. Its anthem, *Mijn Drenthe*, is deeply rooted in history (find it in HMV or on Amazon – go on, you know you want to).

For those of you who like facts and figures, Drenthe's total area is 2,756.97 square kilometres and its population in 2002 was 478,695, giving a population density of only 173 per square kilometre.

It lies in the northeast of the country, with the Province of Groningen to its north, Friesland to the west, Overijssel to the south and Germany to the east.

Drenthe is a Province with no cities and only a few towns. It seems to have survived largely unchanged for many hundreds of years. It still consists primarily of peat bogs, of woodlands and heaths. Even today, it is primarily rural, agricultural and very beautiful. Sheep and cows are everywhere in the large, flat, lush green fields. Some of the farm buildings seem to have frozen in time – real-life picture postcards.

The pub and restaurant where I was staying had a 'trappist monk' theme. Something tells me that it may be the only place in the world to have this. There were cut-out, life-size monks, torch-holders on the walls ready to have flaming torches put into them, mock medieval doorways and so on. The various function rooms seemed to have themed names. This, I think, was because the Abdij de Westerburcht where I was staying sold 'trappist beer' – *La Trappe.*

Whatever the theme, the coffee (non-trappist) was fantastic. As for the *Croque Monsieur*, it was, well, eccentric. Perhaps eccentrically Dutch. The reason I say this is that it appeared with the melted cheese (Edam) and ham as expected, but on Dutch brown rye bread. Tasty, though.

Asking the incredibly helpful and friendly young man on reception, I found out that Kamp Westerbork was in fact around 10km outside the village itself. Apparently, it was common for visitors to expect the camp in the village itself, but it had actually been established for its original purpose in such a way that it would not impact on the local community.

I drove off to find the camp but got lost before I left the village. I ended up driving through some of the residential areas behind the main road. These were well-ordered, well-to-do, bright and, what struck me most, incredibly clean, just like the rest of the village.

Eventually, after lots of opportunities to practise my three-point-turn skills, reversing around corners etc., I saw a map ahead of me. I pulled up and looked at it, working out easily exactly where I was. The only problem was, I didn't know where I was going. Along came my saviour in the form of a jet-black schnauzer, the size of a small horse, walking placidly beside an elderly woman who was as small as the dog was big.

I asked her if she spoke English and she said, 'only a few words'. German, then? Definitely not. This was to become a pattern over the next few days. Firstly, although Drenthe borders Germany, there is clearly no way these Dutch people are going to speak German. Secondly, when a Dutch person says that they hardly speak any English or say they only speak it 'a leetle', this means that they have linguistic proficiency in English well above the level of the average 16-year-old, school-leaving native speaker.

Quarter of an hour later, I had left the main road and driven for a few miles down even narrower, quieter roads through an eerily still countryside landscape, until I had reached the 'Herinneringscentrum Kamp Westerbork', the Camp Westerbork Memorial Centre.

The camp lies 11km south of Assen, Drenthe's provincial capital. It is a place with a dark and terrible place in history, although life at the camp itself was largely bearable. The reason it occupies this place is because it operated as a transit camp for the Nazis for deportation to concentration and extermination camps in Eastern Europe from 15th July 1942 until 13th September 1944. During this period, 93 trains left the camp, carrying more than 100,000 people – mainly Jews but with a contingent of gypsies – to camps in the East, notably to Auschwitz. Yet during this time conditions at Westerbork were reasonable. The food was passable, there was recreation and entertainment and the hospital was well equipped.

Westerbork's history – and indeed the place today – are full of ironies, in my view. Not least of these ironies is that the camp was built not by the Nazis but rather by the Dutch Government using largely Jewish funds. It was built to shelter refugees, but ended up a link in the chain leading to the gas chambers.

As early as 1933 the first refugees from Nazism had begun to arrive in the Netherlands. The 'Committee for Particular Jewish Interests' was set up in response, funded largely by the Dutch Jewish community, with the aim first and foremost of offering help and advice.

The trickle of refugees, though, became more like a flood across the Dutch border after the *Kristallnacht* of 9th to 10th November 1938 when anti-Jewish action became more overt in Germany. Many of those crossing the border did so illegally. At the time there were twenty or so small refugee camps around Holland, but the government took the decision that it would be more sensible and effective to bring all of these together onto one large site. Eventually, the site was found. It had to be near enough to facilities to allow for supplies, health care and so on and yet sufficiently isolated that the camp didn't impinge on local people or that refugees became integrated into local society. This was quite purposeful. People here were just passing through on the way to settle elsewhere, after all. You can't help but be struck by some of the parallels within immigration and asylum centres in the UK today.

Drenthe was the ideal location for the camp and 25 hectares of ground was purchased to build what would become Kamp Westerbork, using, again ironically, over 1 million guilders from the Committee for Jewish Interests.

Building work began in July 1939 with the first German Jewish refugees arriving in October. These first inmates helped with the completion of the camp and there were reports of good barracks and a thick broth to welcome them.

The intention was to house 2,500 people in total when the camp was complete, but by May 1940 there were just 700 there. One of the main aims of the camp at this time was to offer training. Indications are that the training was in fact very good. At the same time, life there was frustrating as there appeared to be little hope for the inmates of emigrating.

It was in May 1940 that Germany invaded the Netherlands. Understandably, there was considerable panic at the camp, being, as it was, close to the German border and with many German refugees having experienced the Nazis at first hand. In an attempt to escape, the camp inmates boarded a train, hoping to flee to England. A bombed bridge put paid to this, though, and by the end of May most were back in the camp. Whilst under Dutch control, refugees had been allowed to come and go to the camp largely as they wished, but this now stopped under German administration.

As far as Dutch Jews were concerned, nothing really changed initially and life went on. However, in summer 1941 the *Entjüdung*, the de-jewification of Holland was planned and this began in 1942, with Dutch Jews being concentrated into ghettoes. The ultimate plan, though, was to rid the Netherlands of all Jews, sending them to labour camps in Eastern Europe.

Just imagine the Nazis' delight in having Westerbork already established and set up. It was a perfect transit camp for their intentions. To meet an operation of the size and scale that the Nazis had in mind, though, a much bigger camp was needed and a huge expansion was undertaken financed by funds confiscated from Jews.

In 1942, the Nazis worked up the final piece in their plan: the so-called *Endlösung* – the final solution – which was to be the systematic extermination of all Jews. With this new impetus, the Germans took over the running of the camp themselves in 1942, with the first train leaving for the death camps of Poland in July of that year.

Initially, the camp had been run by the Dutch – firstly by Mr D A Syswarda, who had previously been an administrator for an organisation responsible for psychiatric patients, and then by a Captain of Reserves in the demobilised Dutch Army Reserves, Captain Jacques Schol, who had previously run a large refugee camp.

It was Schol who introduced new regulations and an organisational structure to the camp in 1942. As most of the inmates were German, that language was used for this work. It was the early inmates – the Germans – who took up all the significant positions in the internal camp administration and as a result they and a disproportional percentage of their compatriots survived the camp.

One of the organisations set up was the *Ordnungsdienst*, initially operating as a fire brigade and using the stronger, fitter, younger men. As time went on this became the internal security force – maintaining law and order. In effect, they were the internal Jewish police force – even loading people onto the death trains later in the camp's history.

Barbed wire and watch towers were now erected at the camp and the Camp Commandants were now Germans. The first such commandant was a Major in the SS, Dr Erich Depper. He stayed only three months, causing riots with his brutality. He was replaced by another SS Major Josef Hugo Dischner, an alcoholic who was fond of using his whip on detainees. Neither of these men created the conditions the Nazis wanted. They wanted a compliant and unsuspecting population, much easier and much less resource-intensive to work with, and so after six weeks Dischner was replaced by another SS man, Lieutenant

Colonel Albert Konrad Gemmeker who remained as commandant for the rest of the war. He was a gentleman, and much more manipulative and dangerous than those who had gone before him.

As in Auschwitz and the concentration camps themselves, the SS kept their hands as clean as they could at Westerbork – delegating the dirty work to the Jewish camp organisations themselves. For much of the time, the SS only actually patrolled outside the camp, leaving the inside to be run by the Jews. The SS Commanding Officer's only concern was to meet his targets – just like in so many businesses around the world today. As long as the targets for deportations were met, how they were met was largely immaterial. In this way they left the Jewish organisations to do their own dirty work and determine the deportation lists. The overall head of the Jewish administration in the camp, a man by the name of Schlesinger, not surprisingly survived the war, left the county and was never seen again.

While by this stage many of the normal Jews were living in overcrowded and unsanitary conditions in barracks, people occupying the prominent positions in the Jewish administration had homes of their own and lived quite extravagantly. Many of these had assumed power when the camp truly was a refugee camp for German Jews. They now had power over life and death. How the Nazis achieved this is quite fascinating. They seem to have really understood exactly how to divide and rule and how to appeal to the basic survival instincts in man to do terrible things to other members of their own communities.

Mentally, I am sure, this allowed the Nazis to distance themselves from the real horror of what they had done, and enabled them to live with themselves, seeing themselves almost as efficient production managers rather than makers of death. Quite fascinating psychological techniques.

A lot of the Nazis' tactics depended on creating a semblance of normality and even care. There was ballet, music, theatre and cabaret in the camp – to entertain detainees as well as the Germans. There were sports competitions. Ironically (that word again) the camp had one of the best hospitals in the country. At one time this hospital had no fewer than 1,725 beds and 120 doctors. In the small book available at the memorial centre entitled *Camp Westerbork – Symbol of Destruction*, Dirk Mulder recounts the tale of a premature baby brought to the camp.

The Camp Commandeer, Geneker, went to great lengths to have an incubator brought in and required a Professor of Paediatrics to attend and work on saving the baby. Seemingly no expense was spared until the baby was brought to the stage where he could survive without an incubator and drink from the bottle. Geneker visited on most days. And yet, a few days later, the baby was deported to the death camps. It seems this behaviour borders on the schizophrenic.

The deception perpetrated on the Jews included telling them that all would be well, that families would be kept together and that conditions in the East were harsh but survivable. Even at their destinations the deception continued. At one of the extermination camps, Sobibor, the railway platform had a clock but it did not work and the hands never moved. There were departure timetables, but no departures. All in all, 19 cattle-wagon trains were sent directly from Westerbork to Sobibor. These trains carried 34,313 people to that death camp – only 18 survived. Despite the deception, people feared deportation and were desperate to say. Many tried to become part of the internal Jewish administration machine, while others tried different ways to become indispensable, through music, cabaret or skilled work. In all the time, although many still worked outside the camp, only 210 people tried to escape – not least because the Nazis made sure that those working outside the camp left relatives behind.

Initially, trains were sent from nearby Hooghalen, with the first trains carrying 2,030 people leaving on 15th and 16th July 1942. By November of that year, though, the tracks had been taken into the camp itself to make things easier and more efficient for the Nazis.

By February 1943, the deportations had regularised, with trains carrying around 1,000 people in cattle trucks departing each Tuesday. It was the Jewish camp organisation which would decide who was deported. The lists would be produced late in the day to minimise disruption and while the trains were loaded (by the Jewish internal police) everyone else was confined to barracks. Sixty-five trains, carrying 58,380 victims went direct to Auschwitz, most of the others going to Sobibor. Most of the victims were Jews, but around 250 of them were gypsies.

One of the last trains to leave Westerbork in September 1944 carried Anne Frank and her family members. They had been brought to Westerbork following their betrayal in Amsterdam one month earlier. Within the camp they had been kept in the punishment barrack – the prison within a prison – because they had been in hiding, so they would have been among the first to be loaded on to the trains to the East. In December, Anne and her sister were transferred from Auschwitz to Bergen-Belsen where they died of sickness.

Camp Westerbork was officially liberated on 12 April 1945 by Canadian troops. Just 876 prisoners were still there.

Appropriately, it seems to me, the camp was first used after the war as an internment camp for Dutch Nazis. Later it became an army camp, but its last use, to my mind rather unfortunately, was as a reception centre for people from the Dutch East Indies – largely South Moluccans, who stayed there under the name 'Camp Shattenberg'.

In 1971, the camp was finally demolished and the desire seemed to be to forget the whole dark chapter in Dutch history.

Nothing was there at all until the National Westerbork Memorial, created by a camp survivor, Ralph Prins, was erected in 1970. This consists of a stretch of rail at the terminus, with the rails bending up at the end towards heaven, carried on sleepers which symbolically get more and more torn-up as they go eastwards. It is in the original position of the terminus, built from original rail. A heap of boulders looks like a pile of skulls at the other end.

This was all there was on the site for years as it became a site for a radio telescope observatory.

In 1981, though, a small group was founded which ultimately became the Former Camp Westerbork Foundation. Things got moving from then on and the Memorial Centre was built in 1983, originally in the shape of a barracks, although this subsequently had to be expanded because of the ever-growing number of visitors. The actual site of the camp now has areas mown and raised to show the outline of the different buildings. Corner fragments have been erected in grey stone, looking almost like bombed-out ruins, to give a sense of the layout and, it has to be said, this arrangement really is effective in giving you a feel for the place as it was.

As you approach the camp, memorials looking like large tombstones give the bare, horrific facts surrounding the camp and its deportations. Clear statements which make you weep.

I started by visiting the memorial centre. Light, neat, clean and modern. I'm a linguist by training and certainly not one of those Brits who think everyone should speak English, but I was really disappointed that all the exhibits, photos and artefacts were labelled and explained only in Dutch. Not even German or French. Similarly, there were no guidebooks or historical works in English, other than Dirk Mulder's brief booklet which I have already mentioned.

By this stage, I had learned just how open and friendly Dutch people are. I had found that, quite understandably, the key to this seemed to be not just starting off talking in English but rather beginning by asking them, '*Spreekt u Engels?*' The receptionist at the centre was so friendly and helpful – and also incredibly apologetic about the lack of materials in English.

Even using pidgin Dutch and a combination of English and German to make sense of the captions and information, it was a hugely moving and informative place to visit. There were photos, authentic documents stamped with the Star of David, clothing and mementos from the day, even a part of an original barrack with three bunks on top of each other. There were theatre programmes from the camp theatre and lists of 140,000 Dutch dead from the Second World War in 42 volumes, for those who didn't get a grave of their own. There were personal effects from camp inmates, drawings done in the camp by detainees and original film footage from 1944. It wasn't too busy there except for some teenagers, I think on a field trip of some sort.

Even here, strangely and perhaps unforgivably, I found myself looking at the photos of detainees working on farms and in the countryside for dogs – any dogs, but particularly of course the Dutch Partridge dog. To no avail.

It wasn't until I'd finished looking around the centre that I realised I had seen no sign of the camp itself. I actually felt quite cheated. Impressive as it was, I needed to feel the atmosphere and see where this camp had been. I was relieved to find, having visited the helpful receptionist again, that there was a camp to be seen, some three kilometres away, through woodland paths.

The good news was that, although it was quite feasible to walk, there was a bus. I found this a little surreal, I have to say. The bus service was a minibus, running only from the Memorial Centre to the camp and back every fifteen minutes or so. What struck me as odd was that the bus wasn't run by the Centre itself, but by Arriva. I couldn't imagine how this would come about. Was the franchise advertised in *Euro Bus Monthly*? or were there shadowy dealings behind it? You know the kind of thing – an anonymous phone call in the middle of the night to a top Arriva executive from a well-placed informant: 'Psst, there's a new money-spinning route becoming available in a former concentration camp. If you look after me, I'll look after you …'

The journey to the camp was down a narrow lane passing through extensive woodland. It was completed at some speed, it has to be said, with many a narrow scrape for the hardier walkers and cyclists making their own way to the camp. The memorial centre had felt fairly remote and the camp itself was even more so.

Getting off the bus by the camp gates – one of those horizontal red and white candy-striped barriers, surrounded on either side by fences complete with barbed wire – the first thing I saw were the tomb-like memorials. There was a row of them bearing instructions for me to decipher in my Anglo-German Dutch. It proved easy actually. One said: 'In Auschwitz-Birkenau more than 56 500 Jews from the Netherlands and more than 200 gypsies from the Netherlands were murdered.'

I walked through the gate and followed a grassy path around to some of the reconstructed corners of a building – it was a barrack building first. I just stood there, looking at this empty grassy space ahead of me. The shape of the building had been mown into the ground and what would have been the floor of the building appeared to have been raised by a few inches.

It was so still and so quiet there. Birds sang. The air was warm but there was no sun. It almost felt like time had stood still. It's a remote spot with no traffic noise. I sat on a bench and just stared ahead, trying to imagine people in this space living in squalor and fear.

Surrounded by trees as far as I could see, together with heathland and long grass, this was undoubtedly a beautiful place. A really beautiful place.

The whole camp is a scene of so much irony. There is the irony of the beauty, stillness and tranquillity when you think of the terrible happenings there. There is the irony of it being built by the Dutch and for protection and yet being used by the Nazis as a portal to extermination.

There is the irony of it being funded by Jews for their own destruction. Of Jews choosing who should die and packing them onto the trains.

Even the weather seemed schizophrenic – sun, then warmth under cloud, then a downpour and even thunder and lightning at one stage. It was appropriate somehow.

It was such a huge area that even if there were, say, one hundred people on the site it seemed really empty. I walked on past the Administration building and on to dormitory after dormitory before reaching the punishment barracks, where Anne Frank and her family had been held. Here, there was a barbed wire fence and gate between you and the mock ruins. I had first read *The Diary of Anne Frank* when I was about 12. It had always haunted me – the first time I'd thought properly about the evil of Nazism and Man's inhumanity to Man.

Standing now looking across to the place they had been held – the actual space – looking at some of the older trees that she would have seen, was both incredibly moving and barely comprehensible.

On I went, towards a watch-tower, rebuilt to overlook what would have been the end of the line, the area where the trains were loaded. Here stands the Westerbork monument – a rail track around 50 metres long as previously described. At the other end is a wall with buffers. Several floral tributes lie there, near the boulders which look like a pile of skulls.

Standing taking this sight in and soaking up the atmosphere in the rain, I saw a fairly constant stream of elderly cyclists going past relaxed, enjoying themselves, chatting. Why not, in this beautiful countryside?

I suppose I was on the site for about an hour before I headed back to catch the bus. On the way I passed the parade ground – a large tarmac square where the roll-call would have been taken. A group of German teenagers had arrived and were laughing and shouting as they jumped over the commemorative markers – each mini-sculpture representing a certain number of Jews – laid out on the ground.

I felt really sad as I waited for the bus back to the car park. I don't suppose that that is too much of a surprise. As I waited, a group of younger children on their bicycles, with activity sheets, went by and into the camp.

It was late afternoon now and time to head off. It was on this journey that I did my only really silly piece of driving on the trip (to the accompaniment of Rick Astley again, of course). The road bent round several ways before crossing an unmanned railway crossing and then curving down a hill towards a roundabout. At the roundabout, I wanted to go left, which means, abroad, going three quarters of the way round the roundabout. There was no traffic about to remind me, though, and I decided to approach it as a conventional left turn in the UK – by approaching the roundabout in the left-hand lane – only to be confronted by a rather confused Dutch driver who had done a right turn and now faced me head on. He didn't seem angry – just confused. Needless to say I smiled and waved and moved off at speed. I was shaking, though, from the thought of what could have happened.

Next stop was Assen, Drenthe's provincial capital. Again, the countryside on the way was beautiful. I lived in North Germany for a year and had at first found the expanses of low, flat landscape rather dull. Over time, though, I had come to see the comfort and beauty of it – not unlike Norfolk – and it was this that I was reminded of as I drove the 11km, thankfully without incident, towards Assen. On the radio, again, was some mid-80s pop of the Rick Astley school.

My first impression of Assen was that it looked like a building-site. There seemed to be a number of large buildings going up all around – a bit like your view from the balcony of your last-minute bargain hotel.

I was pleased with how I dealt with the driving in a town – lots of changing lanes, roundabouts, filter systems and so on. I was getting the hang of this.

Parking in a multi-storey car park, I emerged into a row of one-off shops, which reminded me of all the British seaside towns which Tom and I visit so regularly. Quite run-down and non-descript – full of bargain shops.

Assen dates back to the thirteenth century and is quite unusual in that it doesn't lie on a trading route, at a major crossroads or even on a river. In fact, it was established in a sparsely populated, deserted area (you're getting the picture of Drenthe by now, aren't you?). It was founded around a convent for Cistercian nuns. The convent had had to be built by the people of Drenthe as punishment for those naughty folk cutting their bishop's head off.

Over time a small village built up around the convent, consisting mainly of farmers and all the traditional village industries. By the end of the 17th century the regional council had taken over the original convent and the small town of Assen became Drenthe's administrative and governmental centre.

Assen became a city in 1809, when Lodewijk Napoleon (the brother of the famous Emperor and King of Holland at the time) gave the town its city rights. The original forest granted to the new city at the time – the *Asser Bos* – remains today.

In the following years, Assen expanding gradually as it became home to a military garrison.

Since the end of the Second World War, Assen has become a centre of industry, although it maintains very much a small-town flavour. In fact, there was good reason for the building work – Assen is a growing city, increasing its population by a net 1,000 people each year, which is incredible given that the population is only 60,000. Over the next ten years, there are plans for an extra 10,000 jobs to be created in the area.

The provincial government has decided that the much needed economic and population development in Drenthe will be focussed on Assen (the fastest-growing city in the Northern Netherlands) and just one other area. There is a real determination to keep the villages and hamlets rural and attractive, as, in addition to light industry, the future is seen as agriculture and, increasingly, tourism. Drenthe sets very high store by its environmental and ecological credentials.

Apparently, as the regional centre for 200,000 people, the shopping centre is particularly in vogue. There are certainly some lovely pavement cafés and some specialist shops, but to be honest I found it like a rather dull provincial British town.

True, it had a C&A, but that can't make up for everything.

In fact, as I later found also in Emnem, there seems to be a preponderance of shoe shops everywhere. In fact, here are …

10 facts about Holland and the Dutch:

1 There is one shoe shop for each shop of any other type.
2 Toilets have a shelf on which you leave your deposit and you have to use rough, recycled toilet paper.
3 The Dutch are incredibly friendly people. Many have blonde hair and blue eyes, but have open, smiling faces, unlike many of the Germans they physically resemble.
4 The image of the Dutch and their bicycles is true. All other road-users try to avoid them and in the evening bikes take over the villages, ridden by people of all ages.
5 Apple cake and cream is available everywhere and highly recommended.
6 They are obsessed by Rick Astley, closely followed by UB40 and, unaccountably, Leo Sayer.
7 They enjoy fantastic mobile phone signals everywhere (perhaps it's the flat landscape and maybe they're frying their brains anyway).
8 In towns and cities they appear to change language (normally English/Dutch) in mid-sentence without batting an eyelid.
9 It always costs 6 euros to get into public attractions.
10 To overtake, in Holland, you have to get close enough to the car in front to be able to exchange body fluids, pull out sharply and then back equally sharply, even if there is an empty road in front of you. All of this must be carried out without indicating.

I had come to Assen primarily to visit the Drents Museum – housed in the former abbey church together with other historic buildings, such as the *Ontvangeshuis* (1698), the *Drostenhuis* (1778) and the *Provinciehuis* (1885). I was convinced that the Museum of Drenthe would have pictures, paintings, maybe even a whole feature, on the Dutch partridge dog.

The square – as, to be fair, did other parts of the city – had some nice old buildings. Clearly, there had been some wealth in the city as shown by some of the mansions and civic buildings around. Indeed, one of Assen's nicknames is 'the town of mansions', but presumably this is only when measured against other towns and cities in Drenthe.

The museum cost – you guessed it – 6 euros to get into. In the entrance hall, an elderly lady was sitting on a chair with a Chihuahua on her lap. I took this as an encouraging sign.

Having spoken – in a way – to the man on the ticket desk and found out all about the museum (not), I headed off into the first area. This was the modern art area and I passed through it like a rat through a drainpipe. Now I like modern art as much as the next man (or actually a lot more than most) but I held out little hope of finding a Drenthe partridge dog there – and to be honest I hadn't got time to work out if the yellow triangle in a blue square was one of these dogs or a metaphor for the melancholy existence of man or woman living in the alienation of post-modernist nihilism. Anyway, people looked at me as if I was a complete philistine as I went through. Again, everything was only in Dutch, but given that this was a museum dedicated to the province of Drenthe, that was not a great surprise. There was quite an impressive-looking interactive exhibition, based around the creation of the earth, but I didn't hang around for that, either. The museum's speciality was archaeology and I'm sure it would be riveting for an archaeologist, but I'm not one, so again I passed through at speed.

I had real hopes for the *Stijlkamers* – the rooms laid out as they would have been atvarious points in history. The rooms reminded me of those Flemish paintings, very dark with black walls, heavy, dark wooden furniture, delft crockery and dark rugs. They were quite light, but that was because the windows of the museums were large. There were no images of dogs on the pottery and I examined the paintings of rural and agricultural scenes in some detail. At this point, some of the modern art fans went by and you could almost hear them thinking, 'so that's why he was in such a rush. What on earth does he see in that?'

Anyway, no matter how hard I tried, I couldn't find a reference to the Drenthe partridge dog in the museum of Drenthe. The rural paintings were all beautiful, almost chocolate-box scenes, but dogless. Likewise, in the shop, there wasn't a dog to be seen even though it was quite well stocked. They seemed a bit obsessed with images and statuettes of a little lad in pinafore shorts, called Bartje. In fact, I soon learned that his statue was just outside the museum itself and, very disappointed in the museum, that is where I headed next.

Bartje is a little boy who has become a symbol of Drenthe. He is a fictional character from a book written in 1935 by Anne de Vries called simply *Bartje* and subsequently a well-known Dutch TV series. The book is a portrayal of the grinding rural poverty of Drenthe, where there was little more to eat than a staple diet of brown beans. Bartje's famous saying – known right across the Netherlands and spoken in dialect – is: '*ik bid nie vur bruun bon'n*', or 'I will not pray for brown beans.'

Assen is a pleasant enough town, perhaps rather unremarkable. I spent some time looking around the shops, but was unable to find a book on our old friend the Dutch partridge dog. I was beginning to get a really bad feeling about achieving my quest.

Assen is the shopping centre serving around 200,000 people in the region, but I suppose that's not really that many people. Other than for shoes, I think they might have to go a bit further afield.

People had seemed a bit less friendly than in the villages, but then I suppose that's true in the UK, too, where the 'regional capitals' can have a reputation for being a bit unfriendly – although nothing on the scale of the national one. Presumably, the troubled teenagers of Drenthe, together with the more Bohemian set of artists and writers, look to lose themselves in the bright lights of Assen. Well, good luck to them is all I can say – it would be like going wild in Britain and heading off to Bridgnorth.

I was quite down when I left Assen. I couldn't believe that the Museum of Drenthe had no reference of any kind to its regional dog. I was only cheered slightly by my success in navigating my way through the traffic system so that I could leave 'the city in the trees'.

I got back to the hotel without incident, parked the car and felt relieved that I was leaving the car for the day. I walked off in search of a park to see what dogs I could find and glanced in the shops as I went – making a mental note to squeeze in a visit to the Paper Cutting Museum before I left. There was no park to be found, so I decided that my strategy should be to sit on a now sunny terrace of one of the roadside cafés and watch the world (and, with any luck, their dogs) go by.

Once again I got a real sense of well-being sitting there, sipping coffee, watching a happy world go by at a sedate pace. This really suited me. I even had a bit of luck watching for dogs although I saw nothing new. I watched an elderly man and his equally elderly yellow Labrador make slow progress along the street, stopping to talk to someone (the man, not the dog) every 10 yards or so. I also saw my second very large, black schnauzer of the day, but no Dutch partridge dogs.

It occurred to me that my couple of days could flash by and I would be leaving Holland a failure if I wasn't careful.

Urgent action was required, so what with him having been so friendly and helpful, I decided to ask the waiter. In my mind, he wouldn't own one himself, but he would have a friend who did and would arrange for me to go there that evening. In reality, he had never even heard of the breed – something I was to get used to over the next couple of days. A little dejected, I went on with my walk.

I tried to visit the church, which looked somehow very northern European, but it was locked, which surprised me in such an idyllic, peaceful village. The church dates back to 1360.

After a wander to the other end of this beautifully kept, attractive village (which for some reason had a wild west shop were you could buy everything a cowboy could want), I returned to my hotel and decided that I would eat dinner there that evening – especially as there was a regional special dish on that night. When in Rome, do as the Romans do and all that …

An hour later I was sitting in the conservatory area of the hotel restaurant, purposefully sitting so that I had a view of the main road of the village outside – still hoping to see my quarry out for a walk in the pleasant evening sunshine.

It was a good job that I had sat myself somewhere interesting as it took me ages to get served. Luckily, this has never worried me. In fact I revel in time spent eating – quite untypically for the British. I saw whole groups of people out cycling. One group looked like a Women's Institute outing – about 20 elderly ladies cycling two or three abreast, chatting away before pulling over at my hotel and taking possession of the outside terrace. Teenagers went by, two per bike. The village was obviously a draw for people from quite far afield, full as it was with cafés, restaurants and bars. This looked like a pretty idyllic scene and I found myself feeling unaccountably jealous.

There was a small card on the table, listing all the drinks available. It had, of course, a 'trappist' theme and I knew exactly what I was going to have: some *La Trappe* beer.

I was eventually served by a charming young lady who spoke excellent English as usual and whose specialist subject seeming to be smiling in such a way as to brighten up the whole room. I ordered the special and settled back with my beer as the restaurant began to fill up. My *La Trappe* was pretty strong stuff at 6.5% alcohol by volume – also extremely tasty, crisp and refreshing. Others in the range were the *Dubbel* at 6.5%, the *Tripel* at 8% and the *Quadrupel* at 10%. That's as strong as some wines! I tried the *Dubbel* and *Tripel* but couldn't face the *Quadrupel*.

A couple came and sat at the next table. In their fifties, the lady had her back to me, but her companion was tall and thin, with very short blonde hair going grey, a pinched face, clean-shaven and wearing round, metal glasses. Maybe it was the beer or more probably my travels earlier in the day, but I could only think of 'SS Officer' when I looked at him. He didn't smile, looked right through you, was incredibly precise in his movements, and curt in his manner. I found it quite unnerving.

Luckily, my dinner arrived before I was tempted to mention the war, as they say. I was a little bit apprehensive after the *Croque Monsieur* incident, to be honest. My regional special turned out to be a boiled extravaganza. The main feature was lots of boiled white local asparagus (quite a delicacy, I've since learned) with boiled potatoes, boiled ham and a little bit of hollandaise sauce, dressed with a diced boiled egg. Not incredibly colourful on the plate.

I really hadn't eaten much all day and I attacked the massive plate of food with gusto. There wasn't a lot of flavour, to be honest – a subtle nuttiness perhaps to this asparagus, but I wished it had been green or just a little colourful. As I went on, I began to feel quite sick. Meanwhile, these specials were flying out through the kitchen door to seemingly delighted locals. (During the rest of my stay in Holland, I noticed just how big a selling point Drenthe asparagus was.) It was going down a storm – I think I even detected a flicker of emotion on the SS Officer's face.

Whilst I was still ploughing through my part of the European Asparagus Mountain, four older people arrived in the conservatory, chose a table and unpacked some cards and what appeared to be a cribbage board. One of the nice things about cafés and restaurants abroad is that you can just as easily take a paper in and drink a coffee as smoke with a pint in your hand. You can just as soon have a dish of ice cream.

I felt pretty bloated when I'd finished my dinner. I was asked if I wanted the desert menu and, together with another beer, I decided I would. My fear, though, was that everything would be boiled, so instead I asked if they would do me some mixed ice cream.

I wasn't surprised that I had to wait half an hour for it to arrive. In that time, the conservatory had been taken over completely by oldies with board games – eyeing my table covetously. My ice cream arrived and I was overwhelmed. What a creation! It was half a bowl of fresh fruit with a mixture of ice creams of such fruity, subtle flavours. Probably the best ice cream I've ever had.

I had just finished my wonderful ice cream when, from somewhere in the building, the most amazing sound emerged – a male voice choir singing with such beauty. It was like time stood still. There was just this marvellous sound, a beautiful setting sun, a slight alcoholic haze and gorgeous flavours in my mouth.

Just to annoy the oldies, I ordered a coffee and enjoyed the music more. I recognised many of the songs as things you would hear a Welsh male choir sing, but again probably because of the visit to the camp, some of the other songs sounded like the backing track to some of those black and white films you see of marching Nazis. Of course, there is in reality probably nowhere less likely to celebrate Nazism than Holland.

As I made my way back to my room, I saw the huge room where the choir were practising – probably around 70 of them. An impressive sight and sound. What with the choir practice, the older folks getting together to play board games, the cyclists stopping off for a drink and individuals just enjoying a coffee with a newspaper, I thought there was a real sense of community in that hotel and the village in general. I drifted quickly off to sleep, somehow feeling that I was missing something I had in fact never known.

CHAPTER 13

Searching for the Dutch Partridge Dog

The next day was a beautiful, sunny one and started with an all-you-can-eat continental breakfast and an attempt to read a Dutch newspaper, with no success. Still, all the waiting staff were very friendly and word had got around that I was English – still quite a rarity for a tourist there, I guess.

I had no strategy whatsoever to see the elusive Dutch partridge dog. I had sort of thought that it would be quite easy to find one, but again the hotel staff had absolutely no idea what I was talking about. I decided to carry on along the tourist trail, convinced that I was bound to find one as I went.

If you read any guide to Holland, Westerbork will be mentioned primarily for the war-time camp, with perhaps a mention of the church and also a mention for the *Papierschmitt-kunst* museum – the museum of paper-cutting. How could I possibly go without visiting?

It was in a council building and I was waiting for it to open. While I waited I popped to the loo and found what would, not to be too delicate, be a feature over the next few days: the nutty scent of asparagus left behind, whatever the bodily function. I'm sure Jilly Goulden could describe the aroma better – you know the sort of thing: 'I'm getting the aroma of a Victorian Teddy Bear being dragged down an oak staircase in a musty cellar where a bunch of cloves has been left hanging in a corner covered in mildew.'

Anyway, the museum cost 4,50 euros to get in instead of the usual 6 – which was suspicious – and was staffed by two elderly ladies. I tried the '*Spreekt u Engels*?' and the answer was 'no'. These people were lovely – and so was their museum. They did everything they could to show me around and it was quite amazing – I hadn't realised that there was so much to it.

You're probably all familiar with this art from early school years. Basically, you take a piece of coloured paper, fold it in half, draw an abstract shape on it, which you then cut out. When you then unfold it, you have a cut-out which is symmetrical down the middle.

This was something quite different, though. For a start, some of them were six feet by four feet in size. They were also incredibly detailed – fine work at times almost too small for the naked eye. There were landscapes, panoramas, portraits, everything. They could have been drawn in pencil, they were so fine. Some were not symmetrical – I remember one in particular which was a picture of a whole orchestra.

There was a video describing the history of paper-cutting (in Dutch only), which nevertheless showed, amongst other things, that there were schools and movements in this branch of the arts. As I looked around the museum it became obvious that the same trends had occurred as in other visual arts – from the highly representational to the modern figurative. I particularly liked the ones that looked like wooden block printing.

The older of the two ladies did in fact know a little English and a little German, so we got by marvellously. She even made a small picture for me – of a pair of dolphins.

One of the main figures in paper-cutting had retired to Westerbork and that is how the museum had come about. I was disappointed to find out that it was not particularly a

Drenthe art form and my question as to whether there was a partridge dog amongst the thousands of exhibits led to the usual incredulity. In fact there were no dogs at all. She even seemed to doubt whether there was in fact any such dog as a Dutch partridge dog.

Still, it had been a fantastic hour. It was another example of expecting very little and coming away with a lot. I loved it and I loved the people. It was fun and entertaining, just the opposite of the Drenthe museum.

Drenthe is world-famous for one thing, although probably amongst comparatively few people: its megalithic tombs. There are 54 megaliths in Holland and 52 of these are in Drenthe, the other two being further north in Groningen. The Dutch word for megaliths is *hunnebedden* and they are very old indeed – some 5,000 years old in fact – dating to a time when they were built as tombs by the Neolithic Beaker people.

My next visit was to the village of Borger, where the *National Hunnebedden Informatiecentrum*, the National Megalith Information Centre, is to be found. Eight of the 54 megaliths are in and around Borger, including the largest in the country near the museum itself.

In fact, it is possible to complete a 60-mile megalith route on foot, by cycle or car and 'spot' all of the tombs on the way … now there's an idea for a book!

Borger itself is another lovely village. The sun was shining, there's a mixture of old and new buildings, all beautifully kept, and a number of restaurants and street cafés. Some of the buildings were houses converted from Dutch barns. Enough to put some of those presenters of property programmes on cable TV into ecstasy. Everywhere was clean and spotless and the people again incredibly friendly and welcoming. There were loads of dogs, too, and as I forced down yet another piece of apple cake with cream and strong cappuccino, I marvelled at the number and range of dogs on show. Many of them were trotting alongside bicycles, attached by a one-foot-long bendy arm coming from the bike. Not a single Dutch partridge dog, though.

The *Hunnebedden* Centre was a wonderful surprise – I mean, how much would you expect from a megalithic tomb centre? Not much, if you're like me. Somehow, though, this was in line with the understated beauty of Drenthe.

In reality, the centre was fantastic. Modern and light (and, rather comfortingly, costing 6 euros to get into, of course), the experience started with sitting in a small theatre. The lights went down and a five-minute audio-visual began, with dramatic music and a few subtitles in several languages. It began with the Ice Age and showed how the Drenthe landscape had been formed through glacial shift. It ended with the Beaker Folk building these megalithic tombs – for political correctness (at least of a sort) the building group seemed to be led by a young woman, which seems unlikely. She was, however, pretty well-endowed which, I guess, rather undid the political correctness bit.

The audio-visual was full of marvellous photography and loud mood music – I thought it was superb. I took about an hour to look around the rest of the centre. There were montages of Neolithic camps and Neolithic people, stuffed wolves – everything you could want on a day out. I took a picture of one of the fang-laden wolves close up and later tried to convince Tom that I had been 'up close and personal' with a dangerous grey wolf. He pointed out the turnstile and fire extinguisher in the background, though, and that rather undermined my attempt to convince him. There were picture boards, a few interactive displays, a mock hut and, best of all, a recreation of one of the *hunnebedden*. The size of the boulders was incredible and the weight of them immense. Upstairs in the centre was rather more serious archaeology, plotting Neolithic remains around Europe.

Having spent, ooh, minutes in the megalithic tomb gift shop (as you would), I headed off to see the real McCoy, about 100 yards away. Incidentally, I did buy some playing cards with Drenthe pictures on them at the gift shop. The packs were sealed, but they had Drenthe landscapes, rural scenes, pictures of Drenthe animals on them and so on. In short, the sort of gift that any right-thinking individual would welcome with open arms. I already knew what my main source of excitement would be back in the hotel room that night …

The *hunnebedde* itself was pretty big and impressive. It was quite spooky just to sit on a log in this quiet clearing and think that these very boulders had been there in that very formation for thousands of years. I sat there imagining some of the figures from the museum shifting these stones into place, grunting away with effort and wondering if there had been any dogs getting under their feet like there are when I'm trying to do my slightly smaller-scale DIY. The thing is, though – and it's a cause of great personal regret – I may have peaked too early. I mean if you start with the *biggest* megalithic tomb in Drenthe, where else is there to go? Just how good is any megalithic tomb going to be after that?

The first inhabitants of Drenthe arrived thousands of years before the megalithic tombs. They were almost certainly hunter-gatherers, fairly nomadic in lifestyle. To the east and the south, however, were more settled people, growing crops and keeping sheep, cattle and pigs. Bit by bit, our nomads settled into this lifestyle too. The *hunnebedden* are the megalithic tombs which these first agrarian communities used to bury their dead.

It seems that this custom may first have been adopted from Scandinavian and North German peoples around 3400 BC –

a thousand years after the Neolithic Drenthe people had settled into agricultural communities. The massive boulders used to build the tombs had been brought to the area in the Ice Age from Scandinavia, carried by glaciers, so in a way I suppose it is quite fitting that they were put to use in a Scandinavian custom.

These people came to be known, rather oddly, as the Funnel Beaker Folk, after the distinctively shaped pottery that they made. So huge tombs are not the only claim to fame for this impressive culture!

Sitting on a log, marvelling at this particular tomb – the largest in the Netherlands – I was struck by the enormity of the enterprise. This tomb is no less than 22.5 metres long. I had difficulty in thinking how primitive people would have built it.

Building them certainly needed teamwork. The massive boulders would have to be dug out, then manoeuvred using ropes, levers and logs acting as rollers. First of all, two stones would have been placed upright into specially dug holes. Then a capstone would be put on each pair of stones, using ropes, levers and ramps of logs. There would be five such constructions, resulting in a construction of five capstones, with an entrance left in the south side of the tomb. Once complete, the gaps between the stones were filled and the mound largely covered with sand so that grass would grow up the sides.

I was not alone in getting into some pretty strange positions to look under the capstones to see what it was like. Even so, the reconstruction in the museum probably gave a better idea.

So, once complete, these were burial mounds as well as territorial markers. Here the Beaker Folk would be buried with some of their famous pottery.

I don't know why, but I found the whole visit mesmerising

and just felt a tingle down my spine at the age and primeval nature of it all.

Just a few miles away from Borger, a short drive through sun-filled heavy forest, was my next destination: the so-called *Boomkroonpad* – the tree-top walk. I had been dying to visit this place, which was yet another pretty unusual Drenthe attraction. The idea is basically to take you from the roots of a tree, up the trunk and right into the tree-tops – some 410 feet up into the air.

It was another peaceful, idyllic setting in deep, deep forest. Some children were playing in a play area, otherwise there was complete peace, quiet and beauty. The entrance gate was wood and grass and just melted into the landscape.

I was very much in the mood to go underground and see tree roots at first hand, so it was a surprise when they turned out just to be lit-up green tree-root-like displays, with very cheap horror effects thrown in – horrible little goblins jumping out of the dark at you in a tacky way. There was even a human skull whose eye sockets lit up as insects attacked it for no apparent reason. I was more than ready to leave the roots and couldn't wait to climb the stairs up to the treetops. Flight after flight of climbing later, it was certainly worth it. Up aloft, there are suspended pathways from tree to tree, pointing out different types of trees and observation areas giving views across miles and miles of forest. Quite spectacular and again incredibly peaceful.

I was sad to leave the *Boomkroonpad* – there were miles of marked pathways between 3 and 16 km in length through the forest to walk, and just leave the world behind in absolute peace and quiet. This wasn't getting the Dutch partridge dog seen, though, was it?

So, it was back to the hotel to leave the car (what a relief!) and try out the Arriva bus service to Emmen, another of the larger towns in Drenthe. Although it was only about 2 o'clock in the afternoon, it wasn't completely clear to me whether I would be able to get back by bus – it seemed to lose interest short of Westerbork later in the day. So, it was back to my '*Spreekt u Engels?*' in the direction of the bus driver, who seemed to be the first grumpy Dutch person I had met. He did tell me, though, that I had to change buses on the way back. I was the only passenger and sat back a little disappointed.

Things soon changed, though. The countryside we drove through in the sunshine was simply beautiful. We passed through the picture postcard area of Orvelte – wonderful old buildings in a sort of agricultural idyll. It looked like a gorgeous open-air museum – and I later found out that that's exactly what it was. At least I got a really good view from the bus, even if I couldn't stop to take pictures like I would have if I'd been in the car.

Suddenly, Mr Grumpy decided to be chatty. He asked me where I was going and what I was doing and seemed genuinely interested. By the time we got to Emmen he was taking the bus off its route to drop me somewhere convenient as I was the only passenger! That's certainly never happened to me before.

I quite liked Emmen. With a population of 105,000 it is nearly twice the size of Assen, with a wide array of shoe shops. It is also home to one of Holland's biggest tourist attractions, the *Noorder Dierenpark* – Emmen Zoo. I was pretty short of time, though, and couldn't fit in a visit to the zoo. I went straight to Tourist Information and met a charming young woman. I explained my quest – to find a Dutch partridge dog – and her manner changed a little. She was still overtly friendly, but her body language became tenser and she definitely distanced herself from me, even though there was a counter between us. I actually saw her co-worker's eyebrows raise when

I explained my quest, although she wasn't meant to be listening. I could tell she was just going through the location of the panic button in her mind.

Not only did the lady from Tourist Information inform me that she didn't know where I could see one – she went further by trying to deny there was such an animal. And this is the Drenthe Tourist Office. I asked if they had any merchandise with dogs on it, convinced that I would be able to show them the truth. Ten minutes later we had exhausted their stock, despite one or two excited moments where Lady 1 would say to Lady 2, 'Oh, there are dogs on those placemats, remember?' only for Lady 2 to reply something like, 'Yes, there are, but we haven't had those for two years now.'

And then a breakthrough: 'I know what you mean,' says Lady 2. 'It's black and white, isn't it, and farmers use them with their animals?' 'No,' I reply. 'It's definitely brown and white and it's a gundog.' 'Oh no, you're wrong,' comes the rejoinder from Lady 2. 'It's black and white and we have a special name for it – it's not called a *Drentsche Patrijshond*, it's called a *Stabij*.'

This went on for a few minutes with neither of us giving ground.

I thanked them for their time and left – even more frustrated than before. A coffee in a street café didn't bring a Dutch partridge dog past, however much I closed my eyes, crossed my fingers and wished for it.

I liked Emmen and had a good wander around, not least trying to find a bus stop. Beginning to doubt my sanity, I went into various bookshops, determined to find a book on the seemingly mythical partridge dog. This was Drenthe, its home region, after all. Needless to say, I couldn't find any such dog, but got strange looks in one bookshop when I broke the silence jumping up with my fist in the air shouting, 'Y-e-e-s!'

In a general book – *De Grote Honden Encycloedia* by Esther Verhoff – I found a two-page entry for the *Drentsche Patrijshond* and it was, of course, brown and white. I had to buy the book, convinced that my Anglo-German would enable me to read it. I wanted to go running back to the Tourist Office and show the friendly but very doubting ladies what their regional treasure looked like but, pushed for time and by now some distance from them, and not having the Dutch for 'so put that in your pipe and smoke it', I resisted.

By now I was completely lost in quite a large web of pedestrian precincts. I came past the same shoe shop at least three times while time ticked away.

Finally, I found my way to a small bus station and tried to find the stop for a bus to my interim destination – a tiny village by the name of Zweeloo. I couldn't find anything, though, and I had almost resigned myself to a heavy taxi fare when a bus came in marked 'Hoogeveen' and turned out to be the bus I wanted.

It was evening rush-hour now and the bus was packed, but the change in Zweeloo was perfect with one bus sitting waiting for the connection with the other and I was soon back in the hotel in Westerbork. I had already come to view it as 'home'. How quickly that happens!

I took my purchases to the hotel restaurant and enjoyed a cup of coffee as I unwrapped my playing cards to reveal lovely rural and farm scenes – including some dogs which, being typical of Drenthe, were … Border collies.

I also flicked through my rather beautiful new encyclopaedia. The very page before the partridge dog was a black and white dog, a multi-purpose hunting dog from the Netherlands called a *Stabyhoun* or *Stabij*. I'd never heard of it and, thank God, it wasn't in my breed-spotting guide, but there it was – the dog Lady 2 had been talking about!

This was now my last evening in Drenthe. I clearly wasn't going to see a Dutch partridge dog here and I felt pretty dispirited. Even so, it had been a fantastic visit. There had been so much to see and enjoy, so much beauty in such an unlikely place in many ways. Best of all it was really unspoilt. By British standards, Drenthe was commutable from Amsterdam and if it had been in the UK, every second house would have been bought up as a second home, pricing locals out of the market. As it was, but for the absence of the partridge dog, Drenthe was almost perfect.

I had to get back to Amsterdam the next day and had a detour to make. I didn't want to be looking for the junctions and directions in busy traffic, so set off again in the Skoda to find my way – trying to remember the turns I needed to make at the various roundabouts in nearby Beilen to head off towards Hoogersmilde and onwards towards Drachten.

After a few minutes I was seemingly headed towards Hoogersmilde, but down a very narrow road next to a beautiful still canal. It was peaceful and quiet. The odd car coming in the opposite direction meant pulling off the road. I couldn't believe that this was my main route for the morning – there was barely room to overtake the ubiquitous bicycles, the riders of which seemed to stare at me, driving in the twilight in such a remote place.

Eventually, I came to the village of Hoogersmilde, through various narrow lanes and over a swing bridge, then just putting my foot down and going for it across a dual carriageway, hoping I'd looked the right way and was on the right side of the road.

I stopped the car and looked at my map. I'd only been there two minutes when one of the villagers came out of his house, a broad smile on his face, and asked if I was lost. This was no 'neighbourhood watch', just concern for a fellow human being. We were then joined by his wife. He explained that I had taken a tiny country road for the nature reserve instead of the dual carriageway!

Via the dual carriageway I was soon in Westerbork and ready for the next day.

I finished the day with a couple of white beers and the most delicious pizza, made to my own specifications, that I'd ever eaten. The waiter couldn't do enough for me. I sat outside and watched the sun going down – the groups of cyclists from other towns and villages weighing up the various menus of the cafés and restaurants. What an idyllic way to spend the evening.

The only downside was a group of about 10 German teenagers at a neighbouring table taking the piss out of the Dutch, thinking no one would understand them. Still, they were just kids and that's what kids do.

I'd had a great day and went to bed feeling very contented after yet another asparagus-scented visit to the bathroom. I was completely resigned to the fact that I had failed in my quest.

The next morning I woke up full of the joys of spring, even though it was summer. Far from feeling downhearted I felt pretty upbeat and even quite smug. The only thing playing on my mind was finding my way back to the car rental bureau at Schipol Airport and negotiating my way through the traffic. As regards the Dutch partridge dog, I was really excited.

You see, you don't think I'd leave this to chance, do you? I would have loved to see a *Drent* in Drenthe, but my experience in Bedlington had taught me not to rely on these things. So, before leaving for Holland I had been scouring the Web for breeders and one had kindly agreed to be in today so that I could meet her and her partridge dogs. This was really going to happen. My quest would be completed this very day.

I was walking around smiling idiotically at everyone at breakfast. There was some sort of business meeting going on and my table was next to the manager's as he entertained bankers, marketing people or something similar. It was clearly a set-up as the manager interrupted his meeting and made a point of coming over to me, speaking in English and asking me how I was enjoying my break, emphasising I was from England. This was clearly meant to impress his visitors as presumably there had been little British tourism until this point. A pioneer, that's me.

I couldn't believe how cheap my bill was. I even treated myself to three postcards: one of the hotel itself, one of the memorial centre at Kamp Westerbork and one of a beautiful Drenthe farming landscape featuring a couple of lovely Border collies!

I was really very sad to leave the hotel and the village but I was soon underway back to Amsterdam with a pretty significant diversion via Emmeloord in Flevoland in the west of the country, where I had arranged to see the elusive *Drenten* (the plural of *Drent*, the local term for the breed).

I had planned an 'easy' journey of A roads and dual carriageways, travelling northwest towards Drachten, then cutting cross country at Oosterwolde through to Wolvega and then on to Emmeloord. I was feeling great, as happy as proverbial Larry once again, really beginning to enjoy the driving to the accompaniment, inevitably, of Rick, Leo and UB40. In fact rather spookily at one stage I was trying to bring Leo Sayer's hits back to mind (it didn't take long) and started singing 'I feel thunder in my heart'. Within five seconds it was playing on the radio. Strange, but true!

Then the diversions started – miles of them, taking me miles (or rather kilometres) out of my way. There were so many contraflows, temporary roundabouts and diversions through busy little towns that I think I had very soon completed a crash course (no pun intended) in driving abroad.

Let's just say that when I arrived in Emmeloord one and a half hours later I was glad that I had used my Right Guard that morning.

Marjaan de Raad is a lovely, friendly woman. Given that we had only corresponded via the internet, with a couple of phone calls the day before my visit by way of confirmation, she was incredibly welcoming.

On going into her neat suburban house – I had been expecting a house up a lonely lane, where so many breeders in Britain tend to live – the first dogs I saw were not what I expected at all. Small, white, with a medium-length cottony coat, they looked like a cross between a *Bichon Frise* and a Maltese terrier. If I was right they were of the *Bolognese* breed – a rare Italian dog – and it turned out that they were. What a bonus!

Despite my excitement at seeing a *Bolognese* – well two, actually – with lovely welcoming temperaments, I couldn't wait for Marjaan to let in the *Drenten.* And then the door opened and in came Marjaan's two beautiful bitches – Eva and Otje. What wonderful friendly dogs they are. I couldn't quite believe that this was it – I was seeing the dogs I had been searching for and my whole quest was complete. At the same time, in appearance, the Dutch partridge dog is, I suppose, quite unspectacular. Moderate in all things really – as befits an all-round working dog of course. At first sight it looks almost like a larger Springer spaniel – one of our most popular dogs.

The next couple of hours just flew by, talking about these wonderful dogs and Marjaan's obvious love of them. Indeed, when I asked her what it was that she really liked about these dogs, her answers were very revealing. She said that, first and foremost, she experienced an emotional reaction when she saw *Drenten* – the sight of them actually makes her heart beat faster. I don't think she really wanted to rationalise her feelings at all, but she did finally admit that she loved the fact that you can show these dogs as well as teach them to do a practical day's work – best of both worlds, I suppose.

Marjaan told me that she had had *Drenten* for some 30 years. As with many people who later become enthusiasts of particular breeds, she happened upon what would become hugely important in her life quite accidentally. As a newly wed, her neighbours had a *Drent.* She liked the dog so much that she got one herself and this proved to be her way into the world of dogs. She was 'bitten', as it were. When her dog died, she got another male and went on a week's residential training course with her new companion. Meanwhile, her best friend was showing Clumber spaniels and she became interested in the show world, first showing her own dogs in 1988.

To start with she would enter 2 or 3 classes and, if not competing, would go along as a spectator, attending a show perhaps once a month or so.

Her current two dogs, both females, are Eva (7 years old) and Otje (4 years old). These are their pet names. Eva is in fact a Champion, although Marjaan is very modest and never uses the title. If my dog were a Champion, I'd have it tattooed on my forehead.

So Eva is Kamp Eva van Oudsher and Otje (known as Ot) is Mijn Othilia van der Flevomare. Both are absolutely gorgeous dogs with wonderful temperaments. They like a bit of fuss but are incredibly well-mannered, reacting instantly to Marjaan's voice.

Marjaan told me that there would typically be 35 dogs at a show. Obviously, that's not a huge number and it probably makes for quite a close-knit community. There are specialist clubs for the breed in Holland, Belgium, Luxembourg and Denmark, with Championship shows in each.

These dogs are fortunate in that they are not a victim of fashion. I suppose this is no surprise, given the difficulty I had in finding them even in their native country. Indeed they are generally a very healthy bunch who have not been overbred. Even so, there has been some trouble in the breed with von Willebrand's disease – a condition linked with hemophilia, where the blood fails to clot. Indeed this came to light when a pregnant bitch bled to death. To this day, there is no good DNA test for the condition.

Although I suppose it's a bit of a rude question, I really wanted to know how much a *Drent* would cost me. In the past they used only to be available via a particular puppy contact bureau, which would supply only screened puppies. Now, though, puppies can be supplied by anyone. A puppy used to cost typically the guilder equivalent of 700 euros a few years ago, but now the cost in euros was almost what it had been in guilder (a phenomenon I came across several times as I crossed Europe) and they could now easily cost 1,100-1,200 euros. The puppies had become more popular, too, so that you could now expect to wait 4 to 6 months for a female puppy and 2 to 3 months for a male. Nearly all of the puppies stay within the Netherlands, although a male had been sent to Canada the previous year, to be followed by a female this year. So, soon there would be little Canadian *Drenten.*

I had already suspected, and Marjaan confirmed, that there were no Dutch partridge dogs in the UK. So, if I were to get one it would be the first …

Other than the von Willebrand's issue, it seems that the *Drent* is a pretty healthy dog. Epilepsy had been a problem but careful breeding had reduced the problem significantly. Like many breeds, there is a problem with the eyes – PRA

(Progressive Retinal Atrophy), which causes blindness and cataracts. There is now a screening programme for dogs, so that affected dogs can be taken out of any breeding programme. It is a measure of Marjaan's love of and dedication to the breed that she as the breeder pays for the screening to be done at one and a half to two years old. I can assure you that most breeders don't do this – I thought it was just fantastic.

The only other issue in the health of the breed was that of problems around the hip and elbow joints – but fortunately for the *Drent* this isn't very significant. Even so, the matters identified above in a relatively sound breed which hasn't been overbred just go to show the extent of health issues in dogs today.

Marjaan was, perhaps unsurprisingly, not able to explain any particular link between the breed and the province of Drenthe, other than the fact, of course, that this was its place of origin. What she did tell me was that by the end of the Second World War the breed was close to extinction. It was a group of people in Groningen, the province neighbouring Drenthe, who got together to see how many partridge dogs there were to breed from and then establish a proper breeding programme to ensure the survival of the breed.

Of course, the *Drent* is first and foremost 'designed' as an all-round hunting dog (an *Allround Jachthond*), although like most breeds the dogs are now primarily companions. Marjaan's dogs had been taken on a hunting course and learnt the fundamental skills of working in a hunt, but they were not hunting-dogs as such, not least because Flevoland has long since seen its last partridge or pheasant!

So, some facts and figures about this fantastic breed. It was first recognised by the FCI (the International Canine Federation: the overall world governing body for dogs) in the 1940s and it appears in their Group 7 – Gundogs.

It weighs around 50 pounds and is 22-25 inches in height. It always has some white on its coat, with brown, orange or sometimes brown and tan patches.

The origin of the *Drent* probably dates to the first use of firearms, as do most of the spaniel and setter breeds. He works first and foremost to the gun, and now generally hunts animals such as rabbits in the absence of his favourite, the partridge (in a pear tree or anywhere else).

These are said to be around 6,000 *Drenten* in the Netherlands.

In advance of going to Holland, I had got in touch with a couple of groups of professional dog trainers over there, to see if they had any experience of, and views about, the breed. I spent the next half hour or so seeing what Marjaan made of the comments I had received.

One common observation I got about the breed related to its enthusiasm and indeed even over-enthusiasm. Clearly, the owner needs to know what they're doing. The dog can be easily excited and distracted and needs an owner who knows how to focus the dog on him/herself, especially where the environment is particularly stimulating. It seems that they are quite a sensitive breed, needing very clear and consistent handling, involving lots of praise. They need a confident handler, otherwise they soon lose confidence themselves and then become stressed. Indeed, they are sensitive bunnies and will pick up readily on stresses and strains in the household.

The dogs are a hugely attractive breed with beautiful facial expressions and, just like the dogs I see in Britain, this can lead to the wrong sort of owner getting hold of them. There are still strong working instincts in the breed, and trainers and behaviourists in Holland see the same sorts of problem – resulting mainly from boredom and poor handling – as I do with Border collies from working stock. In other words, the dogs' stress levels go up and up, as a result of which the handler becomes less confident and less able to deal with the dog, who then becomes more wilful and apparently disobedient, leading to a complete breakdown in the relationship. Certainly, by the sound of it, this is not a breed for inexperienced owners.

The trainers who responded to my messages suggested that the *Drent* was just about a perfect working hunting dog – quick to learn, agile, speedy, enthusiastic and soft-mouthed. On the other hand they would not choose a *Drent* for obedience competition. Sure, they would do okay, but others would do better – particularly those more willing to toe the line unquestioningly.

They are agile and quick, but probably not precise enough to do really well at agility – which requires concentration and strong self-control at times (there are, for example, very precise contact points which need to be hit and prevent a dog just launching itself off an obstacle). For the *Drent* it is again its unbridled enthusiasm which may work against it.

It excels in all sorts of other activities, though: in fact anything requiring speed, a well-developed chase instinct, versatility, swimming and stamina. Quite an all-round athlete.

Marjaan agreed wholeheartedly with the characterisation of the breed given by the trainers and behaviourists and we spent the next hour, whilst munching a pizza she had thoughtfully provided, watching some of Marjaan's DVDs of reunions she organises for her past puppies and other Drents. Watching 20 or so of them splashing around in a river together is something I could do all day. Marjaan was kindness itself and presented me with a book on the breed – *de Drentsche Patrijshond* – and a copy of the breed club's periodical *Onze Drent* ('our *Drent*'). We also spent time taking pictures of the dogs at play and just fussing the lovely Eva and Otje, who were two of the best behaved and obedient dogs I've had the pleasure of meeting.

It had been the most fantastic few hours and I felt truly privileged to have met not only Eva and Ot, two beautiful dogs, but also Marjaan who, it seems to me, is everything a dog breeder and enthusiast should be.

It was time to leave and head back to Schipol a happy man.

Incidentally, Marjaan's parting-shot took me aback. 'Why didn't you go to see the big breeder of *Drenten* in Emmen, by the way – in Drenthe itself?'

Well, I didn't know, did I? I was really sad to leave Marjaan and the *Drenten.* If you want to meet the dogs, have a look at Marjaan's website. You'll see that Ot had a lovely litter of puppies later that year.

It only took me an hour back to Schipol – passing the longest set of huge wind-farm turbines I have ever seen – but the roads got busier and busier as I went. It was beginning to feel really comfortable driving abroad by now. Anyway, what could go wrong with Leo and Rick belting out of the radio? When I returned the hire car even my scraped hubcap went unnoticed.

I felt quite elated getting rid of the Skoda without anything untoward having happened. This did, though, mean that I had about six hours to kill before check-in for my late-evening flight.

How silly would it be to miss out on Amsterdam when only about 30 minutes away by train?

Having stashed my luggage in a very high-tech locker I was soon on a slightly claustrophobic double-decker train on the way to Amsterdam with a truly cosmopolitan collection of fellow passengers.

I've been to Amsterdam a few times and really enjoyed it. What I wasn't mentally prepared for, though, after the peace and quiet of Drenthe, was the hurly-burly of large, fast-moving crowds. I almost felt physically sick as a sea of faces came towards me. How I wanted to be out in the country and away from this bustle. It was probably psychological, too, but somehow the real mix of people and their differing agendas and destinations came over as quite hostile – even menacing.

The one thing I really wanted to do – ignoring the dubious attractions of the new Sex Museum (what would they have in there, then?) – was visit the Anne Frank Museum. This just seemed to fit in with my visit to Kamp Westerbork. Finding my way on foot from memory – and not wishing to stop and look in my guide too obviously – it took me about 30 minutes to find Anne Frank's house.

How easy it is to take everything for granted. I had been mind-blown the first time I saw the canals of Amsterdam, yet this time it all seemed rather familiar. I was just passing through, quite unaffected by everything.

Round the corner from some incredibly drunken people playing football with a can and another just urinating where he stood, I found the museum. The queue was miles long and I noticed that it was open until early evening, so I decided to go back later in the day.

I was getting hungry and really fancied one of those Amsterdam specialities: a roll-mop herring on a bread roll, which you can buy from stalls on the canal bridges. However, queues here (exclusively of Dutch people) were really long and you seemed to have to speak up and define what you wanted in some detail. My confidence deserted me. This wasn't easy-going Drenthe.

I needed to find something to do to spend a couple of hours and the main criterion had to be that I could do it sitting down. I'm pretty sure that it's possible to do anything sitting down in Amsterdam – but a couple of hours is stretching it. I chose the old favourite, the canal cruise. The downside of this was that it involved walking all the way back to the main railway station.

The canal trip itself was okay but nothing remarkable. I guess I had used up all my excitement earlier in the day. I saw the narrowest building, the hooks to lift the furniture through windows, the hippy houseboats and the rest of it, but really just enjoyed sitting back and watching the landscape go past.

After some of the worst Kentucky Fried Chicken (if that isn't an oxymoron) I'd ever eaten I went back to the Anne Frank Museum. It had acquired an ugly, modern extension since the last time I'd been but despite all the displays and video footage now available, it's the private living rooms, hidden above Mr Frank's spice warehouse, which are the most moving. Creeping around and not daring to creak a floorboard, turn on a tap or flush a toilet, 8 people lived in these few rooms from 6 July 1942 to 4 August 1944, when they were betrayed by people unknown to this day.

Visiting these rooms you can see some original pictures stuck on the walls to brighten it up, scraps of writing and excerpts from Anne's diary to bring the place to life.

It's more than a museum – it's a monument to man's inhumanity to man. It brought me full circle to Kamp Westerbork, where the Frank family were sent to the punishment barracks prior to their onward transportation to Auschwitz and Bergen-Belsen.

I was really moved by my visit to the house. I bought a copy of Anne Frank's diary for Tom, desperate that he should understand.

An hour later I was sitting in a departure lounge, musing over my trip to Holland.

All in all, it had been a fantastic trip. I had seen beautiful places, met wonderful people and finished my dog-spotting quest. I had also found somewhere I loved and knew I would return … maybe to pick up my Dutch partridge dog.

Showing Tom the photos of me with Eva and Ot I had mixed feelings. He had to concede that I had completed my challenge and it occurred to me for the first time that I didn't win anything at all for doing it. Worse still, though, the challenge was over. I had found it all-consuming and it had, I suppose, become an obsession. I was pleased with myself – perhaps unnaturally pleased – but I did wonder what would happen now. I mean, how do you replace an obsession? Unless, of course, you replace it with another one …

Spot-a-long Guide

If you've enjoyed reading *Searching for the Dutch Partridge Dog* you may like to have a go yourself – at a simplified version!

Here's how to do it.

1 Set yourself a time limit – perhaps 3 or 6 months.
2 Set any other rules (e.g. how many dogs you can see at any one dog show) if you want to.
3 Get hold of a small, illustrated guide to dogs.
4 Have a go! Tick off the dogs as you spot them.
5 Score your efforts and see what your score says about you.

1 point each

Golden Retriever	☐	German Shepherd Dog	☐
Cocker Spaniel	☐	English Springer Spaniel	☐
Staffordshire Bull Terrier	☐	West Highland White Terrier (Westie)	☐
Labrador Retriever (any colour)	☐	Yorkshire Terrier (Yorkie)	☐
Boxer	☐	Cavalier King Charles Spaniel	☐

___ / 10

2 points each

Rottweiler	☐	Greyhound	☐
Poodle (any size)	☐	Irish Setter	☐
Cairn Terrier	☐	Schnauzer (any size)	☐
Rough Collie	☐	Border Collie	☐
Beagle	☐	Dalmatian	☐

___ / 20

3 points each

Afghan Hound	☐	Shih Tzu	☐
Belgian Shepherd Dog (any variety)	☐	Weimaraner	☐
Whippet	☐	Pug	☐
Dachshund (any variety)	☐	Doberman	☐
Chihuahua (any variety)	☐	Border Terrier	☐

/ 30

4 points each

St Bernard	☐	Manchester Terrier	☐
Airedale Terrier	☐	Rhodesian Ridgeback	☐
Old English Sheepdog	☐	English Setter	☐
Bull Terrier	☐	Samoyed	☐
Scottish Terrier	☐	Pointer (any variety)	☐

/ 40

5 points each

Bloodhound	☐	Saluki	☐
Sealyham Terrier	☐	Burmese Mountain Dog	☐
Pharaoh Hound	☐		

/ 25

7 points each

Bedlington Terrier	☐	Puli	☐
Chinese Crested Dog	☐	Leonberger	☐

/ 28

17 points

Dutch Partridge Dog ☐

/ 17

TOTAL **/ 170**

0 – 35
You must be in a world of your own – or maybe a cat lover? Get out more and look around you. Watch less TV. Play fewer video games. Remove your head from your rear orifice! Try again.

36 – 70
Perhaps you need to give yourself longer? Spend more time in public places but be careful about hanging around in parks on your own. Be warned, to get the information you need you may actually have to talk to people. You might even get to like it.

71 – 100
You've seen, probably, most of the easily available dogs. If you are going to get serious about this, then firstly ask yourself 'Why?' and, if you come through that process with your dignity and sanity intact, then you're probably going to have to go out of your way to see less common dogs. This may involve, for example, going to dog shows. Be warned, this can be habit-forming.

101 – 150
This is getting serious. Were you a train-spotter as a child? Perhaps you are a member of the Eddie Stobart fan club. Maybe you just love dogs or being out and about. With just a little more obsession you could find yourself in the top category. Wouldn't that be great?

150 +
Welcome to the club. Boy, you've put some work into this. You are seriously obsessed. Pat yourself on the back and seek professional help. There are places and groups for people like you who need to get a life. I'll probably see you there …

AND FINALLY ...

Things We Can Learn from a Dog

Here are a few things we could learn from dogs, which would make the world a better place. Again, this is to be found on the internet and it is not possible to attribute it to anyone in particular:

1 Never pass up the opportunity to go for a joyride
2 When loved ones come home, always run to greet them
3 When it's in your own best interest, practise obedience
4 Let others know when they've invaded your territory
5 Take naps and stretch before rising
6 Run, romp and play daily
7 Eat with gusto and enthusiasm
8 Be loyal
9 Never pretend to be something you are not
10 If what you are looking for is buried, dig until you find it
11 When someone is having a bad day, be silent, sit close by and nuzzle them gently
12 Thrive on attention and let people touch you
13 On hot days, drink lots of water and lie under a shady tree
14 When you're happy, dance around and wag your entire body
15 No matter how often you are scolded, run right back and make friends
16 Delight in the simple joy of a long walk

And my favourite:

17 Avoid biting when a simple growl will do